THE
WOMEN'S
PROJECT
& PRODUCTIONS

ROWING TO AMERICA
AND SIXTEEN
OTHER SHORT PLAYS

A Smith and Kraus Book
Published by Smith and Kraus, Inc.
177 Lyme Road, Hanover, NH 03755
www.SmithKraus.com

Manufactured in the United States of America

Cover and Text Design by Julia Hill Gignoux, Freedom Hill Design

First Edition: April 2002
10 9 8 7 6 5 4 3 2 1

Contemporary Playwrights Series ISSN 1067-9510

Library of Congress Cataloging-in-Publication Data
The women's project and productions : 17 one-act plays, 1975–1999 / edited by Julia Miles.
p. cm. — (Contemporary playwrights series)
ISBN 1-57525-271-6
1. American drama—Women authors. 2. American drama—20th century. 3. One-act plays, American. 4. Women—Drama. I. Title: Women's project and productions. II. Series.

PS627.W66 W66 2001
812'.041089287'09045—dc21
2001054941

To Dick —
Hope all the
talks on
[illegible] + gloom —
Best,
[signature]

THE
WOMEN'S
PROJECT
& PRODUCTIONS

ROWING TO AMERICA
AND SIXTEEN
OTHER SHORT PLAYS

Edited by Julia Miles

CONTEMPORARY PLAYWRIGHTS SERIES

A SMITH AND KRAUS BOOK

CONTENTS

INTRODUCTION

Women's Project & Productions:
Rowing to America
and Sixteen Other Short Plays

For the last twenty-four years, playwrights from the Women's Project have explored a variety of subjects and styles within the concise demands of the one act. We usually produce full-length plays, but we have produced festivals of one-acts to show more work by our talented writers. First Looks, a reading series for new plays, occasionally provides a hearing for one-acts and the Playwrights Lab and Directors Forum, our primary developmental avenues for emerging artists, annually present a series of one-acts. For this anthology, I have chosen a wide range of work from our established and emerging artists that reflects the enormous diversity of their work.

The long one-acts include: Lavonne Mueller's bittersweet *The Only Woman General* (performed brilliantly by the late Colleen Dewhurst) about a general who, for her last tour of duty, must orbit the earth in an Army spacecraft with a full load of plutonium for the next 250,000 years; Julie Jensen's gothic *Old Wives Tale,* which tells of a childless older woman in rural Utah who develops a relationship with her new neighbor and her deformed children; Caridad Svich's minimalist *but there are fires,* where a husband works to get the spark back in his marriage; *The Encanto File* by Rosa Lowinger, a mystery about a Cuban swindle deal; and Sallie Bingham's *Throwaway,* a hopeful story of a young woman who finds healing for her broken family from her wise grandmother.

The short plays, ranging from ten to twenty minutes playing time, are from the Directors Forum and the Playwrights Lab, and most were presented in our annual Tandem Acts, where plays receive a "bare bones" production.

These plays range from studies of a woman's fight for her sanity in *Bread* by Margaret Hunt; the claustrophobic relationship of a brother and sister in Daisy Foote's *Farley and Betsy;* and a test of a mother's feelings versus the demands of the law in *Sentences and Words* by Cindy Cooper, to a probe of a mother's instinct in Sheri Wilner's *Relative Strangers.*

Some of the Tandem Acts series developed from specific themes: multi-culturalism inspired *Rowing to America*, the presence of miracles brought about Lisa Humbertson's *The Nature of Things* and Dana Leslie Goldstein's *Burn;* barriers gave us Juliana Francis' *Box* and Lynda Sturner's *Look What You Made Me Do;* the theme of lust and mayhem inspired Judy Tate's *Mistaken for Genius* and Liz Duffy Adam's *Greeks and Centaurs;* violence evoked Carmen Rivera's *Betty's Garage;* and visions of the future resulted in *Freakish Times* by Lesli-Jo Morizono and Alva Rogers' *the life before/reconstruction/reconstructing whiteness.*

All these short plays were presented in pared-down productions using min-imal sets, props, and costumes. The plays are actor- and audience-friendly and are ideally suited for the stage, festivals, and classroom presentations.

In selecting a title for this collection, I was inspired by the touching opti-mism of Kitty Chen's character who said while trying to row to America, "Everything will be all right." I believe her attitude embodies the spirit of our talented playwrights who keep writing and theaters that keep producing plays despite all economic obstacles, and by doing so make everything all right.

Julia Miles
Artistic Director
Women's Project & Productions

Greeks and Centaurs

A TEN-MINUTE MUSEUM PIECE

by Liz Duffy Adams

For Mathew

BIOGRAPHY

Liz Duffy Adams' plays include *Dog Act* (staged readings at Portland Stage Company and New York Theatre Workshop); *The Train Play* (a Clubbed Thumb production at the Ohio Theater, staged readings at Yale Rep and The Arts Festival of Atlanta); *A Wrinkle in Time* (adaptation commissioned and produced by Syracuse Stage); *A Fabulous Beast* (One Dream Theater); *Teacup for a Shallow Apocalypse* (Santa Monica Playhouse); and the short plays *Greeks and Centaurs, The Last Woman on Earth*, and *Aphra Does Antwerp* (The Women's Project Tandem Acts Festivals; *Last Woman* also at New Georges Perform-a-thon and the Estrogenius Festival). She is a graduate of NYU's Experimental Theatre Wing and the Yale School of Drama, and a member of New Dramatists.

ORIGINAL CAST LIST

Greeks and Centaurs was first presented by the Women's Project & Productions directed by Rebecca Patterson with the following cast:

SALLY	Abigail Lopez
MAN/GUARD	Chris Wight
CENTAUR	Kohl Sudduth

SETTING

Briefly in New York; mostly at the British Museum in London.

TIME

Last November.

CHARACTERS

SALLY
MAN/GUARD
CENTAUR

GREEKS AND CENTAURS

(Sally, a New Yorker maybe thirty years old, is on the phone.)

SALLY: I'm back hi I'm back, how are you, can't wait to see you, London was oh you know it was fabulous, Malcolm was great, we slept till noon every day—his boyfriend has a day job—had coffee for hours and talked and talked while he smoked and smoked and just before everything closed we'd rush out and see stuff and so well they live right around the corner from the British Museum and yes I know "colonial vandalism" and yes OK yes of course but so one day I went there by myself and the freakiest thing happened which is really what I called to tell you, the most tremendous amazing unusual life-altering really sort-of shattering thing—

(Stops abruptly. Quickly punches in numbers.)

Your machine cut me off so anyway at the British Museum it was about to close and I rushed in and I only had time to see one thing except I went right past the Rosetta Stone so I sort of saw that but it's not much to look at, I mean you know there was a little crowd of people standing around it just sort of vibrating at it and you know OK people it's a ROCK I mean the idea of it OK yes but so anyway I rush past the Rosetta Stone— and you know in the gift shop they have Rosetta Stone mouse pads which I must admit is pretty funny —and I rush into the Elgin Marbles gallery and what started everything what struck me as I swung around the room what I really have to tell you—

(Stops abruptly. Quickly punches in numbers. Then resuming, but speaking less rapidly, seeing it. Gradually the phone slips away as if forgotten, as the museum takes shape for her, around her.)

All around the enormous room. A marble frieze. It would have gone around the top. At the Parthenon. At first glance a battle scene. Naked men in helmets, brutal short swords, furious naked centaurs slashing with sharp raised hooves. A mêlée. A rampage. A carnage. Greeks versus Centaurs. But a little closer and. The room was nearly empty. Just before closing on a rainy winter evening, the sky already black above the skylights, pure white light from spots glowing on the white marble. A Greek hand tangles in a Centaur's flowing hair. A Centaur foreleg presses into a taut Greek belly. A hoof nestles into the hollow beside a Greek's curly marble pubic hair. A delicately traced vein along an upraised arm, a velvety equine flank. A Centaur hand grasps a Greek bicep, fingers curling around the tense, swollen muscle as they gaze into each other's eyes, mouths open as if gulping for air. All around me, men and centaurs struggled, embraced, tenderly grappled. I couldn't. Fucking. Believe. My eyes. *(She's in the museum, standing, staring. A Englishman enters, also looking at the sculptures.)*

Oh my God, do you see it, do you? It must be intentional, don't you think? I mean it couldn't have been accidental, it must have been intended; I mean, oh, I mean, look at it, do you want to, uh, what do you Brits call it, how about a fuck? Don't be alarmed, I think it's the only reasonable response, I mean, all around us, in the world you know, sex and violence, sex and violence, from the trivial fun cartoon kind infused with shabby irony to the really really awful kind, the kind no one wants to have anything to do with, even the perpetrators must wish they could wake up, that raping people and killing them and mutilating their bodies could be a bad dream though I suppose that must be sentimental on my part or a failure of imagination but here, but this, but here we are with the pure erotic thing itself, the clean clean lines of it, you know, and don't we have to, don't we really just have to seize hold of someone and deal with that? Don't we?

(Slight pause.)

MAN: I'm sorry, what?

SALLY: You heard me.

MAN: Well, yes, I suppose I did. And you're quite right. So if you'll excuse me I'm going to go extricate my boyfriend from the Egyptians.

(He exits. The sound of echoing hoofbeats, and a centaur enters. He sees Sally; they approach each other and strike a pose from the frieze. He kills her and exits. A museum guard enters.)

GUARD: Closing time, all out please.

(Sally comes back to life.)

GUARD: You all right, miss?

SALLY: Sure. Sure. It's just, it's a world for Greeks and Centaurs. And what am I?

GUARD: *(Falling to his knees.)* A fucking goddess.

(Slight pause)

SALLY: *(To herself.)* No, no, no. Too much. Don't be ridiculous.

(The guard starts over as if for the first time.)

GUARD: Closing time. All out, please.

SALLY: Listen, can I just ask you—I mean, you're here every day, you see all this, is there any effect, does it cast a sort of spell on you, enflame any passions, you know, stir up any chaotic urges, of, you know, any kind?

GUARD: What, this homoerotic filth? Makes me want to go out and inflict some damage, yeah, stomp some fuckin' faggots, I'd take a spanner to this rubbish 'cept I need the job to pay my neo-nazi membership dues, why, what's it to you, you nosy cunt—

SALLY: Stop! This isn't it! I'm sure this isn't right.

(The guard starts over as if for the first time.)

GUARD: Closing time. All out, please.

(The centaur re-enters and attacks the guard. They grapple sexily while Sally watches. The centaur kills the guard and exits. The guard comes back to life.)

GUARD: Closing time. All out, please.

SALLY: No. No, I'm not ready to go. Give me a minute, I'm in the middle of, of . . .

GUARD: Suit yourself. Stay all night if you like. We'll lock you in with the sodding mummies, shall we? Place is haunted, you know. Tormented ghosts of the colonially vandalized. *(Scary haunting sound.)* Woooahhh. . . Frightened half to death, aren't ya?

SALLY: Well, no.

GUARD: Aw, sod off. My feet are killing me.

(He pulls out a hip flask, sits down on the floor and starts drinking. The centaur enters. Sally retreats. The centaur stalks Sally around and around the seated guard. Sally's terror mounts until she suddenly turns, goes back to the centaur, and kisses him. He kisses back. Then kills her and exits.)

GUARD: *(Starting over.)* Closing time. All out, please.

SALLY: *(Getting up.)* All right. All right. I'm going.

(She hesitates, looking.)

GUARD: Big fan of colonial vandalism, are you?

SALLY: Oh, no, but . . .

GUARD: Yeah, I know. It's something, isn't it?

SALLY: Do you get used to it?

GUARD: Well, yeah. Still . . . it sort of pulses at you in this light, doesn't it? Like it could come to life any minute.

SALLY: Yes!

GUARD: Be a mess if it did.

SALLY: Sort of a gorgeous sexy mess.

GUARD: Oh, well. You don't want to go romanticizing. It's only mythological, isn't it?

SALLY: *(Thinking about this.)* Huh.

GUARD: Anyway. Closing time. Fancy a drink?

SALLY: You're pretty mythological yourself, I think.

GUARD: Not a bit. Got a name and everything.

SALLY: What is it?

GUARD: James. See? There's never a myth called James.

SALLY: James. I'm Sally.

GUARD: Right. Sally. Meet you by the gift shop in ten minutes? I'll be the one on two legs.

(He exits. The centaur enters and approaches Sally again. Before he can kill her, she deftly takes his sword from him and holds the point of it to his heart. He surrenders beautifully. She hesitates. She is still thinking about it as the lights fade.)

END OF PLAY

Throwaway
by Sallie Bingham

To Julia Miles

BIOGRAPHY

Sallie Bingham is a playwright, novelist, short story writer, and poet who lives in New Mexico. Her first play, *Milk of Paradise,* was produced by Women's Project and Productions in New York City. Other produced plays include *Paducah* (Women's Project & Productions), *Couvade* (Actors Theater of Louisville), *In the Presence* (Goucher College, Baltimore, and St. Edward's University, Austin), *Hopscotch, The Awakening* (adaptation of Kate Chopin's novel) and *Piggyback* (all at Horse Cave Theater, Horse Cave, KY), and *In the Presence* (revised at Mill Mountain Theater in Roanoke, VA, where it won first prize in their new play competition).

CHARACTERS

    SHEILA

    JAY

    PENELOPE

    DAN

    FRANCES

    MIRIAM

    JOEY

TIME

The present.

SCENE

A bedroom and a porch.

AUTHOR'S NOTE

My aim as a playwright is the slightly sheepish laugh that proves a connection between the audience and what is happening on the stage. I believe people learn, and understand, more when they are laughing. I like to write about twisted-up families and wandering single people, all set in odd corners of a world gone mad.

    Throwaway addresses the question of magic: Can human frailty be cured by nonhuman means? Of course, a witch is never a witch; but Miriam, the grandmother, possesses the confidence that comes from knowing many secrets — the confidence which all the other characters, to a greater or lesser extent, lack. Therefore she provides, if not the solution to their problems, the glue that holds them all together.

    And Penelope, her granddaughter, may yet be saved.

THROWAWAY

SCENE ONE

The curtain rises on a dark stage. Pause.

SHEILA: The extension cord won't reach.

JAY: Want me to turn the lights back on?

SHEILA: No! I can manage . . . There. Get back in bed.

JAY: OK. *(Pause.)* Well?

SHEILA: You sure you really want to do this?

JAY: I wouldn't tell you I wanted to if I really didn't want to.

SHEILA: I know, but it's kind of painful.

JAY: Painful for who?

SHEILA: Well — for me. For one.

JAY: For one?

SHEILA: I think it might be kind of painful for you, too.

JAY: How come?

SHEILA: Look, I know how objective you are —

JAY: I try to be.

SHEILA: But — humanly speaking, for once —

JAY: Yeah?

SHEILA: I mean, you weren't part of any of this.

JAY: Look, I'm not going to start being jealous now . . . Start the thing, will you?

SHEILA: OK. Remember, though — will you? It was all a long time ago.
    (Screen lights up with a slide of a bride and groom, fifties style, leaving church in a hail of rice.)

SHEILA: Me, and Dan.

JAY: You look . . . pretty.

SHEILA: It was a pretty dress.
    (Need slide: a couple on a beach.)

SHEILA: Bermuda. Everybody used to go to Bermuda.

JAY: Looks overcast.

SHEILA: We had rain, the whole week. The trouble with rain — it seemed like we had to spend more time in bed. I mean, we'd been spending plenty of time in bed already, we'd been having snacks, drinks, meals, everything, in bed — they'd bring the trays up and leave them outside the door, they wouldn't even knock. Half the time, the food'd be cold by the time we remembered it.

JAY: What's wrong with staying in bed?

SHEILA: Nothing.

(Another slide: A Christmas tree.)

Our first Christmas. We'd just moved into that apartment on the Boston Common. There was a really big tree on the Common and Dan wanted to let it go at that. He didn't have good memories of Christmas. But Mother sent us all the old ornaments — little elves on skis, silver balls with initials on them

JAY: So you got your tree. You look happy.

SHEILA: I was fat! I went on a diet, right after Christmas.

JAY: You look pretty, though.

SHEILA: I weighed ten pounds more than I do now!

(Slide of a newborn infant.)

JAY: Well, it figures.

SHEILA: I wasn't pregnant, our first Christmas! We'd only been married two weeks!

JAY: Sorry.

SHEILA: I was a virgin when I married. You may find that hard to believe.

JAY: I didn't say . . .

SHEILA: People used to say that if a girl was promiscuous before she got married, she'd start again, afterwards. I didn't want Dan to have that on his mind.

JAY: You don't believe that now, do you? I mean, with Penelope —

SHEILA: I don't know whether I believe it or not. Sometimes, when I see the way my daughter is living —

(Slide of a woman holding a small child.)

JAY: That's Penelope, isn't it?

SHEILA: Six months old. When she sat on my lap, I'd put my nose in her hair — she had little short fluffy hair, pale, like the tailfeathers on a baby duck: and she smelled all . . . powdery, golden, sort of.

(Lights up. We see Jay and Sheila, sitting side by side in a folded-out sofa bed; Jay wears a golf cap; Sheila wears a flowered church hat. Both wear pajamas.)

JAY: Why'd you turn on the lights?

SHEILA: It's enough.

JAY: Enough, for who?

SHEILA: Enough for me.

JAY: You said you'd show me the whole bunch!

SHEILA: From here on it's only Penelope's birthday parties . . . That what you want to see?

JAY: I want to see it all — everything that happened to you, before I knew you . . .

SHEILA: I don't want to, Jay. It hurts, more than I thought it would. I haven't looked at those slides in years! The past — it's just — you know, it's a throwaway — like those yellow flyers they hand you at the supermarket . . .

JAY: I don't believe that.

SHEILA: Where's your past?

JAY: I've told you about that.

SHEILA: Two words, maybe three . . . That's fine! I don't want all those pictures of your past running through my mind. Besides, we ought to get up, dress. Penelope's coming to get her things.

JAY: So?

SHEILA: I don't think she ought to find us in bed.

JAY: She doesn't mind.

SHEILA: You talked to her about that?

JAY: Just to be sure she wasn't feeling funny about it.

SHEILA: I asked you not to talk to her about that!
    (Getting up, putting on her robe.)

JAY: Look, I have to talk to her.

SHEILA: I mean, our sex life is our sex life, even if —

JAY: I didn't go into details.

SHEILA: I should hope not! Get up! Put something on! Help me fold up this bed!

JAY: *(Getting up.)* She said she was happy to see us happy together.

SHEILA: *(Wrestling with bed.)* It sounds like you asked her permission.

JAY: If she'd said it bothered her, or something —

SHEILA: Then what? Here — help me fold this blanket.

JAY: I told you, from the start, I wouldn't do anything to make Penelope unhappy.

SHEILA: You left her, didn't you?

JAY: Look, we both agreed to the divorce. She wanted a fresh start.

SHEILA: Give me that corner! Didn't they teach you how to fold blankets in camp?

JAY: I never went to camp . . . Penelope tells me she's perfectly happy.

SHEILA: But you and Penelope have only been divorced six months!

JAY: She's your daughter. You both know how to make do.

SHEILA: I was always telling you two to get back together — get back together and have a kid!

JAY: I didn't want a kid. Neither did Penelope. Where're my pants?

SHEILA: Over there, where you threw them. Oh God, I wish you hadn't persuaded me to look at those slides!

JAY: I didn't persuade you, Sheila. You've been wanting to show them to me ever since you and I —

SHEILA: Got it together? Is that the expression?

JAY: Don't start acting your age. Look, you're upset. Come here. Let me hold you . . . *(He puts his arms around Sheila, who stands stiffly.)*

SHEILA: At least put on some clothes!

JAY: I've got my pajamas on . . .

(Enter Penelope, carrying a backpack.)

PENELOPE: Hey, you guys . . .

SHEILA: *(Backing off.)* Good morning, Darling. I didn't hear your key.

PENELOPE: Sorry. I need to get some things for my trip.

SHEILA: Let me help you.

(Begins to open bureau drawers.)

It'll be hot, in Mexico. You'll need your cotton prints.

PENELOPE: I don't have any cotton prints, Mom. I'll take these cut-offs —

SHEILA: You can't wear shorts down there! Men in that culture aren't used to seeing ladies in shorts.

PENELOPE: I won't be going anywhere, Mom.

SHEILA: Now, Honey, you never know . . . Take this blouse — pink's becoming to your shade of skin; even before you tan, pink won't make you look so —

PENELOPE: Blah?

JAY: I told you I'd foot the bill if you wanted to go to Club Med —

PENELOPE: Look, I'm going for a rest, right? Not for an instant replay.

SHEILA: Penelope, you sound so hard . . . What about these slacks?

PENELOPE: Hard?

SHEILA: Maybe determined is the word.

PENELOPE: I've got to go, haven't I?

SHEILA: What?

JAY: Of course you don't have to go. I just offered it as an idea, a sort of random suggestion. I mean, you've been working hard all winter —

PENELOPE: Is that it?

SHEILA: Honey, what else would it be?

JAY: I just thought, after all this snow, you ought to have a little change of scene . . .

PENELOPE: I'm not in the way, here?

SHEILA: Darling — how could you think — !

PENELOPE: I thought from the way you and Jay always wear your hats when I drop in —

SHEILA: Honey, that's just a mannerism!

PENELOPE: I thought you only put them on when I was coming.

SHEILA: Why would we do that?

JAY: We wear them all the time.

SHEILA: They're — they're kind of our badge.

PENELOPE: Badge?

SHEILA: Even at our age — at my age! — There are always possibilities . . .

PENELOPE: But Jay never played golf.

JAY: I might want to try it.

PENELOPE: And you haven't been to church in years!

SHEILA: I'm thinking about going at Easter. . . . Here, you'll want to take your leghorn — that Mexican sun is fierce!
(Pops straw hat on Penelope's head.)
Most becoming!

PENELOPE: You mean, even in bed —

SHEILA: We won't discuss that.

JAY: Let me explain. In bed, we're our real selves, we're kind of boiled down to our essence. There isn't any question in bed: I mean, I'm Jay, your mom's Sheila — even in the dark. It's different when the light's on.

PENELOPE: *(Removing hat.)* I don't think I'll need this hat, Mom.

SHEILA: That sun is terrible for fair skin! Take it, for my sake.

PENELOPE: I don't want it.
(Puts the hat back in the drawer.)
There — that's it . . . I have everything I need.

SHEILA: She's mocking us, Jay.

JAY: What?

SHEILA: In a very subtle way, she's mocking our insecurity. She's telling us she doesn't need a hat.

JAY: Oh, come on, now.

SHEILA: She's telling us she knows who she is.

PENELOPE: Look, Mom —

SHEILA: I've asked you not to call me that.

PENELOPE: Sorry, Look — She —

SHEILA: You picked that up from Jay!

JAY: Penelope heard me call you she ever since we were married.

SHEILA: Ever since who were married?

JAY: Penelope, and me —

SHEILA: That doesn't explain it. You used to call Penelope Lovebird. I don't call her Lovebird.

PENELOPE: Look, I'd be delighted to call you Sheila —

SHEILA: Everything isn't catching! Everything can't be catching! *(To Penelope.)* Your father used to call me Feather — I don't know why. You never call me Feather! Jay never calls me Feather! Certain things just can't be passed along!

PENELOPE: I'm losing the thread.

JAY: Look, if I can say something . . . I think your mom's trying to tell you she loves you.

PENELOPE: Is that it?

SHEILA: Darling, I'd do anything in the world to make you happy.

PENELOPE: But I am happy, Sheila.

SHEILA: How can you expect me to believe that, when I know what you've lost? *(Pause.)*

PENELOPE: You mean . . . Jay?

SHEILA: Of course I mean Jay!

JAY: Sheila, you astonish me sometimes.

SHEILA: I'm glad I still have the power! Oh, I know you two — you think you're the only ones who have the courage to speak frankly. But it's not so.

PENELOPE: Look, Mom, the traffic getting out to the airport is going to be terrible.

SHEILA: I just want you to know I understand.

PENELOPE: Please — don't.

JAY: Sure you've got enough cash?

PENELOPE: I can always cash a traveler's check.

SHEILA: And I want you to know I did everything in my power to prevent your divorce.

JAY: The banks down there are closed a lot. Here . . . *(Giving her money.)*

PENELOPE: Thanks . . . *(To her mother.)* Anything else?

SHEILA: *(Crumpling.)* I don't want you to go. I'll be all alone —

JAY: I'm here, She.

PENELOPE: Mom —

SHEILA: With Penelope gone . . . What'll we have to talk about, Jay?

JAY: Plenty of things, She! We've got to get the apartment painted — change the atmosphere, as you said. We've got to decide where we're going on our winter vacation . . .

SHEILA: But the substance, Jay! The emotional substance —

PENELOPE: I'll only be gone a week.

SHEILA: Honey — at least — just for me — take your hat!

PENELOPE: I can always get one down there, if I need it.

SHEILA: But Penelope, a Mexican hat — they have donkeys on them . . .
    (Penelope takes the hat.)

JAY: Good-bye, Penelope.
    (He embraces her, kisses her forehead.)
    Be good.

SHEILA: *(Embracing her.)* Good-bye, Darling! Remember, don't drink any water.
    And fruits in stalls — no matter how luscious they look —

PENELOPE: *(She shoulders her pack, leaves.)* Take care of her, Jay. Good-bye.

SHEILA: I feel like we've driven her out.

JAY: She wanted to go. She wanted a break . . .

SHEILA: Alone down there in a hotel room.

JAY: She'll go to the beach —

SHEILA: She felt she had to get out of our way!

JAY: Look, I raised that with her —

SHEILA: When do you have all these discussions?

JAY: She said she felt perfectly comfortable about you moving in here; she said
    it didn't bother her at all. She wants to get herself a studio apartment,
    down in the village. I told her I'd help her . . .

SHEILA: That proves it. She feels we don't want her here.

JAY: She's happy for us, Sheila. I don't like to say this, but you don't give Penelope
    credit.

SHEILA: Credit?

JAY: Credit for her generosity. You don't know how pleased she is we've found
    each other.

SHEILA: I don't know if I like that.

JAY: She knew for a long time it wouldn't work — I mean, our marriage.

SHEILA: Whose marriage?

JAY: Hers and mine. And as soon as that was clear to her — she wished me
    better luck, next time. You can't imagine how generous Penelope is.

SHEILA: Jay — tell me something. Aren't you still a little bit in love with her?

JAY: I admire her.

SHEILA: I don't think you admire me.

JAY: I can get close to you. With Penelope, there're always these drafts blow-
    ing around between us. Maybe that's the way it is, when you admire some-
    body. It lets in an awful lot of air.

SHEILA: I see what you mean . . . I'm starting to feel better, Jay.

JAY: Let's go out on the balcony and find a little patch of sun . . .

SHEILA: I'll fix us some Margaritas.

JAY: And then we can go have lunch at that new place you like . . .

SHEILA: With the pink napkins and the geraniums?

JAY: Yeah.

SHEILA: Maybe they'll have Salad Nicoise. I've been longing for anchovies. It's become almost an obsession. You know, when I was pregnant, I used to think all the time about oranges. I had a positive fixation on oranges! Dan brought me home oranges, every day, after work — but they were never the right ones. They had that dye on their skins, or they wouldn't peel, or they were sour . . . One day he even went to Brooklyn, because he'd heard about a fruit seller there who got his oranges from Majorca . . . You know what, though? Even those oranges from halfway around the world weren't what I was looking for . . . They didn't have any taste.

(Exit, arms around waist, for the balcony.)

(Lights out. On the screen, a slide of Dan, an eagerly smiling young man, holding out an orange. Curtain.)

SCENE TWO

The same. The bed has been replaced by a kitchen unit. At rise, Dan is seen standing at the counter in front of an open waffle iron. He is prying around the edges of the waffle with a fork.

DAN: Franny!

FRANCES: *(Offstage.)* I'm coming.

DAN: *(Prying at the waffle.)* I forgot to grease the waffle iron!

FRANCES: *(Offstage.)* What?

DAN: I forgot to grease the waffle iron! It's sticking! It's sticking all over the place!

(Enter Frances, dressed for work, carrying a briefcase.)

FRANCES: Problems?

DAN: All I've got is shreds!

(He removes shreds, pours in more batter.)

FRANCES: Don't worry about it, Dan. I really only have time for a piece of toast.

DAN: *(Pouring batter.)* I like you to have a good solid breakfast before you leave the house. I know what you have for lunch.

FRANCES: Only when I can't possibly leave the office.

DAN: Cottage cheese! How can you live on cottage cheese!

(Closes waffle iron.)

This one's going to be good.

FRANCES: I only want a cup of coffee.

DAN: You're drinking too much coffee. Five, six cups a day. It's terrible for the bladder.

FRANCES: I'm not having trouble with my bladder, not anymore.

DAN: Now look, Angel, it wasn't me fucked up your bladder. Frankly, I'm getting tired of the way you're always throwing it in my face. Even at breakfast.

FRANCES: All I know is I never had any trouble with my bladder before we got married.

DAN: Look, I had those tests. There's nothing in my . . . I don't have any germs, or whatever! Whatever you have you're giving to your self. It's that coffee — six, eight cups a day. That's a terrible strain on —

FRANCES: Look, would you just fix me a piece of toast? It's almost eight — the subway's going to be impossible.

DAN: We're out of bread.

FRANCES: Out of bread! How can we be out of bread?

DAN: That's why I'm making you waffles. This one isn't sticking. I don't think it's sticking. Of course I won't know for sure 'til I open the damn thing up . . .

FRANCES: How much longer is it going to take?

DAN: I have to wait 'til the light goes off.

FRANCES: What light?

DAN: The light on the waffle iron! You mean you never looked at the light?

FRANCES: It never occurred to me to look at the light.

DAN: You know every detail about health insurance, you can tell me just how much I can get to fix my teeth if something happens to them, you've got all forty one —

FRANCES: Forty-nine.

DAN: — Pegged in your mind, and you never even bothered to look at the light on the waffle iron.

FRANCES: Look, Darling, I've really got to get started. I know you wanted to make this a special breakfast —

DAN: Yeah. I did.

FRANCES: But really, the truth is, I want to get to the subway. Let's save the waffles for Sunday, OK? Sunday we can have breakfast in bed . . .

DAN: Look, just give me another two minutes will you? Two, two and a half minutes. The light's starting to fade . . .

(Doorbell.)

FRANCES: You expecting somebody?

DAN: No!

(Goes to the door; lets in Penelope.)

Why, Honey! I thought you were on your way to Mexico.

PENELOPE: Hello, Dad.

(They embrace.)

FRANCES: Good morning, Penelope.

PENELOPE: Good morning, Frances. I'm not disturbing you, am I?

FRANCES: I'm just about to leave.

DAN: *(At waffle iron.)* The light's gone off!

PENELOPE: What?

DAN: The light's gone off on the waffle iron!

FRANCES: Look, Darling, I can't stop now. You and Penelope divide it.

PENELOPE: I want to talk to you, Frances.

FRANCES: There's nothing in the world I'd rather do than sit down and have a really good talk. I've been thinking about you, as a matter of fact —

PENELOPE: I've been thinking about you, too.

DAN: *(Prying off waffle.)* There — perfect! What do you say to that! I used to get by with the mix but not anymore after I read what they put in it. Chemicals, preservatives — into plain old waffle mix! I said, to Hell with that. If I'm going to make waffles, I'm going to make the batter, from scratch . . . Penelope, here's the maple syrup (real stuff, Frances and I picked it up in the White Mountains last summer). Frances —

FRANCES: I really don't have any appetite.

PENELOPE: Look, Frances, I know this is inconvenient for you, but I need your help. You're in a kind of special position, from my point of view.

FRANCES: What?

PENELOPE: I mean, you're the only married woman I know.

FRANCES: Look, I don't pretend to be any kind of example.

PENELOPE: I want to talk to you both about my life.

FRANCES: Please, Darling, not before nine in the morning.

PENELOPE: I can't help what time it is. These things come when they come. I was in the taxi, I was on the way to the airport, like a good little sheep, following directions, doing what Mom and Jay planned, and then I saw this little tree growing out of a cement playground by the East River Drive. It was a nothing sort of little tree, it had about three leaves left at the top, and the branches looked stunted. But there it was, in the dead of winter, with its three leaves, growing up out of that concrete playground . . .

DAN: I'm going to make another waffle. *(He pours batter.)*

PENELOPE: And I said to the taxi driver, "Look, take me back, will you? Just turn around as soon as you can and take me back." And he said, "Where? Where you want me to take you back to? I thought you was going to the airport." And then I started to think about you two — the way you always have breakfast together, and Daddy always fixes something hot and makes you eat it — the last time I was here, he was making porridge —

FRANCES: Filthy stuff.

PENELOPE: And I said, Take me to my father's. He lives on East 84th Street. I want to see him and his wife, before I leave town . . .

FRANCES: So — what's it all about? Are you in some kind of trouble?

PENELOPE: No, the thing is — I'm worried about Mom.

DAN: What's the matter with her?

PENELOPE: She got scared when I was going out the door. She just kind of collapsed.

FRANCES: Look, Penelope, you can't sacrifice yourself to your mother.

DAN: She's got a case of insecurity nobody's ever going to cure.

FRANCES: I've known women just eaten up by that kind of thing — always nurturing, always taking care of some kind of —

PENELOPE: What?

FRANCES: Oh, just some kind of unhappy person. It can eat you whole!

DAN: Honey, the best thing you can do is to get out and let Jay handle it.

PENELOPE: I don't think Jay can handle it.

DAN: He's said he's going to redo your apartment. He's going to do all the painting himself. If that's not commitment —

PENELOPE: He doesn't understand Mom. She needs a lot of stroking.

DAN: Sure does. Here, have another waffle. This one is the right color — right texture, too. I'm getting the hang of this thing.

PENELOPE: No, thanks, Dad.

DAN: *(Shoveling waffle into garbage.)* Why is it nobody ever wants to eat in this house?

PENELOPE: *(To Frances.)* You see, I know Jay.

FRANCES: Of course you do.

PENELOPE: He's got the best intentions of anybody in the world. He'll be fixing up the apartment, breaking his back to get just the right shade of eggshell coral, or whatever, and Mom'll be saying it's fine, just fine, and she'll be starving to death, underneath, she'll be locking herself in the bathroom and running the faucets so he won't hear her crying.

FRANCES: What exactly is it she wants?

PENELOPE: She wants to be loved.

DAN: Look, Penelope, if that's what she wants, she's got it. I mean, Jay left you for her. What more proof does she need?

PENELOPE: Mom's like a sieve, it all runs through, she's got to have it piled up again every day.

FRANCES: I've got to get going.

PENELOPE: I think their sex life is kind of fucked up.

DAN: Don't tell me she's got bladder trouble.

FRANCES: Look, I'm going.

DAN: I always used to get her to drink cranberry juice. It really works.

FRANCES: Good-bye, you two.

PENELOPE: Frances, I need you.

FRANCES: Look — I'm not up for this kind of discussion. I mean, your mother's sex problems, before nine in the morning . . . it's just a little more than I can handle.

PENELOPE: Just ten more minutes. Then you can zip up your briefcase and go out to do battle with the world.

DAN: Frances, stay — the girl's asking you.

FRANCES: Look, exactly what do you want me to do about your mother?

PENELOPE: I want us all to get together.

FRANCES: What, all five of us?

PENELOPE: Yes, I want us all to get together and work this out. You know when an elephant is wounded, the other elephants all gather around and support it . . .

DAN: I don't think your mother would care for the comparison.

FRANCES: Where do you imagine this little get-together taking place?

PENELOPE: I worked that out in the taxi. I know how important place is . . . There's only one house that has the right feel. Grandma's.

DAN: You mean Miriam?

PENELOPE: Yeah. The old family place, in Knott County, Kentucky.

FRANCES: But from what your father tells me, your grandmother doesn't even admit your parents are divorced.

DAN: Whenever I bring it up, she just changes the subject, goes right on about birds, or mushrooms, or whatever.

PENELOPE: That's exactly why we ought to go there. Grandmother's a healer. She doesn't see the things that hurt in the world. She just sees the things that heal. She can help us — all of us, if we go down there to see her. The way she used to help me.

FRANCES: When are you planning for this to happen?

PENELOPE: Right away. I mean, it's Friday, we could get Mom's car and load up and be down there tomorrow.

FRANCES: Penelope, Knott County's another world. I've never even been there —

DAN: You're right. It's another world.

PENELOPE: That's exactly why we need to go. It'll be like a pool of clear water. We'll be able to see our reflections.

FRANCES: Our reflections?

PENELOPE: The way we really are, without all these distortions. That's what she did for me, the summer I was eleven: showed me my reflection.

DAN: It's getting on for blackberry winter, down there, we might even have some mild weather.

FRANCES: I don't even know what clothes to take.

DAN: I've been meaning to take you down to Knott County, but you're always so tied up.

PENELOPE: Look, I know how busy you are here, but if you could just for once let it all go . . .

FRANCES: You think your grandmother would accept me?

PENELOPE: Grandma accepts everything she sees.

FRANCES: Dan, do you think —

DAN: She'll love you, Honey.

FRANCES: I've always been curious . . .

PENELOPE: Look, I'm going to go over and get Mom and Jay organized. You two pack. I'll be back in, say, an hour. We'll meet you downstairs. I'll call Grandma —

DAN: Look, Honey, wouldn't you really rather go to Mexico?

PENELOPE: Rather go to Mexico than put this family back together? *(Exit.)*

FRANCES: Back together?

DAN: Well, you know, in a way, you could say we're all related.

FRANCES: *(Double take, laughs.)* I have to call the office . . . *(Curtain.)*

SCENE THREE

The porch of Miriam's house in Knott County, Kentucky. The next afternoon. At rise, Miriam and Joey are sitting, intent on their work on the table. They are wearing matching denim outfits. Joey has on a fisherman's hat into which he sticks his flies as he completes them. Grandma carefully adds them, like brooches, to the front of her dress. They work together meticulously, silently, each tying a fly on a tiny vise.

MIRIAM: There! That's the wings on!

JOEY: You sure they're the right shade of blue?

MIRIAM: I thought I'd make this one a little different.

JOEY: I'm sticking to what it says in the manual. We haven't caught a fish yet. It's too early to start experimenting.

MIRIAM: I think the manual is stingy.

JOEY: Stingy?

MIRIAM: Lacking in imagination . . .

JOEY: It's too early for imagination. We need to get the groundwork down first.

MIRIAM: I've always found mine works best at the early stages.

JOEY: Your what?

MIRIAM: My imagination. Wait 'til the late stages, and you know too much. It cramps your style. Now for instance, if I wait to try blue wings until after we've mastered this sport, I probably never will try blue wings because by that time I will have seen a lot of insects and none of them will have blue wings. So you see, it would cramp my imagination.

JOEY: You want to catch fish, don't you?

MIRIAM: Yes, I want to catch fish, but I also want to do it the way I like to do it. It was just the same way when I was learning about mushrooms. I used to pick every mushroom I could find, look it up in *The Golden Book of Non-Flowering Plants,* and if it didn't look like a deadly one, I'd cook up a mess on my hot plate and eat it. Now, I never got sick, not once, and nobody I served the mushrooms to got sick, either. But gradually I got to know more and more mushrooms, and then I bought a magnifying glass, and a big book and I started to see a lot more poisonous varieties. I was looking for detail, you see, and it's the detail that shows whether a mushroom is poisonous.

Pretty soon I couldn't see the forest for the trees. Why, the Death Cap looks just like an ordinary supermarket mushroom, except for that little ring around the stalk. Now, how would I have noticed that when I was just starting out? So, I started avoiding a lot more mushrooms, and it got to the point where I could hardly find enough mushrooms to feed myself . . .

It was the same thing with midwifing. First I worked from a library book called *Normal Childbirth* — it had diagrams and pictures and so on. But mostly I worked from feel. You can feel more from the shape of a laboring woman's womb than you can from anything else, just like you can tell a lot more about her condition from the color of her skin and the look in her eyes than you can from any plug-in tests. I used to deliver every child anybody wanted me to deliver, and I never had a blade of trouble. Breech cases, I'd just reach up and twist them around. Never had to cut, never had to call in a doctor. But then I went to the midwifery school down at the hospital, and they showed us a lot of horrible pictures of babies born wrong. After that, I got to be picky. Anything looked the least bit funny to me, I'd refuse the case. I lost my natural knack, you might say.

JOEY: Lordy, Lordy. What has gotten you started this morning? You were going it in the bathroom before you even brushed your teeth, you were going it over coffee, you kept right on through the scrambled eggs; I couldn't get a word in edgewise when we was washing dishes, and you are not finished yet.

MIRIAM: I have to start getting into practice. Dan called. Penelope's bringing them all down for a visit.

JOEY: I thought she was set up to go somewhere down south.

MIRIAM: She was. They arranged to have her sent out to Mexico but at the last minute, the poor thing revolted.

JOEY: Why'd she revolt?

MIRIAM: They were trying to get her out of the way. Parents are always trying to get their children out of the way.

JOEY: Penelope's grown.

MIRIAM: There's no limit to the selfishness of parents! That poor child was shipped off to Florida every winter just so her mother wouldn't have to get up and make breakfast!

JOEY: So . . . Did she tell you what she plans on doing?

MIRIAM: She plans on coming down here.

JOEY: By herself?

MIRIAM: She's bringing the whole kit and kaboodle.

JOEY: What about food! We've got to have food in the house!

(He stands up.)

MIRIAM: I thought we were going fishing.

JOEY: You can't have your whole family come down here and find nothing in the refrigerator but a mess of mushrooms and an old placenta you haven't gotten around to burying yet.

MIRIAM: Have to wait 'til the full moon or May'll start hemorrhaging again.

JOEY: Well, I'm going down and buy some eggs! Anyway!

MIRIAM: But I want to go fishing!

JOEY: You can wait and go fishing with your granddaughter. Somebody has got to get some food in the house!

(Exit.)

MIRIAM: No matter what you say about them, they're just little boys at heart. He couldn't get over me putting blue wings on my fly.

(Enter Penelope.)

Oh, Lord, Penelope — is that you, already?

PENELOPE: Grandma!

(She runs up onto the porch. They embrace.)

We got here as fast as we could. The others are down below on the path, helping each other with the suitcases.

MIRIAM: Suitcases! Penelope, my Lord! Get yourself right back down there and help your ma —

PENELOPE: She doesn't want my help, Grandma — not anymore, not since she's got Jay.

MIRIAM: Penelope, a daughter's job is never done — come along, now —

(They start towards exit as Sheila enters, dragging a suitcase.)

SHEILA: Ma, that hill is still impossible!

MIRIAM: You know we built on top to keep people away.

(She embraces Sheila.)

Honey, you're thin as a rail!

SHEILA: I have to keep up with Jay. Where can I put this?

MIRIAM: Why, put it right on in the guest room.

SHEILA: I'll just freshen up a little. That drive was a backbreaker.

(She exits into the house as Jay enters, carrying a suitcase.)

PENELOPE: Jay, you remember Grandma . . .

MIRIAM: Howdy.

(They guardedly shake hands.)

I ain't seen nothing of you since you and the girl here got hitched.

JAY: Why, I guess that's so, isn't it?

PENELOPE: Grandma!

JAY: *(Aside to Penelope.)* Don't go into all that now!

MIRIAM: Who else you all got with you? I see two more coming up the path.

PENELOPE: That's Dan, and his new —

MIRIAM: Dan? Since when you call your Daddy by his first name, Miss?

PENELOPE: I feel kind of foolish, at my age, calling him Daddy.

MIRIAM: There's plenty other things you can call him without going to his first name. Your ma would have a fit!

(Frances and Dan enter with suitcases.)

JAY: I believe I'll go freshen up.

(Jay exits quickly.)

DAN: Grandma! It's been a while —

(They embrace.)

MIRIAM: Sure has, Honey! Why, I believe you're better looking now than you was when I first seen you looking at my Sheila. I thought then you was one of the best-looking young cusses I'd ever come across, and now I swear, you're one of the best-looking OLDER CUSSES —

FRANCES: Dan —

DAN: Grandma, I'd like you to meet Frances . . .

MIRIAM: *(Suddenly formal.)* Pleased, I'm sure.

(They shake hands.)

Now, Dan — tell me, how is your cooking coming along? Last time you wrote me, you asked for my recipe for mudbottom pie. You made it yet?

DAN: Sure have, two or three times, but I don't believe it's got quite the same bite yours has —

PENELOPE: Grandma, we came down here to get some help from you.

MIRIAM: Why, what kind of help?

(Sheila and Jay enter from the house.) You all make me nervous, standing around staring! At least, sit down . . .

(Everyone sits.) Now, what in the world kind of help — ?

SHEILA: Ma, this was all Penelope's idea; we came all this way down here just to make her feel we do take her ideas seriously.

PENELOPE: *(Urgently.)* Grandma, the truth is, everybody in this family is so goddamned fucked up —

MIRIAM: Well, that's the truth.

PENELOPE: And I thought maybe you could straighten us out.

MIRIAM: I don't know about that, young lady. I don't do magic spells or anything like that.

PENELOPE: We don't need magic. We just need your secret . . .

MIRIAM: My secret, as you call him, has gone down to the store to stock up on supplies. He didn't think it right to entertain family on an empty icebox!

JAY: Why, Grandma, what are you telling us?

SHEILA: You didn't write —

MIRIAM: Don't worry, we don't plan to get married. He has his grandchildren to think of, and I have mine! We just live here together, keep each other company.

FRANCES: *(To Dan.)* Good Lord, isn't she a little old — ?

MIRIAM: Well, Miss, I don't know who you are but I guess you've got a right to your opinion. Only, I guess you might wait and ask my honey when he comes back whether I'm too old. I keep myself in pretty good trim. *(Suddenly, Miriam stands on her head.)* How's that, Miss?

FRANCES: Why, I didn't mean —

DAN: She'll hurt herself!

SHEILA: Ma, come down —

MIRIAM: *(Standing up.)* Just wanted you to see what I can do. It looks like you all didn't come for a visit, after all. And if we're going to have a conference, we might as well get started so we can finish with it before dark. *(She sits down. Others gather around.)* Now, before I can do a thing for you, you have to get rid of your trappings.

FRANCES: What's that?

MIRIAM: All them little doodads you carry around in your pockets and purses. You know what I mean!

JAY: Credit cards?

MIRIAM: That's the ticket! All that kind of thing . . .
(Slowly, they empty their pockets and purses on the table.)

MIRIAM: That's it! Now, don't hold anything back! Don't be shy!
(Jay lays out another card.) The rest of you sure that's all there is?
(Dan lays out another card.) Because I'm telling you nothing will work if you've still got one of them little doodads hidden away!
(Frances lays out a card.) That's it, young lady! Now, we'll just kind of mess these all up together . . . *(She stirs the cards on the table.)* Good. Now, that cleared the air! *(She sits down again.)*
Penelope, you start. What's the trouble, Honey?

PENELOPE: Well, you see, Grandma, since my divorce —

MIRIAM: I don't deal in divorces.

SHEILA: *(To Jay.)* She never has been willing to accept it.

PENELOPE: But Grandma, that's what started it all!

MIRIAM: I don't believe that, young lady! In sin you were conceived —

FRANCES: Oh God, not that!

MIRIAM: And in sin you flourish . . . So don't expect me to deal with your excuses. Get to the heart of the business! Is anybody sick? *(All answer no.)*

MIRIAM: Is anybody bankrupted? Run out of town? *(All answer no.)*

MIRIAM: Anybody lose a child? *(All answer no.)*

MIRIAM: *(To Frances.)* Are you a widow woman?

FRANCES: NO!

MIRIAM: And I know the rest of you ain't lost a man or a wife. It looks like to me, you're all just sour. Just sour as vinegar! It's common, this time of year . . . Blackberry winter, you know.

PENELOPE: But, Grandma, there are a lot of other troubles —

MIRIAM: Not worth talking about, Honey! You just make them big when you talk about them! You all just got the plain old sourness, married a few years, maybe, and it don't look so good anymore, or wandering alone too long. That's just as plain to cure as a wart or a freckle — just as simple as sin! *(She stands up.)* Now, I'm going to tell you what to say, and then you're going to say it. And believe me, you'll feel a whole lot better!

FRANCES: Do we have to?

MIRIAM: Yes, young lady, you do! And if anybody mutters a word or tries to choke it back — well, that just won't work at all! Every word has got to be spoken out clear if you want it to do you any good. Now: here we go: EENY. *(Silence.)* Didn't you all hear me? I told you to say every word I say loud and clear. All right, here we go again: EENY.

ALL: Eeny.

MIRIAM: MEENY!

ALL: Meeny.

MIRIAM: MINY!

ALL: Miny!

MIRIAM: *(Shouting.)* MO!

    (Joey enters with sacks of groceries.)

MIRIAM: That's it! Fine! Wonderful! Come here, Joey — let me show you off to these folks. I want you to meet Joey.

    (She leads him around, introducing him.)

    This is my daughter, Sheila, and her husband, Dan . . .

    (They shake hands.)

    This here is my sweet little granddaughter, Penelope, and her boyfriend, Jay . . . And this here is a lady —

FRANCES: Dan! How can you let her —

MIRIAM: What did you way your name was, Honey?

FRANCES: Frances Kirshorn.

MIRIAM: Well, that's a mighty fine name. I hope to get to know you better!

    (To Joey.) What you got in them sacks?

JOEY: *(Unpacking contents.)* Kale. Green onions. Turnips. Whole-wheat flour — And a chicken!

MIRIAM: Good! Now, let's just get started on making this dinner together. Miss Frances, take these onions, and go inside and chop them. *(She hands onions to Frances.)* Penelope, honey, you take the kale and wash it out real good under the pump. Sheila, Sweetheart, you take these turnips and cut off the tops . . . Dan, I want you to sift this flour, we'll make us some muffins. Jay, I believe you're old enough to know how to cut up this chicken . . . Now, I believe that takes care of everybody.

PENELOPE: But Grandma . . . What are we going to do?

MIRIAM: Why, Honey, we're going to eat!

(Grandma and Joey lead the procession into the house as . . . Curtain.)

SCENE FOUR

The same, late that night. Moonlight. Penelope enters, in pajamas, sits down on the edge of the porch. After a pause, Joey enters, coming from the outhouse.

PENELOPE: Who's there?

JOEY: Me. Who's that?

PENELOPE: Penelope. Sitting in the moonlight. I couldn't sleep — it was coming in my window like a blade.

JOEY: Well, I'm going on in . . .

PENELOPE: Wait a minute. I'm cold — hand me that shawl, will you? *(Joey hands her Grandma's shawl.)*
We never see the moon, in the city. Not that I miss it. I don't think about it, generally.

JOEY: You all planning on staying a while?

PENELOPE: I expect they'll want to be home by Monday. They work, you see — or some of them do. I don't.

JOEY: How do you live?

PENELOPE: Hand to mouth.

JOEY: I done that some, but it ain't wise. You get kind of crippled up inside. When I first met your Grandma, I was driving a truck part-time for the mines. Well, she had me on full time in a week. Don't know how she done it.

PENELOPE: Do you find her very demanding?

JOEY: Miriam? Why, no. Just do things her way, she's as sweet as a little red wagon . . .

PENELOPE: How long have you two been together?

JOEY: Well, let's see now. She was putting in her corn.

PENELOPE: Last spring.

JOEY: I was passing on the road, thought she maybe needed help. She took one look at me, and that was it. Told me right off to pack up and move in.

PENELOPE: Why did you?

JOEY: Living in a trailer at the time.

PENELOPE: That was the reason?

JOEY: I didn't know Miriam then. Thought she wanted the usual, which is not a bad situation for a young man on part-time work. But then it turned out she wanted the unusual, and I got interested.

PENELOPE: Which is?

JOEY: *(Finally sitting down.)* Nothing.

PENELOPE: Nothing?

JOEY: She don't want help, she don't want money, she don't even want the . . . other.

PENELOPE: You mean sex?

JOEY: You can call it that. I don't call it that.

PENELOPE: What do you call it?

JOEY: *(Jumping up.)* Hugger-mugger! But she don't want it. Just wants me to sit at that table, there, and work on them durned flies with her. Hasn't even been fishing, yet. Tell you the truth, I think she just wants me to listen to her go on. And she can go on! She can tell some stories! You know people around here claim she's a witch?

PENELOPE: She used to be kind of proud of that.

JOEY: Last time she delivered a baby, they claimed it turned into a bear. Her midwife business fell off pretty smart after that.

PENELOPE: You don't believe any of that stuff, do you?

JOEY: I believe what's convenient. When I'm mad at her because she won't make cornbread with drippings, I believe she turns babies into FROGS. Tell her so, too. She just laughs . . .

PENELOPE: Aren't you looking for something?

JOEY: What?

PENELOPE: Love, or something.

JOEY: I leave that for you people. I'm satisfied.

PENELOPE: Without any sex?

JOEY: Why, you all got plenty of that, and you look green as little apples! But I bet not a one of you has somebody to sit at the table with you and tie flies . . .Pretty blue-winged ones, too, like God himself never made.

PENELOPE: I don't believe I'd be satisfied.

JOEY: You ain't made to be satisfied. Look at all them little fine bones. Them fine little yellow hairs! You was made to rack yourself with every kind of worry, rise up in the morning to plead for night to come on. You're too little to do much else but keep yourself in shape, fuming about all the things you can't change. *(Softly.)* I hear you and that husband of yours split.

PENELOPE: Grandma tell you that?

JOEY: She don't believe a word of it. Cussed me out the time I tried to tell her . . . I read your ma's letters.

PENELOPE: Yeah, we split.

JOEY: Well, that's too bad.

PENELOPE: I don't know. I like my freedom.

JOEY: Now there's one thing you got a right to fuss about, and you ain't fussing. My God. What is a woman but a woman . . . My uncle used to say that.

PENELOPE: What does it mean?

JOEY: Damned if I know. You want a little hugger-mugger?

PENELOPE: Grandma would die!

JOEY: She don't care.

MIRIAM: *(Off.)* Joey! Come on in here. My feet are cold.

JOEY: That's another thing she likes me to do. Warm her feet. Well, let me know if you change your mind.

PENELOPE: Look, we came down here to get straightened out —

JOEY: Real foolish idea, if you ask me. What would you all do if you got straightened out? You wouldn't have nothing left to talk about.

(Miriam enters, in nightgown.)

MIRIAM: Joey, I tell you, my feet are cold.

JOEY: I'm coming.

MIRIAM: Go in there and warm the bed.

JOEY: It'll be hot like a potato pancake by the time you pop in.

(He exits.)

MIRIAM: That you over there in the dark, Penelope?

PENELOPE: I couldn't sleep.

MIRIAM: Not much point in sleeping, at your age or mine. I've done all the sleeping I need to keep me going for the rest of my life. And you haven't done anything to justify wasting the time.

PENELOPE: That's why I need to talk to you.

MIRIAM: *(Sitting down.)* And brought all those others with you. I was listening to them sleeping just now, and even the way they breathe tells me there ain't a thing I can do for them. They breathe regular as trains. Now people you can do something for, they draw one breath, like this, and then they hiccup or toss or something — they show you that way they are ready for change. Those in there, why they breathe like a fleet of locomotives! I wish to hell you hadn't brought a single one of them down here.

PENELOPE: I'm sorry. You know how I am. I get an idea and —

MIRIAM: Just promise me one thing. Haul them out of here tomorrow. I got to have my own house back by tomorrow night.

PENELOPE: So all that stuff with the credit cards —

MIRIAM: I had to do something, keep up my reputation. People around here find out the family came and went off empty-handed, it wouldn't be good for me, professionally. You know I advise a lot of people.

PENELOPE: Joey was telling me about that old witch stuff —

MIRIAM: That's fine.

PENELOPE: You mean it helps you?

MIRIAM: Draws in a lot of trade. Course, I had to quit working miracles — they was going to set the church on me. No more wishing off warts and waving off wrinkles, though you know as well as I do, if you can convince somebody they don't see it, they don't see it — at least for a while, and by the time they see it again, I've already eaten the chicken they brought to pay.

PENELOPE: Grandma, can you do something for me? I don't have a chicken to give you, though.

MIRIAM: Just promise me you'll haul them off.

PENELOPE: Even your own daughter?

MIRIAM: Your Ma is at that stage. She's not ripe and she's not raw. She'll be better later on, after she gets over thanking God for that fool she's hooked up with.

PENELOPE: So you do know.

MIRIAM: I see what I see. I may not admit to it.

PENELOPE: I think that's where all the trouble started.

MIRIAM: Well, then, you are a fool.

PENELOPE: Don't call me that, I might believe it.

MIRIAM: You never noticed what it was like before? The way your ma and that husband of hers had clammed up on each other? Why I never heard a word out of that man the entire time they was married! Just crawled to that office every day and crawled on home! Because neither one of you needed a thing he could offer. Now, with this new one he's got, he can do something for her because she can't do a damn thing for herself. Except get dressed, maybe. So Dan has found himself a goal in life.

PENELOPE: I'm more worried about my mother.

MIRIAM: She'll be fine soon as she stops trying to make everything all right.

PENELOPE: You mean she'll get to be like you and Joey?

MIRIAM: She won't be that lucky. But she may learn to hush up, and that'll be an improvement, for sure. That young man of hers ain't too bad. He knows enough not to complain.

PENELOPE: But how come I've been feeling so sick in my heart?

MIRIAM: Go on off somewhere. that'll do it.

PENELOPE: Just as simple as that?

MIRIAM: You keep staring at all these relatives of yours, it'll make you pie-eyed.

PENELOPE: Can I come down here and stay with you, Grandma?

MIRIAM: Ain't a blade of work for you here. And you'd be into it with Joey soon as my back was turned.

PENELOPE: You heard.

MIRIAM: I didn't need to hear. Truth of the matter is women prefer men that's been broke for them. Broke by a sister or a mother, that's the best of all . . .

PENELOPE: Sorry.

MIRIAM: Sorry about what? Joey's a good-looking boy. You'll find one of your own, after a while. And then you'll be down here fussing he didn't do this or he did do that. You need to find yourself some work, or a good hobby.

JOEY: *(Off.)* You coming, or not? This bed is about to burn up.

MIRIAM: *(Standing up.)* I'm coming.

PENELOPE: I guess this junket was just a complete waste of time.

MIRIAM: It was not. I got to hear that fleet of locomotives.

PENELOPE: Go home and get a job, or a good hobby. Forget the relatives, quit plying from door to door, from crisis to crisis. My god, what would be left? *(She puts her hand out into the moonlight.)* Just light, and my hand in it . . . *(She turns towards the exit as . . .Curtain.)*

SCENE FIVE

Early next morning. Penelope is asleep on the porch, huddled under a blanket. It is barely light; a rooster crows, off.

MIRIAM: *(Off.)* Burning me up! Man don't have a call to be this hot . . .
(She enters, wearing a nightgown.)
Whew! Need to breathe some fresh air . . . *(She sees Penelope.)* Now, if that ain't the dangest . . . See here, young lady — don't you believe in going to BED?

PENELOPE: *(Waking up.)* Why, Granny —

MIRIAM: Don't granny me! I ain't never been partial to it — least of all at six in the morning. *(Rooster crows again.)* You hear that varmint? He's saying the night's over — you done lost your chance for a decent sleep, laying out here in the cold . . . Who covered you?

PENELOPE: I don't know.

MIRIAM: That Joey's sweet on you. I bet he came out here with my good afghan . . . *(She snatches it up, looks at Penelope shivering, relents, wraps the afghan around her.)* Here, now, don't look so peaked . . . What's a man between a woman and her granddaughter? Less than moonshine. You look like you could use a good cup of something hot.

PENELOPE: I'd love that, Grandma. *(Miriam looks at her but does not correct her.)* You have some of that sassafras tea?

MIRIAM: Might have. Now, you comb your hair and wash your face while I heat up the water.
(They exit together. The rooster crows again, the light brightens; Miriam is heard singing and rattling pots in the kitchen. Frances enters, dressed, with her suitcase, and heads purposefully towards the exit.)

DAN: *(Off.)* Wait a minute, Franny! *(He enters, in pajamas.)* You can't just take off like that — there's no bus out of here for another hour anyway.

FRANCES: There's a spider in the corner of the guest room ceiling — it watched me all night! A great big black spider with long hairy legs! You wouldn't do a THING about it!

DAN: Oh Lord, Franny, what was I going to do? Knock it down with my bare hands? I'm a city person —

FRANCES: I'm getting out of here before this place catches up with me.
(She exits, pursued by Dan who is still arguing.)
(Penelope enters, having dressed. She hears the commotion and looks offstage, bewildered.)

PENELOPE: Granny, it sounds like some of your guests are leaving. You better come out here and see.

MIRIAM: *(Off.)* Let them go.

PENELOPE: I thought coming down here, just the sheer act of coming, would do us all some good.

MIRIAM: *(Entering with tea.)* Too much to expect. Honey. Some of these folks LIVE on trouble. They wouldn't know what to do with themselves if things straightened out.

PENELOPE: At least Frances and Dan seem to have worked things out. I mean, he takes care of her, and she works — that makes sense.

MIRIAM: Yes, it does. Too much sense, maybe. Here — drink this while it's hot. That's got sassafras root in it, and the old two-legged root they dig around here and send to China; sposed to be good for your natural urges.

PENELOPE: I don't believe I want any more of those.

MIRIAM: Puny as you look, and white, you could use some strengthening in your blood. Drink . . .

(She hands the cup to Penelope and watches her drink. Dan enters, running, and enters the house.)

What're you up to, in the name of God?

DAN: Got to get some clothes on, and catch her. She's heading down the road . . .

(He goes into the house.)

PENELOPE: Well, it did change some things for those two, maybe.

MIRIAM: Proved he'd run after her. That's always worth knowing. Here — drink that up.

PENELOPE: I expect Sheila and Jay will want to leave today, too. I guess I'm going with them.

MIRIAM: Not if you don't want to.

PENELOPE: Oh, I don't know . . .

MIRIAM: I know you don't, Honey, but you could pretend.

PENELOPE: I'd never do that. It wouldn't be honest.

MIRIAM: When you were little, you were such a sour little thing. I used to play this game with you . . .

PENELOPE: *(Remembering.)* Faces?

MIRIAM: That's it. *(She sits down beside Penelope.)* We'd put on all the different kinds of faces — sad *(She makes the face.)*, angry *(Penelope joins in.)*, greensick, ready to beat up the world . . . Now, the one I want you to try is this one that shows you know what you want even when you don't. *(Penelope tries several expressions but Miriam is not satisfied.)* Get your eyebrows to move a little, Honey — eyebrows tell a lot. And don't let your mouth just kind of hang . . .

(During this instruction, Sheila enters and stands watching.)

SHEILA: You two are up bright and early.

MIRIAM: I'm teaching your daughter how to fool.

SHEILA: Well, good luck.

MIRIAM: There's hot water on the stove if you want to wash.

SHEILA: I'm not even thinking about it. Penelope, we're starting home, just as soon as Jay can get himself organized.

(Dan enters, on the run with a suitcase. He is nearly offstage when Miriam calls him back. He returns, apologizing, kisses everyone, and exits rapidly.)

I didn't know Dan could move that fast.

MIRIAM: Never saw him move like that for you. I'm sorry, he — I didn't mean to draw blood. Let me pour you a nice hot cup of root tea.

SHEILA: *(Accepting cup.)* This got any of your potions in it?

MIRIAM: No.

SHEILA: You swear?

MIRIAM: Well . . .

SHEILA: Fess up, Mama. I never knew you to serve something hot that didn't have a spell in it.

MIRIAM: Why, it's just a little old happiness thing. Never does much good but it can't do any harm.

SHEILA: Happiness! *(She laughs.)* You are taking risks!

PENELOPE: Oh, Mom — it's not going to work, you don't have to be afraid.

(As Sheila, shaking her head, pushes the cup away.)

What did you put in it, Grandma?

MIRIAM: Just a little skunk cabbage juice, distilled by the light of the new moon. It's supposed to fix any kind of sourness.

SHEILA: Penelope, you better pack.

PENELOPE: I think I may stay on here a little.

MIRIAM: See — what did I tell you? Act like you know what you want, and before you know it . . .

SHEILA: But you were going to Mexico, Penelope — that's what we planned.

PENELOPE: I don't want to go.

MIRIAM: Let her stay on here with me, Honey. You've got your hands full.

SHEILA: Now don't you go belittling Jay.

MIRIAM: Why, he's my favorite of all the men you —

SHEILA: Hush, Mama!

PENELOPE: Mother, I know about all that — there's nothing to worry about.

SHEILA: Your grandmother always has to have her finger in every pot. Well, if you're determined to stay —

MIRIAM: Let's see that face, Honey.

(Penelope shows her mother a determined face. Miriam claps.)

SHEILA: Now, if you could show that face some at an employment agency . . . Why is it mothers can't do a thing with daughters?

MIRIAM: You have to let somebody else, some other woman, get in between, to soak up some of those rays.

PENELOPE: What rays?

MIRIAM: Why, all that love, Darling. It burns.

SHEILA: Just don't start hating me, Penelope. I couldn't stand that — God knows you have a reason.

PENELOPE: Have I?

SHEILA: The way some people would look at it, I took your husband.

MIRIAM: Never would have happened if she hadn't been ready to let him go.

PENELOPE: That's true. Jay's much nicer since he's been with you.

SHEILA: One thing I learned in this weary world: how to treat a man. *(She exits.)*

PENELOPE: What are we going to do, first?

MIRIAM: We already did first.

PENELOPE: Well, then — second?

MIRIAM: We're going to wash.

(She and Penelope exit. After a moment, Jay enters, half-dressed, arguing with Sheila, who is following him with the suitcase.)

JAY: You sure you want to leave her down here alone?

SHEILA: She won't be alone, Darling. She'll be with her grandmother.

JAY: That old —

SHEILA: Say it. I've thought it a thousand times.

JAY: *(Whispers.)* Witch.

SHEILA: *(Whispers.)* Witch.

JAY: *(A little more loudly.)* Witch!

SHEILA: *(Shouting.)* Witch! Well, I hope so — I surely hope so, I hope so with all my heart . . . *(She takes Jay's hand and they exit, laughing.)*

(Miriam is heard, off, singing, "Washed in the blood of the lamb." She enters, with Penelope; they are carrying a large tin tub of water.)

MIRIAM: Set it down here . . . Now, where is that soap? *(She takes it out of her pocket.)* Get the sponge — it's over there on the sill. Sponge gets nasty if you don't lay it out in the sun. All right, now — take off that thing and get it in this good hot water.

PENELOPE: *(Beginning to undress.)* What if somebody comes?

MIRIAM: There's nobody left — we run them all off.

PENELOPE: There's Joey.

MIRIAM: If he comes snooping around here, you just look the other way and he won't see a thing.

PENELOPE: *(Climbing into the tub.)* How does that work?

MIRIAM: By this time you must have noticed men don't see you if you don't see them.

PENELOPE: This feels good. *(As Miriam begins to sponge her back.)* What did you put in the water? It feels . . . prickly.

MIRIAM: Just a little something.

PENELOPE: More of that happiness stuff?

MIRIAM: I just said that to rile your ma. I'm terrible, that way — I can't stop myself goading her. Guess I need a dose of something myself to get rid of my evil. *(She begins to sing "Washed in the Blood of the Lamb" as she continues to wash Penelope. Joey enters, carrying his fishing pole. He stands watching for a beat, then exits quietly.)* See what I mean?

PENELOPE: What?

MIRIAM: He's come and gone, and you never seen him.

PENELOPE: How do I know he didn't see me?

MIRIAM: Maybe he did. A cat can look at a queen. Now, don't mistake me, Honey: I'm not aiming to let you have Joey. He can look as much as he wants, it's me he'll be warming up tonight . . . *(Shivering.)* Snow coming, I can feel it.

PENELOPE: You're washing me like there's something to wash off.

MIRIAM: That sickness you brought here.

PENELOPE: Sickness?

MIRIAM: You weren't born with it, and you sure didn't catch it here. I fumigate this house every week to run it off. You caught it up there in the city. I smelled it on you the minute you walked in the door.

PENELOPE: I smelled!

MIRIAM: Sour. Real sour. I knew then . . . *(She take a packet out of her pocket and sprinkles some powder in the bathwater.)* you'd need this.

PENELOPE: What is it?

MIRIAM: The root of the tree that grows in the center of the world. I don't have much to teach you, Honey, and that's the honest truth — but if you'll let me wash you in this water you'll feel better for a few minutes, for sure. Now . . . *(As she bathes her.)* just pretend this is your day . . . Your time.

The time of your time. The time that won't come again. Just lay there in the warm water and count your fingers and toes. You'd be surprised how much pleasure you can take in your bodily parts once you start noticing . . . Washed, just washed in the blood of the lamb. *(She continues to sponge and sing as . . .)*

END OF PLAY

Rowing to America
by Kitty Chen

This play is dedicated to all women
who have had to diminish themselves or been
diminished to preserve the harmony

BIOGRAPHY

Ms. Chen is an autodidact and the recipient of playwriting fellowships from the National Endowment for the Arts (1992–1993), New York Foundation for the Arts (1989 and 1998), Emerging Playwrights Award (Urban Stages), among others. She is a member of Dramatists Guild, the Women's Project, and the three actors' unions.

Blessings of Chairman Moo (work-in-progress), a dark comedy about embalmment and totalitarianism, read at Ma-yi/Vineyard (twice) and Women's Project, for which she received 1998 NYFA.

I See My Bones (1994), about aging and hope. Produced, Urban Stages, 1997. Developed, Playwrights Theatre of NJ, Madison, 1995. Read and workshopped, Playwrights Preview Productions and the Women's Project. Toured NYC libraries 1995.

Eating Chicken Feet (1992), a comedy about divorce, abandonment, and the abasement of Chinese women. Coproduced Off-Broadway in 1993 by Women's Project and Pan Asian Repertory, and in 1997, Kumu Kahua Theatre, Honolulu. Readings: East-West Players (LA), the Women's Project (NYC), Westside Theatre (NYC), Playwrights Theatre of NJ, all in 1992. Finalist for the 1992 Humana Festival. Published by Dramatic Publishing Company.

Rosa Loses Her Face (1989) produced March 1997, Luna Stage, Montclair, NJ. Library tour with Urban Stages 1997 and 1998. Readings: Playwrights Preview Productions, Manhattan Theater Club, Hudson Guild, and Double Image. It is being translated into Egyptian for the theater journal *Al Masrah*.

On Good Terms (1986) (the basis for *Eating Chicken Feet*), read at Second Stage, NY, and Summer Solstice, Amagansett.

Body Parts Trilogy: 3 Short Metaphoricopsychoanatomical Plays. Comprised of *A Change of Heart, So To Speak* (Pegasus, Dallas, Love Creek, and New Georges, NYC); *She's Not My Relative* (readings Ma-yi, the Women's Project); and *Taking It Under the Chin* (reading the Women's Project). *Rowing to America* (produced PTNJ and Immigrants Theatre Project at Lower East Side Tenement Museum; published by Dramatic Publishing Company; to be published in anthology by Smith and Kraus). *If I'm All Grown Up* (the Women's Project). *Looking for Lottie Newmar,* Roots and Branches.

Born in Shanghai, China, and raised near Philadelphia; came to New York City after receiving a BA in math from Brown University. Scholarship student at Martha Graham School and later a professional actress for many years. Reader/panelist for the NEA, NYFA, NYSCA, NJCA, and Bronx Arts Council.

ORIGINAL PRODUCTION

Directed by John Pietrowski at Playwrights Theatre of New Jersey, 1997.

GIRL . . . . Millie Chow
SISTER . . . . Felicia Wilson

CHARACTERS

GIRL: About twelve, bright and inquiring, an enchanting, playful quality; she is special.

SISTER: About seventeen, serious countenance interrupted by an astonishingly beautiful smile; more mature and responsible than her years.

NOTES

Both characters may be played by older actors who have an intrinsic youthfulness. They should be Asian, African, or Latino, but the two need not be the same race. They must be totally comfortable with the lyrical, nonnaturalistic speech and physical style.

A heavy dramatic interpretation should be avoided, as should any temptation to ennoble, politicize, or victimize these characters and their situation. They are women in a tough situation who have the imaginative power to see their way out.

There is a magical, playful quality about this world. Simplicity and clarity should be the guiding principle.

ROWING TO AMERICA

SCENE ONE

The stage is bare. The sky is midnight blue, with a crescent moon and a few stars, the sound of waves slapping the side of a boat. Girl sits on a simple box or bench, rowing with oars. if possible, real ones. All objects may be mimed or suggested. She is a little weary. Sister is in shadow.

GIRL: I'm rowing to America. The only thing I brought with me is a picture of a smile. Here in my head. Strong and radiant like the sun. The smile of my sister.

"When we grow up and go to America, everything will be all right," she would say to me. She told me all sorts of things about America. Have you heard them too? She said the streets are paved with gold lamé. A dollar a day keeps the doctor away. Apple pie and huckleberry finn for breakfast. Milk and honey flow down the avenue Fifth Avenue. A chicken in every pot-pie. Where the sun never stops shining, and spacious skies are blue, and amber grains are always waving at you . . . When we get there, we will wave back. Look, Sister — they're come to greet us! Hello! We're here — we've come to America —

(Lights come up on Sister, who is waving Girl away.)

SISTER: GO! Please go! You'll understand when you're older. Now row! And sing! For me!

GIRL: Don't leave me!

(Lights fade on Sister. Girl watches until she disappears from sight.)

All right all right! I'll row — I'll sing! *(Sings and rows.)*

Row row row your boat,
gently down the stream,
merrily, merrily, merrily, merrily,
life is but a dream . . .
Row row row your boat,
gently down the stream,
merrily, merrily, merrily, merrily,
life is but a dream . . .

I'm tired. I wonder how far America is. Maybe I'll wash up. You must always look your best, sister said. What if I should suddenly run into America without warning?

(Sister appears and combs Girl's hair.)

     I catch the rainwater to drink and wash my face and my hands. I've learned to be like a cat. It's important to stay clean and neat. She would comb and braid my hair with her strong quick hands. Two neat fat braids, like sausage twins. She never pinched or pulled, the way Mother did.

(Lights brighten. Girl breaks away from Sister, laughing. They are younger.)

SISTER: Hah! Now I've got you! If you don't sit still, I'm going to pinch and pull your hair so hard you will long for Mother to pinch and pull!

GIRL: You would never hurt me.

SISTER: No. I would never hurt you.

(Sister gives her a sudden pinch, they both laugh.)

GIRL: You're smiling! I made you smile! The sun has come out! Why don't you smile all the time? Like you used to.

SISTER: I'm not as I used to be. Soon I will no longer be young. When a girl is no longer young, they take away . . . *(She pauses.)*

GIRL: What do they take away? You look so sad.

SISTER: When you're older you'll know. Now sing my favorite song! About the little fishermen.

GIRL: Only if you smile. I want to count your teeth! How I wish I had your shining teeth. Like a string of the finest pearls.

(Sister gives her a huge, goofy smile. Girl laughs in delight.)

     Will you pinch and pull my hair when we go to America?

SISTER: Of course. When we grow up and go to America, everything will be all right. Now warm my heart, dear sister. But softly. For safety's sake.

GIRL: *(Sings.)* Wynken, Blynken, and Nod one night
Sailed off in a wooden shoe,
Sailed on a river of crystal light
Into a sea of dew.
"Where are you going, and what do you wish?"
The old moon asked the three.
"We have come to fish for the herring fish
That live in this beautiful sea;
Nets of silver and gold have we!"
Said Wynken, Blynken, and Nod.

(Lights change back. Sister recedes into shadow.)

GIRL: Where is your smile now, dear sister? Does it still hurt?

SISTER: Row.

GIRL: I better row.

     Row row row your boat

gently down the stream
merrily merrily merrily . . . *(Etc.)*
(She sees something float by.)
Oh. Another piece of paper!
(She fishes (mimes) a magazine out of the water.)
(Reads.) "Among the universe of component CD players, it seems sense-
less to buy a single-play model for $100 when it's possible to buy a changer
for as little as $125." The "universe of component CD player." What does
C-D stand for? *(Searches page.)* The D is for disk. The C is for . . . cos-
mic? What else could it be? A universe of cosmic disks.
(Sings.)
Hello, Moon
Good night, Moon
I row by your light
I sleep in your arms
I sing to your charms
A cosmic disk in the sky.

A thrill of hope
A glow of hope
I keep on rowing
But why am I going?
Hello, Moon
Good night, Moon
Good night, Moon. Good night.

SISTER: "Such a lovely voice — it made you feel," they always said. "Better
not to sing too much."

SCENE TWO
Girl catches a fish.

GIRL: Come on, little fish. What's the use of fighting? I'm famished! Aha! Now
I shall wrap you in seaweed, and what a tasty sandwich!
(She watches the fish thrash in the moonlight.)
Pearly little fish. How can I eat you? *(Starts to throw it back.)*
SISTER: Eat! — or you will not live to see America.
GIRL: I have to eat you. Forgive me!
(She proceeds to eat it. She sees another magazine float by.)

More paper! "Tests show how you can eat real eggs again. Egg World's eggs are better than other eggs." WHAT DOES THAT MEAN?!! Why can't people in America eat real eggs? What are real eggs? Why do they need tests to show how to eat an egg?

SISTER: Always so many questions! You must row!

(Girl, annoyed by ad, turns the page.)

GIRL: "Lascivious Lucy lurks in every lustful heart. Call 1-9-0-0-L-U-S-T-F-U-L." *(Horror turns to curiosity. She examines Lucy's face.)* Her smile. It's so false! It makes her ugly!

SISTER: It's a custom in many countries, when a young girl is no longer young . . . they take away her crowning glory, her greatest gift . . .

GIRL: IT HAS NO STRENGTH.

SISTER: They take away her strength. That way people will love you more and fear you less.

GIRL: People will love you more if you have no strength? That doesn't make sense.

SISTER: One or two modest gifts in a girl is safe. But to shine like a star, is to arouse Fear. Envy. Lust . . . And disrupt the harmony.

GIRL: We should get more love! Make more harmony!

SISTER: This is how it is!

GIRL: HOW do they take away our gifts?

SISTER: Peoples of all countries have devised their own way. It is always painful.

GIRL: *(Fearful.)* Me too? What will they take away from me?

SISTER: Shhh. Not you, my dearest heart. I won't let them hurt you.

(Sister fades into shadow.)

(Girl sits quietly staring, as if at her past and future. Sounds of wind and rough seas grow. She starts up as if from a dream.)

GIRL: WHERE ARE YOU TAKING HER? Then I heard my mother's voice. "Go to sleep, we're taking a walk." I am not a child! We don't take walks in the middle of the night. *(Looking out window.)* My sister, my mother, and all the other mothers march across the moonlit field, like a procession of ravens . . . smaller and smaller. I wait by the window all night. Deep inside me, in a place that has no name, I begin to feel afraid.

(Morning. Sister enters.)

They're coming back. Why is that old woman wearing my sister's clothes? Her body bowed in pain, mouth split wide in silent grief. It's Sister! She lifts her head to look at mother. I see . . . not the moonlight glistening against her teeth . . . but blackness. Her mouth . . . HER MOUTH IS EMPTY! SHE HAS NO TEETH!

(Lights change. Girl bangs on a door.)

Please let me see her. I won't disturb her rest. I WANT TO SEE HER! I hate you, Mother! How could you do that to her — your own daughter? *(Pause.) Your* mother? *(Pause.)* When *you* were no longer young? *(She begins sadly to understand.)*

(Lights change. Sister enters.)

SISTER: They gave me false teeth, cast from a mold of Little Brother's mouth. Now I am ugly and invisible.

GIRL: *(Touches her mouth.)* No, my precious sun. You are beautiful. Does it still hurt?

SISTER: Harmony is preserved, the people are safe.

GIRL: I hate the people! I hate their harmony! Their harmony is wrong!

SISTER: Hush. Come quickly.

(They run to the boat.)

GIRL: America?

SISTER: Yes. Good-bye, dear sister.

(Sister hugs her fiercely for a long time.)

GIRL: Wait! No!

SISTER: GO! Do as I say!

GIRL: No! Not without you!

SISTER: It's too late for me. You're still young and whole.

GIRL: I won't go without you!

SISTER: Do you want them to slit your throat? Turn your larynx to a hard knot of scar tissue? Smother your voice forever?

(Girl starts to cry at Sister's harsh assault.)

GIRL: You said you would never hurt me.

SISTER: Please forgive me, dear sister.

(Sister pushes the boat off. They stand in exact same postures and relationship as in first scene.)

GO! Please go! You'll understand when you're older. Now row! And sing! For me!

GIRL: Don't leave me!

(Sister fades from sight. Girl sits, starts to row.)

GIRL: I'm rowing to America. Where the streets are paved with gold lamé, and I can shine like a star. But deep inside, in a place that has no name, I feel the sun has died.

(Something floats by.)

Another American shopping paper. Every day, I see more and more. I must be getting closer.

(She flips through. She stares at a picture.)

It's her smile! My sister's smile! *(Reads.)* "Smile whenever you like! Never feel self-conscious about less than perfect teeth. Get laminated!" I'll get her smile back for her — I'll take it back to her! You can get anything in America!

(Rows with renewed spirit.)

I'm rowing to America. I'm doing it for her!

(Sings.)

Smile, smile, whenever you like.

In America everybody smiles.

It is good if you smile.

If you smile, you are good.

(Repeat verse.)

(Lights of city skyline appear and grow bigger and brighter.)

Look, Sister. Look at all the lights. Shining like your smile. You haven't left me. I see it everywhere. All around me like the sun. Here in my head, and in my heart.

SISTER: Good-bye, little sister. Please forgive me.

(Sister exits.)

GIRL: They've come to greet us! Hello! — We're here! We've come to America! . . . Now everything will be all right.

END OF PLAY

Sentences and Words
by Cynthia L. Cooper

Dedicated to the many who work quietly
to bring about change

BIOGRAPHY

Cynthia L. Cooper has written nine full length and a dozen short plays, which have been produced across the United States, as well as internationally. *How She Played the Game* was produced off-Broadway by the Women's Project and by Primary Stages, and in Boston, Reno, Vancouver, Budapest, Helsinki, Los Angeles, and schools, colleges, theaters, and museums. *Sisters of Sisters* was produced in Minneapolis, Kansas, and New York; *Dirty Laundry* in Denver, New York, and Minneapolis; *Beyond Stone* in New York at Lincoln Center's Clark Theatre; *Slow Burn and Strange Light* at Wings Theatre in New York; *The World at Your Fingertips* (co-author) at the Promenade in New York and twenty states; *Comrades in the Kamasutra Zone* at West Coast Playwrights. Several short plays have won awards, including *Fox and Hounds,* winner of the Off-Off Broadway Short Play Festival, and *Works of Art,* winner of the Nantucket Short Play Festival. Twice a Jerome Fellow at the Playwrights' Center, her work is included in ten anthologies, including *Women Heroes, Hit the Nerve, The Great Monologues from the Women's Project, Baseball Monologues.* She is a journalist in New York City who has written for *Ms., Women's Enews,* and numerous other publications and is the author of several nonfiction books, including *Mockery of Justice: The True Story of The Sheppard Murder Case,* featured on *Dateline NBC* and made into a CBS TV movie. She is a member of the Dramatists Guild and Authors Guild.

ORIGINAL PRODUCTION

Sentences and Words was produced at La Mama La Galleria by the Women's Project. Original cast list:

Karla . . . . Betty McKinley
Maggie . . . . Susan Peters
Director . . . . Gail Noppe-Brandon

CHARACTERS

KARLA: A lawyer, mid-thirties.
MAGGIE: A teen's mother.

TIME
Now.

PLACE
A small community in a "death" state.

SENTENCES AND WORDS

A woman stands on the porch of a house that crosses between ramshackly and neat. The setting is small southern Ohio town, which is more southern than northern, and more rural than populated. The woman on the porch, Karla Jackson, wears a suit, glasses, blouse, and heels. She carries a purse and a little file folder.

Karla walks up to the door. She bangs loudly on the door several times.

KARLA: Mrs. Denton! Mrs. Denton, I know you're in there.

(There is no answer.)

(Karla looks at herself and quickly takes off her shoes and exchanges them for beat-up loafers that she is carrying in her purse. She takes off her jacket and stuffs it away in the same purse. She knocks again.)

Mrs. Denton. I'll stay here all night if I have to.

(Karla bangs again, profusely. Now, she becomes conscious of her hair and ruffles it. She takes off her glasses and puts them away. She bangs again!)

MRS. DENTON!

(The door opens. A furious Maggie Denton stands at the doorway. She is dressed in a very unfancy skirt with a shirt over it. The shirt hangs outside the skirt. She seems a bit disheveled although she has attempted to be neat.)

MAGGIE: Get away from here. Get AWAY!

(Maggie quickly slams the door.)

(Karla, undeterred, immediately pulls her shirt out from her skirt.)

KARLA: I've got to have a word with you, Mrs. Denton. Tomorrow's the hearing date. For the sentencing. And I've got to talk to you before then.

(Maggie opens the door one more time. Karla, immediately, and with determination, puts her foot into the door opening to prevent Maggie from slamming it shut again.)

MAGGIE: You get away or I'm gonna tell my husband to chase you away. You saw what he did last time.

KARLA: He's gone, Mrs. Denton. I saw him drive away. This is just something for you and me.

MAGGIE: We don't have nothing between us, Lady. Nothing.

(Maggie tries to slam the door and to push it shut. Karla's foot does an admirable, if painful, job of preventing the door from closing entirely. Karla speaks through the slight opening in the door.)

KARLA: This is a death state, Mrs. Denton. You know what that means, don't you?

MAGGIE: I know what you did in court. I heard what you said about my Tommy. And that was plenty enough for me. Standing up for that dirty old FILTHY OLD SCUZZY OLD SLIMY ROTTEN NASTY DISGUSTING Franklin Miller. I seen plenty.

KARLA: Don't stop, please. Tell me. More. I want to hear.

MAGGIE: You're a whore.

KARLA: You can call me Karla.

MAGGIE: I ain't calling you nothing.

KARLA: May I call you Maggie?

MAGGIE: I'm gonna call the sheriff, you don't get off my porch.

KARLA: I don't think so.

MAGGIE: You don't think what?

KARLA: I don't think you like the sheriff any more than I do.

MAGGIE: You think you know so much. All that education you got.

KARLA: Look, Maggie. My foot's about to break. You know that defending Mr. Miller was my job. It's my job tomorrow at the sentencing. I'm not pretending anything different. All I want is one minute of your time.

MAGGIE: He never give Tommy one minute. One minute my Tommy's pitching stones into the field and the next minute he's stabbed behind the shed.

KARLA: You don't have to talk. We can sit. I just need to sit with you before I go back into that courtroom tomorrow. Is that too much to ask? Please? *(Emotionally.)*

MAGGIE: My husband wouldn't allow nobody like you in the house.

KARLA: On the porch then?

I'm begging you, Maggie. I know your husband won't speak to me. But, one day, in the courtroom, one day you were sitting in the back, and I turned around, and you looked me straight in the eye, and we started to say something that day, just you and me, something silent, something that hasn't been said, and I just have to finish that off.

MAGGIE: I don't recall none of it. If there was any such thing, I probably was making a prayer for you, lady.

KARLA: Will you do it again, then? I know you're a real kind-hearted woman. Maggie?

MAGGIE: One minute.

(Maggie reluctantly steps out on to the porch.)

KARLA: Thank you, ma'am. Thank you very much.

(They sit on a soggy couch and moldy chair set out on the porch. There is silence.)

KARLA: I do have one thing to say.

MAGGIE: You said we didn't have to say nothing. I'm not much for talking with you, lady.

KARLA: Okay. If you could just listen. I'd like to talk.

MAGGIE: I'm just going to pray like I agreed to. That's all. You can say whatever you like, but I'm just going to pray.

KARLA: I'll make it real short. The judge set tomorrow for the sentence. Now, you know, this is a death-penalty state. And the judge could sentence Mr. Miller to die. Or he could send him to prison for the rest of his life.

MAGGIE: I'm praying.

KARLA: And as Mr. Miller's attorney, I'm asking that he be sentenced to prison, Maggie.

MAGGIE: I don't have no use for that man. I don't care what they do with him. I don't ever want to hear his name again.

KARLA: And the judge said . . . ahh . . . he said that he would leave it to the family about the death penalty. He said if someone from Tommy's family came forward at the hearing and said that Mr. Miller should not get the —

MAGGIE: I said I didn't ever want to hear his name again.

KARLA: You've known Franklin Miller a long time.

MAGGIE: Too long.

KARLA: Thirty years, I think. I remember something from the file. I thought you might have some feeling of sympathy toward him.

MAGGIE: Towards him! I don't have no feeling of nothing towards him. Let him rot in a pit with birds pecking at his bones, for all I care.

KARLA: You don't care if he's executed?

MAGGIE: NO. NO. I DON'T CARE. AFTER WHAT HE DONE! You want me to care about THAT! I DON'T CARE. ALL I WANT IS MY TOMMY BACK. THAT'S ALL.

KARLA: All right, Maggie. Okay. See, that's it, then. It's okay. I felt I had a duty to ask. Since that was the condition the judge set . . . I had to try. I hope you understand.

MAGGIE: I don't understand nothing, lady. NOTHING.

KARLA: Karla. I'm Karla.

MAGGIE: You want to know what was I thinking that day, lady?
I was thinking I was glad I didn't have some big-time education so that

I didn't have to stand up there like you and defend a dirty vile rotten old man that killed my thirteen-year-old boy. That's what I was thinking.

KARLA: I see.

Sometimes it's not so easy. Especially . . . I know this doesn't make much sense . . . but Mr. Miller — I mean I don't say that there was anything right about what happened — but now I've gotten to know him. He's a friend . . . in a way. Maybe I just hate to see people die. Especially clients. Kind of makes me feel like a failure. Like that big-time education isn't worth a tire track in the mud.

MAGGIE: Comes with the territory, I imagine.

KARLA: I've never had it happen before. You know, that a client was sentenced to death. Can't make sense out of it.

MAGGIE: There's no sense in this world, lady. If there was any sense in this world, Tommy would be hollering out back right now.

KARLA: *(Preparing to leave.)* Yes. *(Standing.)* And one thing, Mrs. Denton . . .

MAGGIE: I've had enough.

KARLA: I did want to say — while I'm here, and all — I want to say, I'm very sorry. About Tommy.

MAGGIE: You're a liar!

(Turns as if to spit.)

KARLA: What? This is too much. I AM SORRY ABOUT YOUR SON. Good evening, then.

MAGGIE: *(Grabbing her.)* Why you telling me that now, lady?

KARLA: What do you mean?

MAGGIE: No body said that. *(Emotionally)* Not no body.

KARLA: Said what?

MAGGIE: "Sorry." I can't hardly believe it myself. Sure, he wasn't no saint. But nobody said they was sorry. Not the funeral man. Not the sheriff. Not the judge. Nobody sitting down there at the county. And nobody 'cept one church lady come knocking out here neither to say their sorries.

(Karla reaches out to Maggie.)

KARLA: Maggie . . . I am sorry. And other people — were. People . . . just plain act . . . stupid . . . sometimes.

MAGGIE: He had a little trouble. So'd his daddy, once or twice. We don't belong to no country clubs or nothing. But they don't have to treat us like we're some trash and it don't mean nothing to us . . . do they?

KARLA: Listen to me: You didn't deserve to be treated that way.

MAGGIE: I just want to die, lady. I didn't tell no one this. Not even my husband. I just want to die as soon as have all those cold-hearted people talking about my baby and asking questions and have Tommy gone like this.

KARLA: Please. I am so sorry. Oh God.

I know . . . how it hurts. It's going to hurt. Like a big ball in the middle of your stomach. But, it'll start getting smaller. Over time. Things will get better. Slowly. Believe me.

MAGGIE: What do you know? This sadness is so thick, I don't know where to put it. I never had nothing like this in my life.

KARLA: I . . . had . . . there was something . . . just last year . . . something like it.

MAGGIE: You had a child stabbed bloody?

KARLA: No, I didn't have that. It was something different.

MAGGIE: Then you couldn't know. Something different isn't the same.

KARLA: Of course it's not the same. I just know how the hurt feels. It's not the same. Was my little brother, Jack, actually, last year. It was different, of course, and well, he wasn't so little, but he was younger than me. And he got real sick, and they were talking about treatment and other help and . . . there are things they can do for people . . . you know, it's an epidemic and all, national . . . and I don't know, well, he decided he didn't want to go through with it, he just gave up. He ahh . . . he ahh . . . went into the cellar and . . . and . . . and . . . you ever seen anyone who's hung themselves? It's a hideous awful sight . . . a horrible . . .

MAGGIE: There, there. Stop now.

KARLA: . . . and he didn't have to go that way. Not saying good-bye or anything. And I miss him so much. If he were alive, right now, today, I'd be calling him on the phone, crying my eyes out to him. And this is very hard on me . . . with Mr. . . . with my client and all.

MAGGIE: No . . . No . . . Karla. It won't be so bad. I didn't mean to set you off. Shhh. Shhh. Calm down.

KARLA: *(Straightening up.)* Oh, this is so stupid. Here I am, supposed to be the big professional, and I'm sitting here blathering to you.

MAGGIE: That day . . . that day . . . when I looked at you. I saw you say you were sorry to me. I saw that in your eyes. You was the only one. And I was a-trying to say thank you.

KARLA: *(Preparing to leave again.)* I appreciate that.

(Turns to exit.)

Well, I'd better be taking my leave before your husband returns. He practically threw the couch at me the last time I came by.

MAGGIE: He's not so bad a man. Everyone hurts.

KARLA: Sure. I understand.

(Starting to exit.)

MAGGIE: *(Catches Karla's arm.)* When would they do it? . . . to . . . him.

KARLA: Mr. Miller? Oh, I don't know. I'll still argue, tomorrow, on his behalf. You know, they'll be some people there. His mother, other people. And then there are appeals and all.

MAGGIE: She must be old by now, his mother.

KARLA: Oh, gee. *(Looks in the file.)* Doesn't say exactly. Seventies, I imagine. She's coming from West Virginia . . .

MAGGIE: I know where she's coming from.

KARLA: Sure — that's your country, too. Well, you probably know more than me. *(Shakes Maggie's hand.)* Well, thank you for coming out on the porch.

MAGGIE: I bet your brother Jack walks right along side you sometimes.

KARLA: He does, sometimes.

MAGGIE: I bet he'd be telling you to remember that part where they talk about an eye for an eye and a tooth for a tooth.

KARLA: Jack wasn't much for religion.

MAGGIE: Yep. I bet Jack'd tell you that's one of the stupidest parts he'd ever heard. I told the preacher that one time too. I think that's stupid I said. That don't accomplish nothing. Just blood on both hands. That's what Jack would say, I bet.

KARLA: He might.

MAGGIE: He'd a probably say what about that part that says thou shalt not kill. What about that? How come nobody talks about that in court?

KARLA: Well, it's a matter of law, you know . . .

MAGGIE: And when they wrote that "thou shalt not" there wasn't no 'ceptions in there for this or for that. I bet he would tell you to bring those things up tomorrow.

KARLA: Well, sure. I can try.

MAGGIE: Good.

KARLA: Right.

MAGGIE: I'd like to come by and hear that. I don't have any fancy court clothes or anything, but, I'd like to know what the judge says to that.

(Karla turns to exit.)

KARLA: Yes, well . . .

(Karla stops, wheels back to Maggie, pulls her jacket out of her bag, and eventually puts it on the porch.)

It's not new or . . . but . . .

MAGGIE: Oh, no. My husband might not approve any business like that. I'd have to . . . well, I'd have to set out . . .

KARLA: Well, I leave it to you. Jack always liked this jacket. He thought the color was calming. Maybe, I'll just put it here on the porch. All right then. Thank you.

(Karla now exits hurriedly.)

MAGGIE: *(Alone, Maggie stands, thinks, picks up jacket, tries it on.)* I'd like to know what that judge says to old Mrs. Miller. I'd like to know that.

END OF PLAY

Farley and Betsy
by Daisy Foote

To my husband Tim Guinee

BIOGRAPHY

Daisy Foote was honored with the prestigious Roger L. Stevens Incentive Award, in association with the Kennedy Center Fund for New American Plays, with support from the American Express Company and in cooperation with the President's Committee for the Arts.

Ms. Foote's plays include *Living with Mary; God's Pictures* (developed at the New Harmony Project and had its world premiere at the Indiana Repertory Theater); *Farley and Betsy* (produced by the Women's Project in its First Look series; Martin Shakar as Farley, Elizabeth Stearns as Betsy); *Darcy and Clara; The Hand of God* (developed with a commission from Wind Dancer Productions and workshopped in the summer of 2000 at the Eugene O'Neill National Playwrights Conference); and *When They Speak of Rita* (developed with a commission from the American Conservatory Theater in San Francisco and produced at Primary Stages in New York in the spring of 2000).

Ms. Foote's screenplays include an adaptation of Elizabeth Jolley's *The Last Crop* for Destiny Productions, which will be directed by Terry Kinney. She has also adapted T. C. Boyle's intricate novel *Water Music* for Earthbourne Films and has just completed an adaptation of John Steinbeck's *The Winter of Our Discontent* for Steppenwolf Theater's new film division.

Recently Ms. Foote acquired the rights to Lucy Grealy's *Autobiography of a Face,* which she is now adapting into a screenplay. She is currently serving a writing fellowship at the University of the South in Sewanee, Tennessee. She is a proud member of both the Dramatist Guild and the Writers Guild of America East.

CHARACTERS

FARLEY COOK: Late forties.
BETSY COOK: Early fifties, his sister.

FARLEY AND BETSY

Lights come up to the kitchen-living area of the Cook House located in Tremont, New Hampshire. Typical of an older New England house. It is low-ceilinged and dark. The room is filled with old furniture including a long trestle dining table, straight back chairs, and two wing chairs. The kitchen half of the room is equipped with outdated kitchen equipment and in one corner of the room is a wood stove. Also are piles and piles of books — paperbacks and hardbacks, all written on the subject of the Civil War. Also, many collectibles from the Civil War era displayed around the room. The jacket of a union officer hangs on one wall. The cap of an enlisted man on another wall. Knives and sabers are in abundance and an original musket used in the battle of Gettysburg hangs above the wood stove.

Farley Cook, late forties, sits in front of the television. It is late in a fall day, and the room is starting to get dark. It should be noted that he breathes, raspy, shallow breaths — the breathing of an asthmatic. He is surrounded by medicines for his condition. He is a rather sour-looking man. He is watching soap operas, which is evident by the type of dialogue and marked music coming out of the box. As he watches, fascinated, he shakes his head and clucks his tongue against this teeth. He then sighs, coughs, and leans back.

FARLEY: Takes all kinds. All kinds of people. That's for sure. All kinds.

(A book drops to the ground. A large thud. Farley jumps. He looks around.)

FARLEY: Who's there?

(He hears nothing. He leans back to enjoy the television again. Watches for a few more moments and then just as suddenly turns his head.)

FARLEY: Is someone there?

(He reaches over to the television. It is an old-fashioned set with no remote control and a knob that controls the volume and turns the television on and off. Farley goes to turn the television off. But instead of doing this he turns it up, way up. It blasts through the house. He is frantic. He reaches over and turns the knob the other way, finally turning off the power. He stands up again, looking suspiciously around the room. He hears someone's footsteps outside the front door. He quickly picks up a book. Opens it to the middle and settles back into his chair.

His sister, Betsy Cook, walks through the door. She is four years older than Farley. She is a strong woman with a resolute air. She carries several ledger books. She puts them on the table. She indicates the television.)

BETSY: Take that into your room if you want to watch it.

(Farley looks as if he doesn't understand.)

BETSY: The television. Go ahead and watch it. Just watch it in your room. I'll call you when lunch is ready.

(She begins to clean up her brother's mess. She throws away used tissues, puts dirty dishes into the sink, and so on. She does everything in a quick, efficient manner.)

BETSY: Farley. . . Farley. . . Farley. . . what you can do in one day.

FARLEY: I wasn't watching anything.

(Betsy continues to clean. She heaves a big sigh.)

FARLEY: I wasn't.

(She looks him straight in the eye.)

BETSY: It's all right. I know you like your soap operas.

FARLEY: I do not.

BETSY: Yes you do.

FARLEY: I would never watch one of those things.

(A beat.) (Disgusted.) Soap operas . . . smope operas . . .

(Betsy goes over to the kitchen area. She opens up a cupboard and takes out soup and crackers for lunch.)

BETSY: It will have to be soup from a can today. I don't have time for anything else.

FARLEY: Fine with me. Don't need to fuss on my account.

(She starts to prepare the soup — opening cans and heating them in pan.)
(Farley starts to pace around the room. As he talks his voice gets more raspy and labored.)

FARLEY: Soap operas! For the housewives and the old people. I'm a working man. Working men don't have time for that kind of nonsense. No they do not.

(Betsy starts to stir the soup on the stove.)

BETSY: *(Laughing.)* Well Mr. Working Man, let's not forget those several days every month you're home with an attack.

FARLEY: Not that much . . .

BETSY: At least several days every month when you're home for the bad breathing. Just like when you were in school there. All those days off from school with your bad breathing. Uncle Edward feeling sorry for you. Bringing that thing . . . *(Indicates television.)* home from the dump for you.

FARLEY: Gave it to all of us.

BETSY: Father and I didn't want it. Fine without it. Perfectly fine. You were the one. Something to keep you occupied. Father and I could have cared less.

(As she talks Farley takes one of the small civil war knives off the wall. He picks it up. His sister's back to him he simulates a stabbing attack. Lifting the knife high up and viciously tearing at the air.)

BETSY: Well . . . there you are. Got me off on the ancient history.

(She starts to turn to face him. He quickly puts the knife back.)

BETSY: Point is, Farley, when I'm here, I want you keeping it in your room. Keep it there so I don't have to hear it. All that silliness.

(The soup splatters. She turns back and starts to furiously wipe the stove as if attacking the enemy. She is as neat as her brother is messy.)

(She then starts to set the table with bowls and spoons. She also puts out crackers.)

BETSY: Important we start being open and honest about our habits as we'll be spending a lot of time in the house together. Open and honest. Only way to go.

(She looks up at her brother and smiles. He merely ducks his head.)

Would you mind serving the milk?

(Farley goes to do this as Betsy serves the soup. She then takes a seat. She starts to eat her soup. Farley gets the milk out of the refrigerator and two glasses out of the cupboard.)

BETSY: Pardon me for starting without you. Don't have a lot of time.

(She looks around the room.)

BETSY: Rush. Rush. Rush. I'm so tired of rushing.

(Points to her favorite chair.) Sit in that chair there. My chair. All kinds of things about the Civil War still to learn.

FARLEY: Mother's chair . . .

BETSY: What's that?

FARLEY: That was mother's chair.

(He indicates the other wing chair.)

FARLEY: And that was father's.

(Indicating Betsy's chair again.) Mother died in that chair. She was holding me in her arms there, and she just died.

BETSY: Yes Farley, I know all about it. I was on the other side of the room watching her. Just a baby you were. Last thing Mother says to me . . . a small girl of just four years old. She said, "Take care of your brother and father. Take care of them, Betsy. *(Sighs.)* And then that blood clot exploded in her brain. She was gone. *(Repeating.)* Take care of your father and brother, Betsy girl. Take care of them.

FARLEY: *(Barely.)* I know. I was there.

BETSY: But you were barely a year. It's my memory . . . not yours.

> *(As she talks, Farley slowly pours the milk into the glasses.)*

How's that milk coming?

> *(He takes the two filled glasses over to the table.)*

Thank you.

> *(He takes a seat and starts to eat.)*

How are you feeling?

FARLEY: Okay.

BETSY: Breathing better?

> *(He nods and continues to eat. He glares at his sister.)*

FARLEY: I don't watch soap operas.

> *(His sister grabs for some crackers. She crumbles them in her soup.)*

BETSY: All right. Have it your way. You don't watch soap operas. *(A beat.)* But keep it in your room when I'm here. That's my point.

> *(They eat in silence. Farley indicates the books.)*

FARLEY: Catching up on your bookkeeping?

> *(Betsy looks over to where he is pointing.)*

BETSY: *(Sounds annoyed.)* Don't be sarcastic, Farley.

FARLEY: Just wondering.

BETSY: The first Monday of every month. That's when we do the bookkeeping. The first Monday. *(A beat.)* What day is today?

> *(Farley says nothing. Sullen.)*

BETSY: Farley, what day is today?

FARLEY: *(Barely.)* Wednesday.

BETSY: Wednesday. Not Monday. *(A beat.)* Told you, Farley. Told you on Sunday that Doug Granger had requested to see the store books. Paid his five hundred dollars. And that gets him a look at the store figures. I told you. He wanted to see them today. Wednesday. I told you, Farley. *(A beat.)* I have a good feeling about this. *(A beat.)* I think he might even give us our full asking price.

FARLEY: I don't want to sell the store.

BETSY: *(Ignoring him.)* Might even give it to us in one payment. One hundred percent. $500,000. Ours. In the bank. No payments. No installments. Just sign the dotted line and hand the money over.

> *(Farley eats his soup.)*

FARLEY: I've been thinking further about my ideas for expansion. We need to think about selling the wine and cheese. You know . . . the gourmet sorta stuff. *(A beat.)* Like the general store over in Francestown there. Move out of the dark ages. Get chic!

(He reaches for his milk. His sister grabs it before he can do this.)

BETSY: Maybe you shouldn't have that . . .

FARLEY: Why?

BETSY: The dairy, Farley. You know all about it. When you have an attack . . . it's best to stay away from the dairy for a few days. Keep your pipes from clogging up.

(She picks up the glass of milk. She carries it over to the sink. As she pours it down the drain in the sink:)

If Doug likes what he sees and I think he will, I bet he'll want to tie things up right away. No messing around.

(She turns back to the table and takes her seat again.)

FARLEY: I believe the time is right for expanding. Develop the larger vision. A lunch room. On the second floor. Course . . . we'll have to bring it up to code first. But that shouldn't be a problem. A new floor. Some rewiring. Shouldn't be a problem. We'll serve the soups, sandwiches, salads. The homemade fare. Simple but good. *(A beat.)* And then once we've got a leg up, we'll bring it even farther. *(A beat.)* An idea I have to bring in the special sort of customer.

(Pauses dramatically.) Tea. You know. How they do it over to England there. Crumpets, scones, cucumber sandwiches. Serve it around four o'clock. You could do that raspberry layer cake of yours and your trifle.

(Betsy leans back. She sighs.)

BETSY: Someone's been watching too much television.

FARLEY: *Yankee Magazine!* I read about it in *Yankee Magazine!* All the really nice places are doing it.

BETSY: *Yankee Magazine.* How I hate *Yankee Magazine.* Everyone's quaint idea about New England living. Well, times have changed. And they will continue to change.

FARLEY: *(Barely.)* Voted us the number one General Store in New Hampshire.

BETSY: Don't start with that, Farley. Don't remind me of that disaster. After Father asked you not to send in that entry blank. But you did it anyway. And every tourist this side of the Connecticut and the Mississippi started coming in to the store. Wanted to have their picture taken. Didn't want to buy anything. Just a picture. *(A beat.)* Don't tell me about *Yankee Magazine.* Have no use for it.

FARLEY: Well, I think it's a good idea. Opening a restaurant. Keeping up with the times.

BETSY: And just where may I ask will you get the money to pay for these great schemes of yours?

FARLEY: Get a loan.

BETSY: Uh huh. And just who is going to give us this loan?

FARLEY: Yes . . . Betsy . . . I believe that would be the bank.

BETSY: I see. Which bank would this be?

FARLEY: Yes . . . Betsy . . . I think you also know the answer to that one. Our bank. The Amoskeag.

BETSY: The Amoskeag?

FARLEY: That's right. The Amoskeag.

BETSY: You think they'll loan you the money?

FARLEY: Soon as they hear my idea. They'll give me more than enough.

BETSY: More than enough?

FARLEY: That's right.

BETSY: I see. The Amoskeag Bank will give you more than enough.

FARLEY: Oh sure. Pick up the phone tomorrow. Set the whole thing up with Parker Owen.

BETSY: Mmm . . . well then I guess I can forget all about that conversation I had with Parker last week.

FARLEY: Which one is that?

BETSY: The one where he told me that there is no future in the general store business. It's all SUPER SAVERS AND PRICECOS. The one where he told me to take the money and run. *(A beat.)* Now I wonder why he would tell me that, Farley, when you're so sure he'll just hand the bank's money over? I wonder why?

(With that Betsy stands up. She takes her empty soup bowl.)

Just finish up here and then it's off to see Doug with my books.

(As she starts to wash the dishes, Farley takes his soup bowl from the table. He brings it over to his sister at the sink.)

BETSY: Don't know whether I should leave the books with Doug overnight . . .

(Her brother is behind her now. As she talks and does dishes he puts his hands above her neck and pretends to strangle her. He continues to make the strangling motions as his sister continues with the dishes. She then shakes out her hands and turns. Farley quickly drops his hands to the side.)

BETSY: What do you think?

(Farley looks vague.)

BETSY: You have no opinion.

FARLEY: I don't want to sell, so why should I have an opinion?

(His sister lets out a large sigh. She turns and starts to wipe off the counter areas. She does this for a few minutes before speaking.)

BETSY: Let's see . . . what would Father do? *(A beat.) (As if listening.)* Stay with the books. That's right. Stay with them. Watch out for any funny business. *(She gives one last wipe with a flourish. She turns to her brother.)*

So I may be awhile. Supper will probably be late tonight.

FARLEY: Who's watching the store?

BETSY: Why Darcy of course. Do you think I would have left the store if Darcy wasn't there?

FARLEY: No.

BETSY: I see. You just wanted to hear yourself talk.

(Betsy turns back to her cleaning and busy making. Farley's breathing becomes shorter and more labored.)

Just like Father always says . . . Farley's got to hear himself talk. Asking a lot of questions. Because . . . Farley's trying to make himself seem important.

(His breathing gets worse.)

FARLEY: *(With difficulty.)* Father says . . . Father says . . .

(Betsy suddenly whips around to face her brother.)

BETSY: What?!

(Farley pulls back. He is clearly afraid of his sister.)

FARLEY: Would be Father *said* not says.

(She reaches for her brother's pills. Puts them in his face.)

BETSY: Time for your medicine.

(Her brother's hands shake as he opens his pill bottle. As he takes his pills with a glass of water . . .)

BETSY: That fat Nazi . . . Deidre Gunter was in the store today.

(Doing a bad German accent.)

"Oh Betsy, I think I might have a buyer for the store. And willing to pay much more than Doug Granger."

(A beat.) (Back to her own voice.)

More than Doug is paying, Deidre? And how would you know about what Doug is paying?

(She turns to her brother whose breathing is worse again.)

BETSY: *(Back to German.)* "Because Betsy, sweetheart, Farley told me."

FARLEY: No.

BETSY: Don't play innocent with me, Farley Cook. Father told me. He warned me to be careful of you. "You know, Farley. You know how he likes to flap his lips in the wind. Always willing to bend someone's ear. Flap. Flap.

Flap." *(A beat.)* I'll tell you I won't miss it. Flap. Flap. Flap. Talk. Talk. Talk. Like it were part of the job. We buy our milk at your store when we could be buying it for a cheaper price at Shop and Save. So we expect . . . we demand conversation. Chit chat. Flap. Flap. Flap. All for the price of a goddamn quart of milk.

FARLEY: I like talking to people.

BETSY: Sure you do. Getting us all into trouble. And this time you've really done it. Fat Deidre Gunter driving me crazy with her real estate lies. What she'll do for us if we sign her broker's agreement. No thank you, Deidre. I don't think so. *(A beat.)* Father says . . . whatever you do, Betsy, don't let the real estate scavengers get a hold of the store.

(Farley looks worried.)

FARLEY: He said that to you? When did he say that?

BETSY: You know how he felt about real estate people, Farley. You know how he hated all of them.

(Farley nods weakly. Betsy picks up the ledger books. She goes to the door.)

BETSY: Wish me luck . . .

(Her hand on the door knob.)

If you're feeling up to it, would you please light a fire in the stove later. Our fuel bill was through the roof last month. Can't have that again. We'll soon be living on a *fixed* income.

(She exits. As soon as the door closes behind her Farley runs for the old rifle/ musket hanging on the wall. He pulls it down. He pretends to cock it and shoot it at the door.)

FARLEY: Listen up, you silly bitch, and listen good. I'm the man of the house now. You better believe it.

(He lifts the gun as though he is pointing it at her head.)

FARLEY: Father's dead. I was there. I tossed the dirt on his coffin. He's dead. And Farley here is number one.

(A beat.)

There will be no more talk of the civil war. "Pull up a chair, Farley. Time to hear the latest biography of Grant." Ulysses S. Grant! You know what I say, Father? You know what I say, Betsy? I say he wasn't half the man Robert E. Lee was. No sir. Abe Lincoln offered the job to him first, didn't he? Not that idiot Grant. He was second string. Drunken idiot. Almost lost the war.

(He jumps as if he's heard something. Raises his gun higher.)

FARLEY: I'll say it if I want to. I'll say anything I want because I'm the man of the house now. I'm number one. *(A beat.)* And we won't sell the store. We won't. Will not!

(The door to the kitchen suddenly opens. Betsy walks in. Farley drops the gun. It tumbles to the floor. A loud crash.)

BETSY: Farley, what on earth are you doing?

FARLEY: What are *you* doing?

(She goes over to wear a hardback sits next to her chair. She picks it up.)

BETSY: I wanted to bring something to read in case I was there a while.

FARLEY: A new biography of Grant?

BETSY: Yes, as a matter of fact it is. How he really was a better general than Lee. Much better. Lincoln only offered the job to Lee first for political reasons. Thought it might win him some converts. And Mary, of course, was putting pressure on him.

FARLEY: Mary?

BETSY: Mary Todd Lincoln, Farley. She was enamored with Lee. Her Kentucky roots and everything. She thought he hung the moon. Bit of a southern snob. Got her into all sorts of trouble.

(Looks down at the gun.)

What are you doing with father's musket? That's not a toy, you know.

(Farley picks it up.)

FARLEY: I was cleaning it. It needs to be cleaned.

(She reaches over and takes the gun. She puts it back on display.)

BETSY: Better leave that to the experts.

(She opens the door. A small smile on her face. She looks beyond her brother.)

Yes, I know. And he's to pay all the closing costs too. Don't worry. It's all under control.

FARLEY: *(Panicked.)* Who are you talking to?

BETSY: See you later . . .

FARLEY: Betsy . . .

(She goes through the door and closes it behind her. Farley runs to the door. Opens it. Yells after her.)

FARLEY: *(Screaming.)* Betsy . . . who are you talking to? Betsy?!

(Lights come down. Black.)

(The lights come up.)

(Early evening of the same day. Farley sits in front of the television. He watches one of the more sordid news programs like "Hard Copy" or "Inside Edition." As he sits in front of the television he keeps leaning over to turn the volume up. Again and again. Each time he does this he looks around the room as if

someone might say something. One final turn on the volume. The television
blasts through the house. He sits back to watch. A few minutes go by.)
The door to the house opens. His sister comes in. She carries ledger books, some
official looking papers, and her biography of Grant. Farley ignores her.)

BETSY: *(Annoyed.)* Farley . . .

(He doesn't turn to look at her. He continues to watch the television. She comes
over to him.)

BETSY: Farley . . . I could hear it in the driveway.

(Farley still won't acknowledge her.)

BETSY: Farley!

(She leans over and snaps off the television. Farley then leans over and turns
it on again. He faces his sister and gives her a taunting smile. She goes and
turns if off again.)

BETSY: Take it to your room.

(Farley looks at his sister. She stands between him and the television. He doesn't
feel quite so brave.)

FARLEY: I wasn't watching soap operas.

BETSY: Television, Farley. I can't stand the television. Any of it.

(She leans over and unplugs it. She picks it up. Farley stands.)

FARLEY: Hey.

BETSY: I'll just do it for you.

(She walks off stage carrying the television. Farley sits back down in his chair,
defeated.)

(As Betsy walks back into the room she is talking . . .)

BETSY: You were right. Stand firm from the start, and they know you won't
be pushed around.

(Farley jumps up.)

FARLEY: Who's that?

(Betsy turns to her brother smiling.)

BETSY: Doug Granger has agreed to everything. To the letter. Five hundred
thousand dollars, not a penny less. *(Laughs.)* A pizza shop. That's what
he'll do with it. Pizzas and subs. Call it . . . A LITTLE BIT OF ITALY.
Not that Doug Granger would know Italy if he fell over it . . . *(A beat.)*
Now . . . how about a celebration . . . cook a few steaks?

(She pats Farley condescendingly on the head.)

Well done, sister dear. Thank you for looking out for me. Bringing me
comfort and security in my old age.

FARLEY: A few meaning three?

(Betsy gives him an odd look.)

BETSY: Excuse me?

FARLEY: You said you were gonna cook a few steaks. A few means three. Only two of us here. You and me.

BETSY: A thank you, Farley, that's all I'm asking for. A thank you . . . if you don't mind.

FARLEY: Father wouldn't like this. Not one bit. His store. The oldest General Store in the state of New Hampshire. Started by his grandfather. A pizza parlor. I don't think so.

BETSY: Oh Farley, you know so little. So very, very little about anything.

FARLEY: Father . . .

BETSY: Don't tell me about, Father. Don't tell me anything. Because you don't *know* anything.

FARLEY: I know I like the store. Don't ever want to sell it.

BETSY: I see. You like getting up at 4:30 every morning?

FARLEY: I don't mind.

BETSY: And you like working every night until nine?

FARLEY: I don't mind.

BETSY: And you like worrying and scraping every month? Wondering if Mrs. Barss will pay her monthly balance or if Mr. Orbit will make up his bad check.

FARLEY: *(Sighs.)* I don't mind.

BETSY: Yes well I do mind, Farley. I mind very much. *(A beat.)* And since I'm the one who does most of the work, and I'm the one who takes on most of the responsibility, then I suppose I should be the one who decides when and if we sell.

FARLEY: We can open a tea room on the second floor.

BETSY: Yes Farley, I know all about it. And I'm not interested. Really I'm not. Not interested in taking on more responsibility. More headaches. Not at all interested.

(She moves in closer to her brother. Challenging. She indicates the official looking papers on the table.)

BETSY: Doug Granger doesn't want to draw this out. After he was finished with the books, we went by the bank. Saw Parker Owen. He drew up the papers for you and me to sign.

FARLEY: No!

(Betsy takes her brother's arm.)

BETSY: Farley . . .

FARLEY: No . . .

(Betsy lets go of his arm. She goes over to the freezer. She takes out three steaks. Tosses them on the counter.)

FARLEY: Three steaks. You have three steaks.

BETSY: So . . .

FARLEY: *(Excited.)* So there's only two of us.

BETSY: They're small steaks.

(She takes the steaks and starts to pound them with a meat hammer. Salt and pepper. She leans over to turn on the oven.)

FARLEY: I'm all you have, Betsy. You're forty-six years old, and I'm all you have. Doesn't that bother you? *(A beat.)* Doesn't it bother you that you've never had a boyfriend? Never been married. Had children of your own? Doesn't that bother you? Make you feel like some sort of freak?

BETSY: I don't think I like this conversation. I think we'll end this conversation. Right now. We'll end it.

FARLEY: That's what we are, Betsy. You and me. We're a couple of freaks. People in town say things about us. Wonder about the two of us. Never going anywhere. Staying tied to our father. Never striking out on our own. *(A beat.)* And now that he's dead . . . now that it's just the two of us . . .

BETSY: Flap, flap, flap, Farley. Flap, flap, flap. Good riddance to all of them. To all their nasty talk. I'll stay in this house now. I will. I'll stay in it. And I'll read my books on the Civil War. So much to learn. Why we haven't even scratched the surface . . .

(She turns away from him. He jumps in front of her.)

FARLEY: No! *(A beat.)* I won't sell! I won't! I like seeing other people. Hearing other voices.

BETSY: You like hearing gossip? You like knowing that people are talking about you? Saying nasty things behind your back? You like that, Farley? You like that?

(He takes his sister's arms.)

FARLEY: I'll take my money. I'll take it, and I'll leave here. I will. I'll go far away and never see you again.

BETSY: Whatever you say, Farley. Whatever you say . . .

FARLEY: You'll be all alone. You'll have nobody. No one!

BETSY: *(Small smile.)* So then you will sign . . .

(Farley hesitates. Realizes he has been tricked.)

FARLEY: No!

(He goes over and starts screaming at her.)

FARLEY: I won't sign. I won't! I won't!

(She turns away from. She starts preparing the rest of the meal for the evening. Making a salad. Boiling water for rice. Measuring out the rice.)

BETSY: It's just like father says. Always doing your little dance. Have to show you're important. All right, Farley. We know you're important. It's been acknowledged.

FARLEY: Are you saying that Father wants us to sell the store?

(Betsy lets out a long frustrated sigh.)

BETSY: I'm talking about family loyalty, Farley. Because in the end your family is all you have. One hundred percent all that you can trust.

FARLEY: What are you trying to say?

BETSY: It's a family decision, Farley. The Cook family has decided to sell the store. And you're a Cook through and through. And your Cook heart is telling you . . . I know it is . . . it is telling you that selling the store is the right thing to do. It's the right decision. In your heart you know that, Farley. You know that.

FARLEY: I'm lonely, Betsy.

(She looks away from him and smiles.)

BETSY: Isn't that right?

FARLEY: Who are you talking to?

BETSY: I think so. I think it's time.

(She turns back to Farley.)

BETSY: Time to sign the paper, Farley.

FARLEY: No.

BETSY: Yes, Farley.

(He explodes.)

FARLEY: No!!!

(He lunges at his sister. He grabs her by the throat and starts to choke her. She screams and tries to pull away.)

BETSY: Farley. . stop. . . Farley . . .

(But he keeps strangling her. She gets weaker and weaker.)

BETSY: *(Barely.)* Farley . . .

(She finally falls to the floor. He looks over at her "dead" on the floor. Triumphant. He walks out of the room. He comes back into the room carrying the television. He plugs it in. He turns it up. He sits down and starts to watch. He doesn't see his sister get up off the floor. She goes over and gets the papers and pen. She walks over to him.)

BETSY: Farley . . .

(He looks up. Startled.)

BETSY: Sign them now . . .

(He looks devastated. Defeated. He takes the paper from his sister. Signs them as she reaches over and turns off the television. Lights go black.)

(Lights come up to Farley sitting in a chair. Betsy is in another chair. She reads out loud from The Biography of Ulysses S. Grant. *Farley looks over to his right to see his Father come into the living room from stage right. A slight pause in the reading as the Father takes a seat. Betsy then resumes her reading.)*

(The lights fade to black.)

END OF PLAY

Box

by Juliana Francis

BIOGRAPHY

Juliana Francis is a writer and an actress. She has worked in New York, Los Angeles, Minneapolis, London, Tokyo, and many European cities. She was a founding member of the late Reza Abdoh's Dar A Luz.

ORIGINAL PRODUCTION

Box was first presented by the Women's Project Tandem Acts with the following cast:

Anastasia . . . . Jill Morley
Mop Man . . . . Michael Casselli
Set design . . . . Michael Casselli

It was directed by Marcella Andre.

Box was subsequently presented by The Ontological-Hysteric's Seven-Minute Series; Reverend Billy's Millennium's Neighborhood Festival; The Sanctuary Theater Company; and PS NBC at HERE, with the following cast:

Anastasia . . . . Funda Duyal
Mop Man . . . . Michael Casselli

It was directed by Tony Torn. Set design was by Gary Wilmes.

INTRODUCTORY STATEMENT

Hold fast, this is most necessary in America. Forget your customs and your ideals. Select a goal and pursue it with all your might. You will experience a bad time, but sooner or later you will achieve your goal. If you are neglectful . . . you will lose your grip and be lost. Do not say, I cannot, I do not know. A bit of advice for you: Do not take a moment's rest. Run.

— *An Immigrant Guidebook, 1891*

BOX

A dim red light reveals Anastasia, half asleep on a stool behind a tall, rectangular pane of Lucite. She is wearing hologram-spangled lingerie, strappy high heels, butterfly clips in her hair, and a fuzzy jacket. There is a plastic Cosmetics Plus bag at her feet. A phone receiver and cord is attached to the Lucite where one would expect a doorknob on a door.

    Sound of a mechanized door sliding open. Light intrudes. Anastasia wakes up quickly, opens her jacket, yanks down her top. She picks up the receiver and addresses an invisible customer.

ANASTASIA: Hello, My name is Anastasia, I am nineteen years old, I am from Ukraine. Oh, okay.
    (She stands up, turns around, bends over, and shows him her ass.)
Oh, yes. Your penis is so big. So big, so hard. What? Oh, okay.
    (She removes her jacket, turns around, and bends over again.)
Oh, you are fucking me. You are fucking me so hard. Fuck me, more, more, more. More. More. More.
What? What? Yes. I am a hor-o-ny slut.
    (She balances on the stool, legs akimbo.)
Hor-o-ny slut. Yes!
    (She smacks her ass against the Lucite.)
Bang me. Bang me. Bang me now.
    (Sound of the mechanized door closing. Anastasia smiles and waves good-bye.)
Thank you. Bye-bye. Thank you.
    (She hangs up the phone and straightens her clothes. Picks up the Cosmetics Plus bag and takes out a can of grape soda with a Krazy Straw and a bag of Utz potato chips. Sips the soda. Reads the chip bag.)
    (Sound of the door opening.)
    (Anastasia quickly replaces her snack, straddles the stool, and picks up the phone.)
MALE VOICE OVER: *(Mildly.)* Close your legs.
ANASTASIA: What?
MALE VOICE OVER: *(Mildly.)* Close your legs.
    (Anastasia recognizes him.)
ANASTASIA: Oh, it's you.
    (She stands up.)
Get on your knees. Get on your knees down on the dirty, dirty floor. What

BOX • 77

makes you think you can come in here and bother me, huh? You are very, very bad. You are a scum sucker. Yes. You should go to my house and clean up my bathroom. Yes. No. You are not allowed to clean off the telephone with your hanky. You deserve dirty telephone. You are very, very bad. No! You are not allowed to take out your penis and play with it. What do you think you are doing with that penis?

(She kneels and rhythmically slaps the Lucite.)

Bad scum sucker! Bad scum sucker! Bad, filthy, dirty scum sucker!

(Sound of the door. Anastasia waves good-bye.)

Thank you!

(Anastasia crosses out from behind the Lucite and looks around. A mop man enters with his mop.)

ANASTASIA: *(To no one in particular.)* Is anybody going to the store?

(She glances at the mop man. He mutters something inaudible, crosses to the Lucite, swabs down the lower half of it.)

ANASTASIA: Shit.

(The mop man exits. Anastasia crosses back behind the Lucite. Picks up her can of soda. Sings an American diva-style pop song about a shipwreck to herself and the can of soda.)

(The end of the song makes her cry; a surprise.)

(Sound of the door opening.)

(Anastasia grabs the phone.)

ANASTASIA: Hello.

(She points to the phone receiver.)

Hello. You have never been in here before. My name is Anastasia. I am nineteen years old. I am from Ukraine. What? Oh, you are a student? In the University? Oh! You are a writer. Oh. Oh. Yes, I think this is a funny place too. Oh, okay.

(She turns around and shows him her ass.)

What? What? Oh no, I don't have any toys. I have fingers. Fingers. What? This is not what you expected? But I have fingers. What? You want me to pee? Oh. Okay. Wait just a minute.

(Anastasia hangs up the phone, pulls off her jacket, and picks up the can of soda. She dances a little as she drinks a big swig. Places the can on the stool and carefully kneels above it. She picks up the phone.)

ANASTASIA: Okay. Give me just a minute.

(Nothing happens.)

I'm trying. Trying to pee. Oh, I wish I could pee. Pee. Pee. Pee.

(Nothing happens. She puts the can down on the floor.)

Sorry. Sorry. What? Oh, okay.

(She sticks her finger up her ass.)

Now I'm sticking my finger in my ass. Oh boy. Look at me, huh? I sure wish I had a big penis to stick up my ass but I just play with my finger until a big penis comes along. Oh, you're finished already? No. I'm not laughing at you.

(Sound of the door. Anastasia hangs up the phone, then knocks on the Lucite.)

This is still not what you expected?

(As the lights dim, she traces a word on the Lucite with her finger.)

(Blackout.)

END OF PLAY

BOX • 79

Burn
by Dana Leslie Goldstein

BIOGRAPHY

Dana Leslie Goldstein has been affiliated with Women's Project & Productions since 1995. In addition to *Burn,* the Women's Project was responsible for mounting the original productions of *Pretend* and *Gateway for Ashes.* Dana's full-length play *Next Year in Jerusalem* was developed, in part, by the Women's Project and is a past winner of The New England New Play Competition. It has been seen at Pulse Ensemble Theatre, The Vineyard Playhouse, and Jewish Theatre of the South. Dana holds Master of Fine Arts degrees in both play-writing and poetry, and she has studied lyric writing in the BMI/Lehman Engel Musical Theater Workshop. Her work has been the recipient of the Harold and Mimi Steinberg Prize for Excellence in Playwriting, The Different Voices New Play Award, The American College Theatre Festival New Play Award, The Henry Hoyns Fellowship in Poetry, The Associated Writing Programs' Intro Award for Poetry, and an Academy of American Poets Prize. *Lady of Copper,* a musical for children which Dana wrote with her singer/songwriter brother, has been seen at The Hartford Children's Theatre, The York Theatre, The Helen Hayes Performing Arts Center, The Bickford Theatre, The Culture Project @ 45 Bleecker, and The Children's Museum of Manhattan. *Lady of Copper* has also been touring New York and New Jersey area schools since 1998. In addition, a feature film version of *Lady of Copper* is in preproduction and should be released in early 2002.

ORIGINAL PRODUCTION

Directed by . . . . .Renee Philippi
Katie . . . . .Brigitte Barnett*
Richard . . . . .Nicholas Martin-Smith*
*member of Actors' Equity Association

CHARACTERS

KATIE: Early thirties.
RICHARD: Her husband, mid-thirties.

AUTHOR'S NOTE

When I was about eight months old, I had a babysitter who took care of me during the day while my parents both went to work. One morning, or so the story goes, I was crawling around on the floor, discovered the cord for a vaporizer that was being used to sterilize baby bottles, and yanked on it until the vaporizer came tumbling down from a shelf and spilled near-boiling water on my shoulder and down my arm. I was in the hospital for several weeks, and the scars are still visible.

If anyone was to blame for this accident, I suppose it was the babysitter, but my mother was the one who felt the guilt of it. She had chosen to go back to work when I was still an infant, and because she wasn't there to watch me (so her reasoning goes), I was hurt. My father felt awful about the accident, but he didn't feel *guilty* about it. This difference between their reactions was the seed for the fictional play *Burn*. Though the mother in the play wasn't even there when the child was hurt, she is consumed by guilt because she wasn't home with her child.

BURN

Morning. A living room. A fire in the fireplace. A piano. A matching couch and loveseat on which Katie sits. After a moment, Richard enters. He is on his way to the kitchen.

KATIE: Hi. Good morning.

RICHARD: I didn't realize you were up already.

KATIE: Dreams. Couldn't sleep.

RICHARD: Don't.

KATIE: I dreamt you were rocking Erica to sleep. You were in our bed. I thought maybe it was a good omen.
(Richard proceeds toward kitchen.)
Where are you going?

RICHARD: To get some tea. Do you want some?

KATIE: Yes. Richard?

RICHARD: Yeah?

KATIE: How are you?

RICHARD: All right.

KATIE: Really. How are you?

RICHARD: What would you like me to say, Katie?

KATIE: Almost anything.

RICHARD: I don't feel particularly well this morning. All right?
(Begins to exit again.)

KATIE: Wait.
(Richard stops.)
Did you sleep okay?

RICHARD: Well enough. My back is a little stiff. I slept on my arm and it has that feeling. Like the skin got twisted halfway around and hasn't found its way back into place yet.

KATIE: No. Not yet.

RICHARD: Can I get the tea now?

KATIE: That bed is too small for you.
(Richard exits.)
(Pause; calling:) Richard?

RICHARD: *(Off.)* What?

KATIE: How long is it going to take?

RICHARD: *(Re-entering.)* I just turned the water on. It'll be a few minutes.

KATIE: No. I mean, how long is it going to take for us to get back to normal?

RICHARD: This isn't normal?

KATIE: Don't be sarcastic.

RICHARD: I'm never sarcastic.

KATIE: Richard.
   (Pause, starts to follow him.)
   It was my fault.

RICHARD: Sit down. Please.

KATIE: Say that it was my fault.

RICHARD: Why?

KATIE: Isn't that what you're thinking?

RICHARD: No. That's ridiculous. You know that.

KATIE: I keep dreaming about her.

RICHARD: I can't hear this.

KATIE: You were so good with her.

RICHARD: Stop it.

KATIE: When she comes home, we'll be fine. Won't we?

RICHARD: Of course.

KATIE: I need to talk about this. Or we won't be fine. When she comes home, you'll move back into our room. *(Pause.)* Richard?

RICHARD: Hmm?

KATIE: You'll move back into our room when Erica comes home. *(Pause.)* Richard, did you hear me?

RICHARD: You know I heard you.

KATIE: Answer me.

RICHARD: It wasn't a question.

KATIE: Richard.

RICHARD: *(Exiting.)* The water's boiling.

KATIE: No, it isn't.

RICHARD: I need to check it. I don't want it to spill over.

KATIE: Richard.

RICHARD: We can't have water spilling all over the stove.

KATIE: Don't be cruel.

RICHARD: I've got to go turn it off.
   (Exits; returns.)
   I can't come back into our room yet, Katie.

KATIE: Why not?

RICHARD: I don't know.

KATIE: You don't know?

RICHARD: You're dreaming about her.

KATIE: Yes.

RICHARD: I'm not.

KATIE: Is that so bad?

RICHARD: I don't know. Maybe.

KATIE: I think you've had a shock. We both have.

RICHARD: You're protecting me. Why don't you say what you mean?

KATIE: I don't know what you want me to say.

RICHARD: I want you to admit it, Katie. It wasn't your fault, it was mine.

KATIE: Don't do this.

RICHARD: And I can't promise that kind of thing won't happen again. Because anything can happen.

KATIE: Come here. Sit by me.

RICHARD: Katie.

KATIE: It wasn't your fault. Look at me. Did you do anything that in any way caused the accident?

RICHARD: No.

KATIE: No.

(Richard sits next to her.)

RICHARD: She did knock it over herself.

KATIE: Yes.

RICHARD: The same thing probably would've happened if you had been home with her. *(Pause.)* Don't you think? *(Pause.)* Katie?

KATIE: *(Pause.)* I don't know.

RICHARD: What do you mean?

KATIE: Nothing. I just — I don't think it's necessarily true that the same thing would've happened if I had been here.

RICHARD: I see.

KATIE: I don't blame you, Richard. I know you had no intention of letting her get hurt.

RICHARD: *(Echoing her.)* Letting her get hurt.

KATIE: I didn't mean it that way.

RICHARD: How did you mean it?

KATIE: I'm not sure. I wasn't here.

RICHARD: But I was. I was responsible for her.

KATIE: Of course you were.

RICHARD: Not responsible enough.

KATIE: That isn't what I meant. It's just that she's only three years old. When I'm home with a three year old, I watch her.

RICHARD: Not every second.

KATIE: *(Quietly.)* I manage to.

RICHARD: You don't have your eyes on her every second, Katie. You know that.

KATIE: You're right; I don't follow her around. I don't see her every second. Not literally. But I know what she's doing. I have a sense of her. All the time. I would have known that she was about to get hurt. I would have.

RICHARD: I knew you thought it was my fault.

KATIE: No. It wouldn't have happened if I had been home with her. That makes it my fault.

RICHARD: What are you talking about? This is definitely not your fault.

KATIE: I think that's why I'm dreaming about her. I should be with her. Right now. In the hospital.

RICHARD: When she's out of Intensive Care, we'll stay with her —

KATIE: And at home. When she's back.

RICHARD: We talked about this. I can take care of her.

KATIE: Not as well as I can.

RICHARD: Up until now — you said it yourself — I was great with her. I was.

KATIE: Even in my dreams the two of you are so sweet together. But I'm always there. I'm present somehow, watching. If I weren't there — If you were taking care of her yourself — I don't know if I can trust you with her again.

RICHARD: Katie.

KATIE: It's just who you are. You aren't always present.

RICHARD: What does that mean? Of course I'm present. I'm in this house twenty-four hours a day. Since she was born. I never leave. At least that's what it feels like.

KATIE: *(Pause.)* Do you want to leave?

RICHARD: That isn't what I meant.

KATIE: Answer me. Do you want to leave?

RICHARD: No. Sometimes.

KATIE: Oh.

RICHARD: That isn't what I meant to say. I — I don't want to talk about this.

KATIE: You already are.

RICHARD: *(Long pause.)* I do love you.

KATIE: That's comforting.

RICHARD: The water's probably boiling again.

(Starts to exit.)

KATIE: I love you too.

RICHARD: *(Turning back to her.)* She is going to be all right.

KATIE: Maybe. If we're lucky.

RICHARD: We are lucky.

KATIE: We were.

RICHARD: You have to trust me, Katie. Please.

KATIE: Or you'll leave?

RICHARD: I'm not going anywhere.

    (Goes to her and holds her.)

KATIE: *(Pause.)* I just want everything to be the way it was.

RICHARD: Never happen.

KATIE: I know.

RICHARD: *(Pause.)* Tea?

KATIE: Please.

RICHARD: Two spoonfuls of sugar and a tiny bit of milk?

KATIE: Exactly.

RICHARD: I can take care of that.

KATIE: I know.

    (Blackout.)

END OF PLAY

The Nature
of Things
by Lisa L. Humbertson

For Susie with love

BIOGRAPHY

Lisa Humbertson is currently a resident playwright at Circle East (formerly Circle Rep) and an associate artist with the Women's Project. She has been working on the development of a full-length play, *Sky Fossils,* recently read at The New Century Theater and SSDC Foundation's CAP 21 series.

An MFA graduate from both the Yale School of Drama, (Playwriting, Dramaturgy, and Critical Analysis) and Carnegie-Mellon University (Playwriting), Humbertson has had productions, workshops, and readings at New York Theatre Workshop, Manhattan Class Company, The West Bank Café, the Women's Project, Urban Stages, The Salon, LaMama Galleria, The Quaigh Theatre, and WBAI Radio, NYC.

Outside Manhattan, Humbertson's work has been performed at The New England Actor's Theatre, Yale School of Drama, International Performance Actions, The Yale Cabaret, The Bowman Ensemble, Voice and Vision, The City Theatre Company, The Pittsburgh Playhouse as well as other regional venues.

Humbertson has won multiple writing awards. She has been both a O'Neill, and a Louisville finalist twice. Additionally, she has received Playwriting Grants from The Pennsylvania Counsel on the Arts, and The Theatre Association of Pennsylvania. Other prizes have been awarded from the Bud Yorkin New Play Festival, and the American Association for Theatre and Education's Unpublished Play Contest. Her radio drama *Boudica* just won first place in the Mind's Ear Radio contest and will be produced in New Orleans in the summer of 2001.

Humbertson has written for television as well as theater, and previous credits include projects with "Wonderworks," Scholastics, and staff writing for a children's television program.

Humbertson teaches at Hofstra and C.W. Post universities and resides on Long Island with her husband, Paul Brady, and their pups, Mac and Molly.

ORIGINAL PRODUCTION

This play was first performed by the Women's Project in 1997, directed by Melanie Sutherland, with the following cast:

Julie . . . . Jo Twiss
Caitlyn . . . . Darra Herman

CHARACTERS

JULIE: A mother, forties.
CAITLYN: Her adolescent daughter.

SETTING
A suburban kitchen. The Midwest. Today.

AUTHOR'S NOTE
I've noticed a strange phenomenon with nieces and nephews. When they became almost teenagers, suddenly they hate to be seen with their parents. In fact, they hate to be seen with older relatives. Parents must walk at least ten feet behind or in front of them, and if a peer appears, family must disappear altogether.

Although this piece explores much more, its original inspiration came from watching my sister and my friends experience rejection from their kids, that odd point when parents become pariahs: despised, yet loved; reviled, yet required; condemned, yet needed.

THE NATURE OF THINGS

Scene: A suburban kitchen. The Midwest. Julie, mother, forties, and her adolescent daughter, Caitlyn, quickly gather up canned goods, flashlight, water bottles, etc.

CAITLYN: I don't know why we have to do this. This is so stupid.

JULIE: Hurry up. The siren went off twenty minutes ago.

CAITLYN: If it's so dangerous, why aren't you down there?

JULIE: I was waiting for you. The school called. They said you left. If something like this ever happens again — stay put. I hope your dad and brothers are OK.

CAITLYN: At least they won't be stuck in the basement with you.

JULIE: Maybe it's good they're in Chicago. The storm isn't hitting there. Did you get the batteries?

CAITLYN: Like about 500 of them.

JULIE: D's, C's, double-A's?

CAITLYN: Whatever was in the drawer.

JULIE: Check — what do you have?

CAITLYN: Mother, I told you.

JULIE: Can opener?

CAITLYN: Yeah.

JULIE: Where's Binky?

CAITLYN: I don't know.

JULIE: We gotta find Binky.

CAITLYN: She's in the cellar — sleeping on the clean laundry.

JULIE: Animals are smart. That's where we shoulda been ten minutes ago, God, I know I'm forgetting something.

CAITLYN: A good TV.

JULIE: There's one down there.

CAITLYN: Yah, but it's screen's about this big. And it's black and white.

(The power goes out.)

JULIE: Won't matter now.

CAITLYN: Why do we have to have these stupid tornadoes?

JULIE: Every place has something. Come on.

(She grabs her daughter's arm, pulls her into the basement, just as pounding rain is heard.)

CAITLYN: *(Wailing.)* I can't believe it's raining.

JULIE: Latch the door.

CAITLYN: I gotta go to the mall tonight.

JULIE: Hurry.

CAITLYN: My hair's gonna get all frizzy.

JULIE: Latch the door.

CAITLYN: Why do I have your hair? Why did you give me the frizzy hair gene?

JULIE: Caitlyn, would you shut the goddamn door?

CAITLYN: *(Noticing her mother for the first time as she lights a lamp.)* You're using kerosene? Why are you doing that, Mother? They kill whales for that, you know. For the oil. Do you know how many whales they killed for you to light that light?

JULIE: They haven't used whale oil for about a hundred years.

CAITLYN: What animal did they kill?

JULIE: I think it's pine pitch.

CAITLYN: Oh great — so now they're killing trees.

JULIE: Would you rather sit in the dark?

CAITLYN: Why do we have to go through this tornado thing? Every year. Every year of my life — locked in the basement — with you — It's like being buried alive —

(Sound of moaning wind.)

What was that?

JULIE: Demented spirits. Looking for peace. *(Then.)* I don't know.

(Opens a bag of cookies.)

Here. Have one. You'll feel better.

CAITLYN: What are you doing, Mother?

JULIE: Eating a cookie . . . ?

CAITLYN: You know you don't want that cookie. That one cookie must be at least 100 calories. It probably has five grams of fat.

JULIE: Bleached flour, sugar, palm oil, monosodium glutamate, 150 calories, *(With glee.)* and seven grams of fat.

CAITLYN: You know you can't afford to eat that. My friends see you, and they'll think I'm gonna look like you.

JULIE: You have a perfect figure: you're thin, you have boobs —

CAITLYN: Don't say that!

JULIE: What?

CAITLYN: *(Julie looks at her perplexed.)* You just love to embarrass me.

JULIE: What did I do?

CAITLYN: Last Saturday. When you were driving me and Jenny to the mall. You said it then. Right in front of her.

JULIE: What?

CAITLYN: You know what you said. You said the B word.

JULIE: Boobs?

CAITLYN: Don't — !

JULIE: They hurt. I was due for my period.

CAITLYN: Well you shouldn't go around talking about it. You just love to embarrass me. But the worst—I can't believe you did it — after I begged you not to — I'll never be able to show my face to Elisabeth again —

JULIE: What?

CAITLYN: She told everyone at school —

JULIE: What did I do? —

CAITLYN: I was horrified — .

JULIE: What are you talking about? —

CAITLYN: *(As if she were killing puppies.)* The radio was on. In the car. And you sang. *(As if her mother's a moron.)* It was the Doobie Brothers.

JULIE: I like the Doobie Brothers.

CAITLYN: I thought I would die.

(Julie giggles.)

It isn't funny, Mother. I've never been so humiliated my entire life.
(Sound of horrible winds.)
What's that?

JULIE: Where's Binky?

CAITLYN: Behind the dryer.

JULIE: Are you sure?

CAITLYN: *(Pounding rain.)* There it is again — What is it?

JULIE: Oh — there she is — I see her tail —

CAITLYN: You care about the stupid cat more than you care about me. Are we gonna die?

JULIE: We should be safe in the basement. *(Not so sure.)* I think.
(Speaking for herself.)
Let's have another cookie.

CAITLYN: Now, Mother, you know you don't want another cookie.

JULIE: Locked up with you, I think I want a drink.

CAITLYN: You really shouldn't drink.

JULIE: I don't drink.

CAITLYN: I see you drink wine.

JULIE: Yah. Sometimes. Once a week, maybe.

CAITLYN: That's how it starts. With one drink. And before you know it, you've become a full-fledged alcoholic. They taught us the warning signs. At school.

JULIE: For Pete's sake, I'm not an alcoholic.

CAITLYN: Denial's another one.

JULIE: If you don't shut up, I'm going to start smoking.

CAITLYN: Daddy said you smoked.

JULIE: Everybody smoked.

CAITLYN: It kills you.

JULIE: Slowly. You want rapid, you have a teenager.

CAITLYN: What's that supposed to mean?

JULIE: Nothing. It doesn't mean anything.

CAITLYN: You despise me —

JULIE: If you don't shut up, I'm gonna start singing —

CAITLYN: 'Cause you blame me — I made you lose your sleep, your freedom, and worst of all — I made you lose your figure. I'd blame you if you did that to me.

JULIE: I lost my figure because I eat cookies. Honey, I don't blame you.

CAITLYN: Then why won't you let me get shoes?

JULIE: Because you just got pants. Oh, so that's what this is about. You have ten pairs of shoes.

CAITLYN: They're ugly.

JULIE: You picked them out.

CAITLYN: They're not in style. People are laughing at me.

JULIE: Then get a job. Buy fifty — Buy a hundred.

CAITLYN: You'd like that, wouldn't you. Have me get a job, flunk out of school. Then I'd have to live with you the rest of my life.

JULIE: I don't want that for anything in the world.

CAITLYN: See? I was right. You detest me.

JULIE: You can't have the goddamn shoes. — We don't have the money. I don't want to discuss this with you. You can't have another pair of shoes.

CAITLYN: You want to ruin me. You want me to be a misfit — just like you. My friends are laughing at you, and they're probably laughing at me, too.

JULIE: Then get new friends.

CAITLYN: I wish I had a new mother.

JULIE: Me too.

CAITLYN: Why do you hate me so bad?

JULIE: When you hate me for everything I am? I can't help but hate you. What have I done to you that's so terrible? You talk as if I'm some grotesque —

am I really that ugly to you? Yes, I'm fat. I need to lose twenty . . . no, thirty pounds. But I have no life. I'm just a chauffeur — I drive you and your brothers to school, to practice, to malls, to friends, and I work. I work at home, and I work at work.

Goddammit, Caitlyn, let me crawl into some dark corner with my cookies and my romance novels, and an occasional glass of wine — and let me just hide there 'til you're thirty. Arrange your own transportation. Just let me binge in peace in my little dark hole, and go pick on someone else.

CAITLYN: *(Caitlyn starts crying.)* You hate me, Mother. You loathe me. I've always known it was true —

JULIE: Now you're being silly.

CAITLYN: You wish I was never born.

JULIE: *(Wondering.)* You know I think you're gonna get your period. Very, very soon.

CAITLYN: It's horrible.

JULIE: It isn't horrible. It's wonderful — being a woman.

CAITLYN: It hurts. And you get cramps.

JULIE: Caitlyn Carrol, did you get your period today? Did it start at school? Is that why you came home?

CAITLYN: It showed on my pants.

JULIE: Oh, honey.

CAITLYN: Everybody saw.

JULIE: Come here, baby.

CAITLYN: They laughed at me, Mommy. They were all laughing, and I ran out of school — they weren't letting us come home cause of the storm — and there weren't any busses 'cause we weren't supposed to leave — and the sky was all black, and I ran and ran and ran —

JULIE: That's three miles — Why didn't you call me?

CAITLYN: You wouldn't have come.

JULIE: Of course I would've come. No storm could ever keep me away from you. But this is a glorious thing — Honey, this is one of the greatest miracles in the world. It's the miracle of life. It lets us — and only us, you and me — women — have babies.

CAITLYN: I was your baby once.

JULIE: And you still are. You always will be. And now you're a woman too.

CAITLYN: Am I gonna be like you?

JULIE: You'll be like yourself.

CAITLYN: I'd rather kill myself first.

JULIE: It's not such an awful thing to be.

CAITLYN: Yes it is — it just isn't fair.

JULIE: Fair?

CAITLYN: All you do is work, and it makes you ugly.

JULIE: Gee, thanks.

CAITLYN: And unhappy. And so busy. Mother, you have no life.

JULIE: You can do things differently. That's your choice. I wouldn't change things. This is what I wanted. You, you are what I wanted.

Listen to that rain. That's me crying for you. Everytime I hear it, I think of the night you were born. I was so scared something'd be wrong with you. I was petrified, but I didn't want to be scared because I thought you could feel what I was feeling. And I wanted you to be calm. When it started raining, I felt like that was God, and Diana, and all the saints, and all the pagan mothers — crying for me . . . so that I wouldn't have to cry, and you wouldn't feel my fear. And they cried, and they cried, and they cried. And finally, after about twelve hours, you came out, so perfect, so beautiful, so loving . . . Babies really don't know anything when they're born, but you knew I was your mother, and you wanted me. *You wanted me.* And God, did I want you. We've always had a psychic link . . . And do you know . . . In those moments before you were born, those hours, you know what I was thinking? I was praying to everything of life, to take from me my life, my strength, my everything — anything of me that was needed, to make it possible for you to come alive. I willed my beauty to you. My hope, my energy. And look at you — You are beautiful. My beautiful little girl. And now you're a woman.

CAITLYN: I don't wanna be. I don't know how.

JULIE: You'll have the whole of your life to figure it out.

CAITLYN: Is the storm over now? I wanna go to the mall.

JULIE: For a short while, sweetheart. We're only in the eye.

(Julie holds out the bag of cookies. Caitlyn reaches for one. Smiles. Fade.)

END OF PLAY

Bread
by Margaret Hunt

For Sissy, who made us all love the theater

BIOGRAPHY

Margaret Hunt has written eight full-length plays and five one-acts, in addition to *Bread*. She is the recipient of a Playwright's Fellowship from the Berrilla Kerr Foundation for her play *Loose Cannons;* two playwright's residencies from the Edward Albee Foundation; and a video-writing grant from the Philip Morris Foundation. A scene from her play *Loon Woman* was published in *Duo: Best Scenes from the 90s* by Applause Books. Monologues from short plays she has written or cowritten appear in *Monologues from the Road, Baseball Monologs,* and *The Elvis Book,* all from Heinemann Books. She is a member of the Women's Project and the Dramatists Guild.

ORIGINAL CAST

> *Bread* was originally produced by Women's Project & Productions on April 29, 1995, at La Mama Galleria in New York City. It was directed by Elaine M. Smith, with the following cast:
>
> Joan Arnold . . . . Caren Browning
> Nellie Cavanaugh . . . . Kerry Metzler
> Abby Arnold . . . . Heather Robinson

CHARACTERS

> JOAN ARNOLD: A divorced poet and writer, forty-one.
> NELLIE CAVANAUGH: Joan's sister, a social worker, early thirties.
> ABBY ARNOLD: Joan's daughter, fourteen.

SETTING

> The time is the early 1990s, late August. The place is a brownstone apartment in the West Forties, near Times Square, New York City.

INTRODUCTORY STATEMENT

People seem to assume that women playwrights write autobiography — unless the play is a period piece or an obvious fantasy. If your main female character is infertile, people will talk to you after the play as if *you* are infertile. They will recommend a drug or a group. The first time I went to talk with a director about *Bread,* she said, "I have to ask you the obvious question." I didn't know what that was because I hadn't yet talked with any stranger about the play. She said, "Have you ever been in a mental hospital?" I wondered why she didn't ask me if I had a daughter or an ex-husband or an imagination.

BREAD

As the lights come up, we see the living room of a brownstone apartment, a Pullman kitchen upstage, two tall windows at right. The room looks like the scene of a war between chaos and order. Dominating it is a well-organized desk, which holds a giant Rolodex, a laptop computer, a cup of sharp pencils, stacks of files, legal pads, and a pile of unread New York Times.

The walls are dotted with 8 X 5 orange and white index cards arranged in an orderly fashion we cannot figure out. On the coffee table stands a paper cutter, blade up. Many surfaces are covered with piles of paper strips neatly organized by size and color. Only the dining table is clear. In contrast to the living room, the kitchen is chaotic. Draped across the kitchen cabinets is a hand-painted banner, "Still Tons o' Fun at Forty-One."

Joan Arnold enters carrying a breadboard with a stainless steel bowl on it covered with a cloth. She is sweating, trembling, and looks exhausted. She wears a clean chef's apron over a filthy bathrobe. She sets her board down on the table, lifts the cloth, holds the dough up to her nose and inhales deeply. Her hands stop trembling.

She seems to calm herself. She smiles.

JOAN: In the winter, on Saturday mornings, Mama would make bread. And all of us would help. Even when we were really little. We'd make breadsticks. Mama called them "ghastlies" because the dough turned gray from our hands. We made them really long — like a foot long or longer — and she let us. She didn't even yell about their being grimy. We made braided bread with poppy seeds. Sometimes we made cinnamon rolls. They made the whole house smell spicy. All the windows fogged.
(The phone rings. Joan freezes. On the second ring, Joan puts down the bowl and covers it again.)
Pick up. *(Ring.)* Pick UP. *(Ring.)* Pick up, pick up, pick up!
(Ring. Then silence.)
God DAMN it!
(She yanks the answering machine away from the phone and throws it out the window. Then she grabs an orange card and writes.)
Buy new machine.
(She stops writing, laughs.)
Yeah, right. With what?
(She tears up the orange card, takes another.)

Start small . . . Breathe.

(She thinks, then writes.)

Find out what day it is.

(Writes again.)

Don't ask anyone — underline that! Then how do I find — buy a newspaper! That's a very normal thing to do!

(Moves to front door.)

People do that all the time. God, it's hot.

(She unbolts and unlocks the door, then whirls around.)

Keys. Keys. Keys. Keys. Keys. Keys.

(She runs back into the room and picks up her purse.)

Where do I buy newspapers? I know that. I'm sure I know that. I've bought millions of newspapers — No, be precise — I've bought thousands of —

(Sees herself in the mirror, drops purse, hurries back into room. Grabs a white card and writes.)

Don't go out in bathrobe! Underline that and put it . . . on the front door.

(She does.)

Oh, shit, that should be on an orange card!

(Tears it up.)

These are for work! Can't you remember anything?

(Begins to cry, stops, takes orange card, writes.)

Get . . . some . . . sleep. Okay, underline that and put it — No! Just do it. Go to bed . . . *(Crying.)* What for? I never sleep — I know! I'll have a drink. Is it after noon? I'll have a drink in bed. I know what I drink. I drink Scotch!

(Opens liquor cabinet and peers inside.)

Well, hell, maybe I drink bourbon. Who gives a fuck.

(Doorbell rings long and loud. Joan freezes, then grabs the bowl and goes out the window. Nellie pushes the door open with a finger.)

JOAN: *(Off.)* Jesus, Nellie, stop right there.

NELLIE: You don't lock your door? In Times Square —

(Joan steps through window, without bowl.)

JOAN: I told you not to come!

NELLIE: You told me not to come yesterday. But when I got back from lunch today, there —

JOAN: Is it today? *(Laughs.)* That's a great question. No, it's yesterday, it's tomorrow, it's next week. It's *always* fucking today, it's never tomorrow.

(Joan begins to cry. She turns away from Nellie and dries her eyes on her apron.)

NELLIE: I had a message to call Joe —

(Nellie is stunned by the room's appearance.)

JOAN: Don't talk to my ex-husband behind my back!

NELLIE: He was calling me because you —

JOAN: If he has to talk to me, he can call me himself. I don't need you to be his mouthpiece — What was I saying . . . I lost my train of — Oh, yeah, want some coffee? It's from yesterday.

NELLIE: Is that a joke? You don't drink old coffee.

JOAN: I'm economizing. Trying to save up money so Abby can get contact lenses —

NELLIE: Jesus Joan! Let Joe buy her contacts —

JOAN: Dancers do not wear glasses — I was going to take one of her dance magazines and draw little glasses on all the dancers before she comes home. *(Laughing.)* But I'm afraid she wouldn't laugh. Milk? Wait — This is espresso. You can't put milk in espresso —

NELLIE: You have rules for drinking stale coffee?

JOAN: Without rules, we live in chaos.

NELLIE: No kidding.

JOAN: Joe already told her he'd buy her the lenses. He'd buy her the goddamn moon!

NELLIE: Is that so terrible?

JOAN: Yes! Cause I have to pay half!

NELLIE: Why? Joe makes a fortune.

JOAN: You don't understand.

NELLIE: Yes I do. You divorced a rich man for a dollar so —

JOAN: Don't start with me —

NELLIE: *(Overlapping.)* — so you could feel morally superior to him. You're morally superior to everybody —

JOAN: It's *my* daughter. It's *my* ex-husband. Shut up! Go take some other mother's kids away from her. That's your job!

NELLIE: That is *not* my job! And you know it! I don't take kids away from their mothers unless somebody's abusing them! You, of all people — *(Nellie reads an index card.)* What is all this?

JOAN: *(Pleased.)* You like the experiment? Looks messy, but it works.

NELLIE: It does?

JOAN: *(Excited.)* Yes, *Miz* Smarty Pants, it does. It's a *system!* I use orange cards to write down everything practical I have to remember and white ones for poems or ideas.

NELLIE: *(Neutral.)* Well, that's . . . terrif — that's just great.

JOAN: It is great! I know you're being sarcastic, Nellie, I'm not dense. I'm just . . . a bit disorganized. So I go through the cards and find out all the things I've been forgetting . . . Everything! It works.

(Joan notices her apron, takes it off, and drop-kicks it out the window.)

I'm doing okay with the old card system. I shoulda been a librarian. Hell, I still could be a —

NELLIE: I've never seen you . . . like this. This bathrobe is . . . stiff with —

JOAN: Pride. It's a new polyester fiber, Nellie. Repels soap and water and well-wishers and well water and well-meaning sisters and swell meaning —

NELLIE: STOP IT! Take a deep breath.

(Joan breathes deeply, then exhales at Nellie.)

My God! You smell like a gin factory.

JOAN: Scotch factory. I drank it to get to sleep. It worked — I passed out, but I had nightmares. Dreamed mother came to New York and started cleaning my apartment, and she did a great job, she threw out all my poems. *(Laughs.)* So I bit her on the neck.

NELLIE: Will you stop it? Joan! You look like death.

JOAN: So? You look like Mother. I think I'm ahead on that one —

(Nellie picks up a mound of paper strips.)

NELLIE: *(Shocked.)* You're cutting up your *bills?*

JOAN: Why not? I can't pay 'em. Why let them live?

NELLIE: Are you *crazy?*

JOAN: Am I? "YOU make the call!"

NELLIE: *(Gently.)* Joan, do you have any idea at all where Abby is?

JOAN: Of course I know where she. . .With her father. HAH! On . . . uh . . . Cape Cod! Joe takes her sailing on Cape Cod, I take her bowling at Port Authority. Oh, God! Abby made that. "Still tons o' fun at forty-one." Do I seem like tons o' fun to you, Nell? What was I — Oh, yeah, we celebrated my birthday the night she left. She wanted to — I was gonna take the banner down . . . Couldn't — God, I miss her . . . especially at night. If I can hear her breathing down the hall . . .

(She snorts.)

Like that, like a pig. She has hemorrhoids — not hemorrhoids — asteroids — No, I —

NELLIE: ADENOIDS!

JOAN: *(Smiling.)* *Le mot juste!* Thank you, Nellie. Adenoids. I think I have a short in my brain — Maybe I'm still drunk, from last night. Feel lightheaded —

(Joan snorts again.)

I love that sound . . . When I hear it? I know I'm not alone . . . Ummm. You cannot imagine how alone you can feel till you wake up in the middle of the night, in the middle of August, in the middle of Times Square. All you can hear are moans. Muffled. What was I — oh, the banner. I thought I'd leave it up till Abby comes home . . . next week or . . . I wrote it . . . somewhere.

(Joan flips through papers on the sofa and finds a rock-hard cake. She knocks on it.)

It's a birthday cake! Abby made it — a giant chocolate chip — we didn't have time to taste it. Joe came early — reminded me of our marriage. I'm saving it till she comes home . . . *If* she comes home —

NELLIE: Why wouldn't she come home?

JOAN: She's starting high school — Performing Arts yet — she needs all these dancer things . . . a thousand leotards, a million shoes . . . she wants to wear makeup, God help us . . . I mean if you had a choice between Park Avenue and Times Square, which one would you choose?

NELLIE: Joe doesn't live on Park Avenue.

JOAN: It's Park Avenue from here!

NELLIE: *(Softly.)* Do you know how long Abby's been gone, Joan?

JOAN: Why are you talking like that? Like I'm some sort of retarded client of yours?

NELLIE: Do you know how long Abby's been gone or not?

JOAN: *(Confiding.)* In days? . . . Well, I would know except — don't get mad, okay, Nellie? *(Whispers.)* I don't know what today is. Is it Thursday?

NELLIE: No, Joan, it's —

JOAN: I MEANT MONDAY! I FELT it was Monday; I KNEW it was Monday, but I just didn't have enough faith in myself to go with my first instinct —

NELLIE: It's Tuesday.

JOAN: Oh, God.

NELLIE: Have you gone outside since your birthday party?

JOAN: *(Considering.)* No . . . I don't think — Oh, yeah, I did — to the deli. Smiler's — where no one ever smiles — bought beer.

NELLIE: Do you remember if —

JOAN: *(Very intense.)* You ask so many *questions*. I just got up, Nell . . . don't even know what time it is . . . I hid my watch somewhere . . . maybe I wrote where on a card . . .

NELLIE: DON'T look for it! . . . Joan, something bad has happened to you. But if you don't tell me what it is —

JOAN: Nothing.

NELLIE: I don't believe that.

JOAN: That's what happened. Nothing. I have such a sense of it now. Nothing. It fills the room.

NELLIE: I do not understand a word you're —

JOAN: *(Cheerily.)* You know, Nell, there comes a time in everyone's wife — God, I think I'm still drunk. I don't mean everyone's wife . . . I mean — What do I mean?

NELLIE: Everyone's life —

JOAN: Yeah! When you have *had* it. I'm living in goddamn Times Square, teaching Rooskies how to maul the English language, working for RUBLES! So I can be free to write WHAT? *(As a Russian.)* "POEMS, Mrs? But vee already haf poems. Ve haf Poosh-keen!" It is totally unnecessary to write poetry. No one needs it. In fact, it just annoys people . . . more than you'd imagine, actually. So . . .

(Joan moves to paper cutter and holds up shredded paper.)

NELLIE: *(Staggered.)* You cut up your *poems?*

JOAN: I call it editing.

NELLIE: You *shredded* all your poems —

JOAN: I don't think they'll be missed. I need a new line of work. I'm thinking confetti. It's hot, but seasonal. Big on New Year's Eve, specially in this neighborhood —

NELLIE: *(Shaken.)* Joan, you're scaring me —

JOAN: I *am* a poet! So what if nobody else knows it?

(Nellie moves to phone.)

I know it!

(Joan chops.)

I know it!

(She chops again.)

I know it!

(She chops. Nellie dials.)

NELLIE: Hi, It's Nell . . . I won't be back today . . . A personal problem —

JOAN: *(Still chopping.)* SHE HAS TO SHRINK HER BIG SISTER'S HEAD. *(Nellie flips through her Filofax.)*

NELLIE: I'm not really free — Right! I'll call you later, let you know — Oh, will you cancel my four o'clock? . . . Mrs. Hernandez? Her number —

JOAN: Now's your chance, Mrs. Hernandez! Grab your kids before the Big Social Worker comes back. Pack the Doritos, Mrs. Hernandez! Get out of town!

NELLIE: One more wisecrack, and I'll hit you. I have to think!

JOAN: I can hear the wheels grinding . . . "exceeding small."

(Joan makes a fan with strips of paper and fans herself.)

NELLIE: Goddamit! Will you shut up!

JOAN: *(In a child's voice.)* We're not allowed to say shut up, Nellie.

NELLIE: *(Panicky.)* Joan, you're not like this!

JOAN: *(Genuinely surprised.)* I'm not?

NELLIE: No! Never. You're on top of things — everything — everyone.

JOAN: I liked you better when we were kids. You were afraid of me then —

NELLIE: I still am. Especially right now.

JOAN: You're getting hysterical.

NELLIE: Well, you *stink!*

JOAN: I take umbrage at that remark.

NELLIE: And you don't . . . make sense.

JOAN: You think Gertrude Stein doesn't make sense.

NELLIE: I'm not arguing. I admit it! You're older, you're smarter, you're *taller* than me. *You're better than me in every way!* You still need a doctor.

JOAN: Are you saying doctor so I won't think shrink? You treat me like a moron.

NELLIE: I want you to see Dr. Stern.

(Nellie dials.)

JOAN: Stern. Nice name for a shrink. Soooo nonthreatening —

NELLIE: I'm not *asking* you. *(On phone.)* Hello? . . . Dr. Stern, please . . . Yes, I'll hold. *(To Joan.)* Do you know that you forget the most basic things — like locking your front door. Like — ugh — like taking a shower?

JOAN: Wait'll you turn forty. You'll forget your name.

NELLIE: Dr. Stern? It's Nellie — No, I'm fine, it's my sister. The one I told you . . . Right, Joan!

JOAN: You talked about *me* in therapy? YOU SKUNK!

NELLIE: Yes, but today! . . . Or tomorrow, if we have to — just for observation. . . . Whichever one will take her . . . It's sort of an emergency, yes —

JOAN: I WON'T BE THERE, DR. STERNO!

NELLIE: So, you'll call when — Fine . . . Can I give her one of my tranks — Thanks. *(Hangs up.)* You have to get cleaned up, in case they have a bed —

JOAN: What?

NELLIE: He's gonna try to get you into a hospital tonight —

JOAN: WHAT?

NELLIE: Or tomorrow. Just for observation.

JOAN: Yeah. And they give me a cute little rubber dress.

NELLIE: You sign yourself in. Come out anytime you like!

JOAN: I'm not going! Therapy is crap. What the hell has it done for you? You've been paying that schmuck a fortune for three years, and what do you have to show for it? You're afraid of waiters, for God's sake! You can't talk to mother on the phone, you get a facial tic. You can't even serve a meal without apologizing all over yourself —

NELLIE: You're right, Joan. I'm just a spineless jellyfish —

JOAN: Redundant!

NELLIE: — And you're superwoman!

JOAN: I don't *need* Freud! I read *Oedipus* — twice!

NELLIE: Do you need your daughter, Joan?

JOAN: What are you talking about?

NELLIE: Joe called me this afternoon. He was supposed to bring Abby back this morning. Do you remember that?

(Joan shakes her head.)

But when they got here, the door was bolted — probably the one time you remembered to lock it. Did you hear someone pounding on the door this morning?

(Joan shakes her head.)

So they went to Joe's. They called all day, but nobody answered. Joe's furious. Abby's hysterical. Are you listening?

(Joan shakes her head.)

Fine. You just stay here and stink, and I'll tell Joe he can keep Abby, that you're giving him custody. Besides, if he saw you right now, he'd take you to court — and he'd win.

JOAN: You missed your calling, Nellie. You should've been a Nazi.

NELLIE: Just get into the shower.

JOAN: A typical Nazi line.

NELLIE: Joan, come on, get cleaned up. I'll help you.

JOAN: What if they call while I'm in the shower? I don't know what to wear. Everything I own makes me look crazy. . . . Do I have time to wash my hair?

NELLIE: Wash everything! Hospitals treat you better if you come clean.

JOAN: *(Laughing.)* Come clean, Nellie. Come clean. *(Pulling on her sash.)* GOD-DAMMIT! I can't untie this stupid sash! I haven't taken it off in so long, it got stuck.

(Nellie takes Joan's sash.)

JOAN: DON'T! Don't touch me! I'm not helpless. I can take off my own clothes, thank you very much!

NELLIE/JOAN: Joan, let me — //Hand me those scissors.

NELLIE/JOAN: Let me help you — //DON'T TOUCH ME!

JOAN: HAND EM OVER!

(Nellie hands Joan scissors. Joan cuts off her sash.)

JOAN: *(Triumphant.)* HAH! And you said I couldn't do it by myself!

NELLIE: Boy, is my face red. Here take this.

(She hands Joan a pill.)

JOAN: What is it? A chill pill? Good, I'm sweating like a pig.

(Joan seems to take the pill.)

Abby must be worried sick! She was supposed to come home — What day is it?

NELLIE: It's Tuesday. Call after you shower. And I'll pick out a very sane-looking outfit for you to wear.

JOAN: Okay. But not like yours. You definitely look like a nut.

(Joan exits. Lights fade for a beat. Lights up. Evening. Nellie cleans the kitchen.)

JOAN: *(Off.)* Was that Dr. Sterno on the phone?

NELLIE: Yes. They'll take you in the morning, at nine. *(Under her breath.)* Thank you, St. Jude, for doing the impossible.

JOAN: *(Off.)* Oh, great . . . Didn't they empty the loony bins in like 1970? Didn't I see a docu — Didn't they close all the — So why is this one still open? And why do I have to wait to be locked up in it?

(Joan enters, dressed, and carrying a quart of beer.)

NELLIE: You're not going to be locked up!. . . It's voluntary. You can come out any time you want to.

JOAN: I didn't ask you to clean my kitchen . . . Did I?

NELLIE: No. But I can't make dinner if it's this dirty.

JOAN: I don't remember asking you to make dinner, either. Why don't you go home and clean your own kitchen?

NELLIE: *(Tensely.)* Because Dr. Stern said I can't leave you alone.

JOAN: *(Crying.)* I'm sorry you hate taking care of me. Believe me, if I could take care of myself, I wouldn't ask you for a goddamn thing . . . I'm sorry I can't keep my mouth shut.

NELLIE: Don't cry now. You were going to call Joe, remember?

JOAN: *(Panicky.)* You called him, didn't you? You told him not to let Abby come here, didn't you? You said you'd —

NELLIE: I called him! But I said you'd call, too, talk to Abby. Try to sound more . . . *up* . . . when you call him.

JOAN: Up?

NELLIE: Okay, normal.

JOAN: To be normal, I need beer.

NELLIE: *(Stunned.)* You never drink beer.

JOAN: I do now.

(Joan holds up the bottle, showing it's empty.)

NELLIE: You drink it by the quart?

JOAN: Just like Grandma.

NELLIE: I'll get it. *(Sweetly.)* Why don't you call Joe now?

JOAN: *(Sweetly.)* Why don't you stop talking to me like I'm a borderline imbecile?

(Nellie hands Joan the beer.)

I'll *do it!* Just give me some privacy, okay?

(Nellie exits. Joan drinks fast and belches loudly.)

JOAN: *(As Hollywood Indian.)* Ah, evil spirit come out. Now you not crazy no more.

(She dials, then hangs up. She tries rehearsing, to sound normal.)

Hi, Joe! . . . The shrink said I need to . . . uh . . . go into the hospital for a few d — for a week, or maybe two.

(She suddenly seems to be talking to the real Joe.)

I did! . . . NO! I asked him about Abby — wait a minute! I wrote it down — Don't let Abby come here. Please don't let Abby . . . I don't want her to see me like this. Nooooo — *(Aware of the break.)* I don't want anyone to see me like this — *I* don't want to see me like this . . .

(She pulls the towel over her head and sits still.)

JOAN: *(Singing.)* They're coming to take me away, ha ha. They're coming to take me away, ha ha, ho-ho, hee-hee. . .

(Nellie enters, sees Joan, bangs her head on the wall.)

NELLIE: *(Sincerely.)* Please, God, please help me —

JOAN: I didn't know you still prayed.

NELLIE: Only in moments of desperation.

JOAN: Oh, God. A desperate woman cooking dinner —

(Nellie serves dinner.)

I'm not hungry.

NELLIE: I don't care. You're eating.

JOAN: If I eat, I'll throw up.

NELLIE: Fine. As long as you eat first. That's nature's way.

JOAN: I think I'd die if I ate anything.

NELLIE: Eat. You'll feel better. You're showing all the symptoms of a starving person . . . who just drank a lot of beer.

JOAN: I never liked beer. Never drank it in my life except when someone forced it on me, like at some goddamn barbecue. I hate barbecue. I hate beer. Except for right now. I used to be quite discriminating about wine, though, after Joe. Joe grew up with shoe trees, with little leather pouches for things. Joe could speak French. Menu French.

(She gulps beer.)

Joe had a lot of class.

(She belches.)

NELLIE: Eat!

JOAN: I'll eat the rice, if I *can.*

(Joan eats one grain of rice.)

Did I ever tell you how to make perfect rice?

NELLIE: A hundred times. Just eat it, okay?

JOAN: I can't. You've served the hamburger so that it's bleeding on the rice — very unappetizing. And you cooked the rice in plain water, when I told you I had a wonderful homemade chicken stock in the fridge —

NELLIE: Okay, *don't* eat. Drink. Throw up! PASS OUT. JUST SHUT UP!

JOAN: Don't get testy about it. If you'd ever listen, you'd be a fine cook. Anyone who can read, can cook —

NELLIE: *(Overlapping.)* CAN COOK! I know. When you're in the hospital, I hope they realize they've got Julia Child locked up in the psycho ward!

JOAN: *(Panicky.)* You said I wouldn't be locked up! You promised! You said I could come out anytime I —

NELLIE: You can, Joan. I'm sorry. I lost my temper.

JOAN: You want nothing but praise from me. Well, I cannot praise a meal that is an insult to the word *meal.*

NELLIE: Fine. I'll be in Abby's room eating my bloody rice.

(Nellie takes her plate and exits. Joan cuts up her food with care, then tosses it like a salad, throwing in any food from table — bread, butter, etc.)

JOAN: I spent ten years of my life, my entire marriage, letting cheeses come to room temperature, chilling champagne ninety minutes, serving hot food on hot plates. Joe knew all the rules. Bake plates at 225 for four minutes for medium/rare plates, right, Joe? You made me a wonderful cook. You *made* me . . . Everybody said so. Everybody but you. You always found the fly in the ointment. "Just a *soupçon* too much garlic, just a *soupcon* too much tarragon." I always wondered if I pissed into the beef bourguignon, what would you say? "Just a *soupçon* too much . . . *Je ne sais quoi.*" What was wrong with me, Joe? Why was I the only one you didn't want to fuck? A *soupçon* too much blue collar? A *soupçon* too much brain? GODDAMIT, ANSWER ME!

(She stops, shivers, looks at mess of food she has made, and trembles.)

(Nellie enters.)

NELLIE: I just thought of something. You shouldn't be drinking. I gave you a tranquilizer —

JOAN: I didn't take it. I palmed it. I don't like drugs —

(Joan grabs her purse.)

It's in here. If you want it, Nellie, you can have it. You seem awfully nervous to me.

NELLIE: NO! Thanks, Joan. But you can't take it either now that you drank all that beer. We'll just have to hope you fall asleep on your own.

JOAN: I never sleep. When I get in bed, my mind races, repeating the same words over and over. If I ever get to sleep, I dream I'm word processing — in Latin — over and over the same words — full of mistakes —

(Abby enters. She wears glasses and carries a bag.)

ABBY: *(Laughing.)* Somebody left the front door open. I bet I know who it was, Mom.

(Joan freezes in her chair.)

Before you yell, wait one second. I brought you a present from Cape Cod that you need for the hospital.

JOAN: *(Trembling.)* Okay. Sure. Fine.

NELLIE: Does your dad know you're here?

ABBY: I left a note. He went running right after you called, Nellie.

(Silence. Abby seems puzzled.)

JOAN: *(Shaken.)* Well, hello, lovey.

(Abby and Joan embrace.)

You look like you grew at least two inches. I think you're almost as tall as Nellie.**

NELLIE: In your dreams!

ABBY: Everyone in this family is obsessed with height.

JOAN: So where's this present, huh? Nellie, could you get me a beer? You can't stay long, you know, darling.

ABBY: I know. I know. Wait until you open this. You will love this present!

(Hands paper bag to Joan, who opens it.)

Lobster slippers! Are they the best, or what?

JOAN: Should I wear these to the hospital? They might move me to the criminally insane section.

ABBY: *(Laughing.)* No. See, you wear lobster slippers and everybody in the place — doctors and patients — will watch their step around you. They mess with you, you pinch 'em.

(Joan puts on slippers, furry red lobsters with feelers that bob up and down.)

JOAN: These are great, aren't they, Nellie? They are definitely a conversation starter . . . If the other patients are able to speak, that is . . .

(Joan begins to cry silently. She stands in her lobster slippers like a statue, tears rolling down her cheeks.)

ABBY: Mom! MOTHER! *(Abby hugs Joan.)* Don't cry, Mom, don't cry! It's okay. You don't hafta wear the slippers.

NELLIE: Abby, I think you should go now.

(Abby strokes Joan's face.)

ABBY: DON'T DO THIS, MOM. DON'T CRY LIKE THIS. *(Abby shakes Joan gently.)* PLEASE, MOM, MAKE NOISE!

NELLIE: Come on, it's late. Your dad will be worried.

(Nellie pulls Abby away from Joan, who remains stiff. Abby shoves Nellie away.)

ABBY: I AM NOT LEAVING. DON'T YOU TOUCH ME. SHE'S MY MOTHER. SHE'S MINE.

(Abby leads Joan to a chair, and seats her gently.)

It's okay, Mom. You don't hafta make noise if you don't want to. It's just when you cry like this without making any sounds, it scares me.

(Abby climbs into Joan's lap, her arms around Joan's neck, begins to pat Joan's face.)

ABBY: I don't need contacts. I don't need anything. Don't worry about money. I can get a job. You don't hafta go away. I can take care of you. I'll come home for lunch. I can make soup and brownies and . . . whip cream. I can vacuum! You don't hafta do anything, okay, Mom? *Okay?*

NELLIE: You have to go home now.

ABBY: DON'T TOUCH HER!

NELLIE: GO! NOW!

ABBY: *You* go! This is my house!

NELLIE: DAMmit, Abby, you're no help if —

ABBY: She's not your Mother!

NELLIE: Yes, SHE IS! . . . I mean, oh, hell . . . It doesn't matter, you have to leave right now!

ABBY: Shut up! Just shut up!

JOAN: *(Flatly.)* Don't say shut up to your aunt. It's rude.

ABBY: Are you okay, Mom?

JOAN: No, my love, I am not okay.

NELLIE: Will you tell her she has to leave, Joan?

JOAN: *Does* she have to leave, Nellie?

NELLIE: Yes. I think we should all go to bed.

JOAN: *(Flatly.)* Some of us have nothing to do there.

ABBY: You don't hafta go to the hospital, Mom —

JOAN: Yes, I do, Ab.

ABBY: *(Wildly.)* No, you don't! There are *crazy* people there!

NELLIE: *(Flatly.)* There are crazy people here, too.

ABBY: *(To Nellie.)* Don't you talk! *(To Joan.)* I didn't say shut up —

JOAN: I want to go to the hospital, Ab. I need them to take care of me. When I come home, you can take care of me. Now go back to Daddy's. I want you to.

ABBY: Okay. But tomorrow, I'm coming to the hospital. I'm going to say I'm sixteen or however old I have to be. And if they don't let me in, I will throw a tantrum like you wouldn't believe.

NELLIE: *I'll* believe it.

JOAN: Go downstairs with her, okay, Nell? Put her in a cab.

ABBY: I don't need to take a cab —

JOAN: That's true. *I* need you to take a cab, okay? Nellie, *please* —

NELLIE: I'm coming. I'm coming.

ABBY: I'll see you tomorrow, Mom, no matter what!

(Abby hugs Joan and exits.)

NELLIE: Thank God. And I always say, "I just love kids." Get ready for bed, okay, Joan? I'll be just a —

(Joan moves to the kitchen.)

JOAN: I can't. I have bread rising. I have to bake it before I can go to the hospital.

NELLIE: What?

JOAN: I made the dough this afternoon. It won't be good by the time I get home again.

(Joan picks up the bowl.)

NELLIE: It's a hundred degrees in here. Are you crazy?

JOAN: Nellie, she's out there by herself — in the *dark!*

NELLIE: Fine. Do whatever you want! You always do.

(Nellie exits. Joan turns out lights and goes to kitchen. She lights candles and sets them at the edge of her table. She oils her hands and begins kneading the dough. As she speaks, she shapes the dough into loaves and other things.)

JOAN: In the winter, on Saturday mornings, Mama would make bread. And all of us would help . . . I don't usually make bread in summer. Or in the dark. But it's cooler now. I have to get it done before I go into the hospital tomorrow. You don't need a lot of light to make bread. You can feel your way. It's soft, smooth, rubbery. You can play with it if you want to.

It's okay. Not like pie dough. "DON'T PLAY WITH THE PIE DOUGH, YOU'LL MAKE IT TOUGH!"

Mama was always happy when we made bread. She didn't work on Saturdays. Or Sundays. Otherwise, she always worked, except when she had a baby. Nellie's the baby. I'm the oldest. I'm in charge here . . .

I'm gonna make some breadsticks for Nellie. Nellie likes to make breadsticks in circles. I like to make long, fat, thick, straight breadsticks. I should tell that to Dr. Stern. *(Laughs.)* I tried to tell him about making bread, but I don't think he understood.

(Nellie appears in the doorway, but Joan doesn't see her.)

I'm happy doing it. I don't know why it makes me cry. Most women cry when they cook. Women throughout history have cooked and cried at the same time. It isn't unusual, and it doesn't affect the taste of the food. My mother yelled when she cooked. Banged pans together. Broke things. But she never cried.

I don't want Mother to know I'm in the psycho ward. She thinks I'm perfect . . . I used to be . . . I used to be . . . perfect . . . won all the prizes . . . made the beds . . . the house was always chaotic . . . everybody's shoes on the stairs . . . I made order . . . I was the mother when the mother wasn't home . . . My mother would be ashamed to have a daughter who blubbered at everything . . . Just because she didn't cry when Daddy died didn't mean she wasn't sad. But she was afraid that if she let herself cry she'd never stop . . . And someone had to go to work and make money . . . to feed us, all five of us . . . buy shoes . . .

Making bread makes people happy, and it's simple to do. You can't make a mistake. Everyone will like it. No one will say homemade bread is bad or dumb or unoriginal . . . When I was in college, I worked in a bakery, made pastry . . . eclairs . . . cream puffs — hundreds at a time . . . But I always liked making bread best . . .

Maybe I should have stayed in the bakery . . . given up pastry . . . made bread.

(Joan scoops up flour in each hand and slowly rubs it all over her face.)

NELLIE: *(Breaking down.)* Oh, Jo-Jo —

JOAN: I need some holder. Hold me, Nellie. Please.

(Nellie wraps her arms around Joan from behind. Silence.)

Remember, we used to say, "Gimme some holder, Mom. I need some holder" . . . NELLIE! Don't let go!

(They remain still, Nellie's arms locked around Joan as the lights fade.)

END OF PLAY

NOTE:

**If actress playing Abby is taller than Nellie, use dialogue that follows:

JOAN: You look like you grew at least two inches. I think you're taller than Nellie.

ABBY: I was taller than Nellie in fifth grade.

NELLIE: Everyone in this family is obsessed with height.

Old Wives Tale
by Julie Jensen

BIOGRAPHY

Julie Jensen's play *Two-Headed*, commissioned by ASK Theatre Projects in LA, was produced by the Women's Project in New York. It has also been produced in Los Angeles and Salt Lake City. *Last Lists of My Mad Mother*, commissioned by Mark Taper Forum, has been produced widely in this country and at the Fringe Festival in Edinburgh, Scotland. It is published by Dramatic Publishing. *The Lost Vegas Series* won the Joseph Jefferson Award for Best New Work. It was produced in Chicago and London. She won the CBS/Dramatists Guild Prize for her play, *Stray Dogs*, and the Kennedy Center Award for New American Plays for *White Money*.

Until recently she directed the Graduate Playwriting Program at University of Nevada, Las Vegas, and is now playwright-in-residence at Salt Lake Acting Company. She is the recipient of a TCG/NEA Residency Grant as well as a major grant from the Pew Charitable Trust.

PRODUCTION HISTORY

The one-act version of this play, *Old Wives Tale*, was produced by the Women's Project in New York and the Theatre of NOTE in Los Angeles. It was also excerpted in the *Georgia Review*.

The fuller version of the play, *Tenderhooks*, has had two professional staged readings, one by Patchett-Kaufman Entertainment in Los Angeles and one by The Utah Shakespearean Festival in Cedar City.

It also won the Norfolk Southern New Play Competition at Mill Mountain Theatre in Roanoke, VA, and was given three professional staged readings there in October 1996.

CHARACTERS

LA PRIEL: (pronounced LaPREEL.) A woman in her mid-sixties, slight of build, rather birdlike and precise. Nervous, frightened, orderly, strong-willed. A piano teacher.

MARGERY: La Priel's older sister, also in her mid-sixties. Rather heavy and slow, a master of folk wisdom which she dispenses freely.

LETHA: (pronounced LEEtha.) A tall (5'3"), lanky nine-year-old girl. Bright in her own way, energetic, disarming. She has only three fingers on her right hand. (Meant to be played by an adult.)

MRS. HICKS: A neighbor. The mother of five children, including Letha. In her thirties but looks older than her years. Direct and slow of speech, she seems both threatening and seductive.

THE SETTING

The immaculately clean kitchen and back porch of La Priel's house, located in a small town in rural America. An archway leads to the living room, a doorway leads to a hall, the bedrooms and the bathroom. The kitchen is practical, with running water and a working stove.

SYNOPSIS

A family with five children, each with a physical deformity, has moved in next door to La Priel. She is both frightened and preoccupied by them. The inevitable collision produces unexpected changes in La Priel herself.

OLD WIVES TALE

SCENE ONE

The setting is La Priel's kitchen with attached kitchenette. A house built in the 1920s, it is not elegant, but it is immaculately clean. There is, however, no sense of style or taste. It is late afternoon.

Margery sits slumped in one of the kitchen chairs in the kitchenette. She is short, heavy, slow, and overly authoritative, in her mid-sixties.

La Priel is near the back screen door, looking out, absorbed, preoccupied, worried. She is about the same age as Margery, possessed of a much more flighty tempo and rhythm, seems always threatened.

MARGERY: The rez-avoy is way low, they say. Ben Marchant and them was out there the other night. Last night, I guess it was. Yes, cuz he was jist tellin' me about it today. And he says it's below the weir. And it ain't been like that since he can remember.
(Pause. A tea kettle on the stove begins to whistle.)
Me and Wesley was out there, oh a week ago or so, see if we could catch us some fish fer dinner. That musta been Wednesday? Yeah, it was Wednesday because Rena and Dutch come on Thursday. And that was the day before. Probably the same day as yer folks next door moved in.
(Pause. Margery notes the tea kettle whistling.)
And I says to Wesley then I didn't ever remember the rez-avoy so low. You could walk out passed them reeds. Well, Wesley could. I don't like to walk through them kinda things. They remind me of snakes. And I says to Wesley I don't want to think about snakes any more than's necessary, and least of all, I don't want to be thinking about snakes standin' up.
(Pause. Noting LaPriel's preoccupation.)
That's what them reeds put in my mind. *(Pause.)* La Priel. La Priel. La Priel, that water's boilin'.

LA PRIEL: *(As if bumped awake.)* Laws!
(Smiles.)
Well then. Postum time, ain't it?

MARGERY: I'd think so . . .

LA PRIEL: *(Getting cups and saucers and putting them on the table.)* Now what is it you take?

MARGERY: A teaspoon of Postum.

LA PRIEL: Oh my land. Yes.

(She gets the bottle from the cupboard.)

Only five more of these left from that case I bought. What else you take?

MARGERY: Hot water.

LA PRIEL: Oh gracious. Well. You see how rattled I am. Some days is better than others. But this bunch next door . . .

(Gets tea kettle from the stove.)

Can ya hear 'em from there yet?

MARGERY: Can't hear a thing.

LA PRIEL: Well, ya will. Them kids will be out soon.

(Returns to table, pouring hot water in both cups.)

First they git in that tire swing. All of 'em. I don't know how many it is . . .

MARGERY: Don't see nobody yet.

LA PRIEL: Then they rough-house around, yellin' and screamin', ya know. Then they'll all scatter. Quiet as nothing. Ya find 'em under the porch, in the lilac bushes, rattling around in the forsythia, I don't know what all . . .

MARGERY: Ya got any sugar?

LA PRIEL: Why? Ya think that would discourage them?

MARGERY: I like sugar in my Postum, La Priel.

LA PRIEL: Oh sure. My goodness.

(She gets sugar bowl. Sits. Pause. They both drink. Margery seriously and intently, LaPriel rather nervously. They alternately look out the window and blow on their Postum.)

MARGERY: Sure is dry. When it's like this, you jist can't keep a lawn up. I says to Wesley the other day, you'd have to keep the hose goin all the time if ya wanted to keep a lawn green in this kinda weather. Even then you couldn't do it.

(Pause. Sips loudly.)

We haven't had the water turn in three weeks. Wes went up again this morning, jist to see. But he jist turned right around and come back, cuz there wasn't enough water to wet the ditch.

(Sigh. Pause.)

It's gonna be a tough time, we don't git some storm.

LA PRIEL: Lookit, here they come. Can ya see 'em out there now? Look at 'em all. How many'd you figger that is?

MARGERY: They all belong to her?

LA PRIEL: So far as I know.

MARGERY: Well, they sure do make up a collection, don't they?

LA PRIEL: What did I tell ya? And ever one of them has got something missing. Jist keep a watch-out. You'll see what I mean.

MARGERY: Like what missing?

LA PRIEL: Pert near anything. Some of 'em ain't got all their fingers. Others missing toes. At least one of 'em's got only one ear. Strangest collection of kids you ever seen.

MARGERY: They look normal enough from here.

LA PRIEL: Well, it's the light how it is now. These long shadows, ya can't see the smaller features. You jist wait, though. They'll finish with that swing, then they'll be spread out more, you can git a look.

MARGERY: They do look a little scrawny.

LA PRIEL: Geneveve Hamilson thinks they're Jehovah Witness or Seven Day Advents.

MARGERY: Well then, ya got yer hands full if it's that. One of them kind don't believe in windows. I don't know which one. And some othern don't believe in doctors er operations. And a course, their kids don't do good in school. They jist don't mix. *(Pause.)* They come from where, did ya say?

LA PRIEL: I dunno. That ole truck they come in's got a California license. 1956 though. And I suppose they *stole* that.

MARGERY: Listen, if they was gonna steal something, they coulda done better an that.

LA PRIEL: But they don't look like a Californian. Not the ones I seen.

MARGERY: Probably from Nevada. One of them little places. Like Pioche or Tonapah. One of them dinky little desert towns. Ain't got a tree, little lean-to shacks fer houses . . .

LA PRIEL: And there's no curtains over the windows.

MARGERY: Well, there wouldn't be.

LA PRIEL: Old blankets and dirty sheets.

MARGERY: Curtains one of the last things come to their mind with them kind.

LA PRIEL: *(Pause.)* Their name's Hicks.

MARGERY: Well, that sure fits, don't it?

LA PRIEL: And the man with them ain't the father. That girl that come over. Member I told you one of them come over? One that's got only the three fingers? She called him Uncle. Gene, I believe it was. Yes, because I thought of Lottie's boy when she said it. The one that shot hisself . . .

MARGERY: If he's their uncle, let's see, that would make him and her brother and sister. Them two look anything alike?

LA PRIEL: They don't. But then I ain't got a very good look at him. He sits in the cab of that truck most the day . . .

MARGERY: With the way them kids have turned out, it might be the cause of it right there.

LA PRIEL: What would be the cause?

MARGERY: In-breeding.

LA PRIEL: Oh.

MARGERY: You think they got all their sense?

LA PRIEL: Well, not by the *look* of 'em, they ain't.

MARGERY: That's yer answer then, ain't it?

LA PRIEL: In-breeding?

MARGERY: Like the people in Parowan, fer example, them in Sigurd. You know why so many of them run around half there? It's in-breeding. Jist not enough people move in. They marry each other. And that's what happens.

LA PRIEL: *(Pause.)* Course. They're pleasant enough. Wouldn't harm ya er nothin'. Them people in Parowan er Sigurd.

MARGERY: Sure they're pleasant. They got nothing to worry about. Church takes care of 'em.

LA PRIEL: But I mean they smile at ya. They're happy people.

MARGERY: Like I says, it's the Church . . .

LA PRIEL: I mean, they speak. They behave quite nicely. Not like this bunch . . . *(Long pause.)*
I always wondered if they knew it.

MARGERY: What?

LA PRIEL: That they ain't all there.

MARGERY: Course not.

LA PRIEL: Then how would ya know if you, yourself, was one?

MARGERY: Ya wouldn't.

LA PRIEL: Well then, how do we know we ain't?

MARGERY: Look at yerself, La Priel. Do ya look like them?

LA PRIEL: But if ya didn't know . . .

MARGERY: If you was one, you wouldn't know it. But if ya ain't one, ya know.

LA PRIEL: Oh. *(Pause.)* Jist look at 'em now, crawlin' up that rope. Listen, one of them is gonna fall out of that tree and right into that water ditch. Serve 'em right.

MARGERY: You can't hurt them kind. Them kind got their own special angel. That's what Mother always used to say.

LA PRIEL: See that one sittin' in the swing now? That's the one that come over. Letha. Ain't that jist a awful name fer somebody like that?

MARGERY: Names usually fit their people, er else the people grow to fit their names.

LA PRIEL: Well now, there she comes. That's her all right. She's mostly normal from what I've seen. Well, I guess she's not coming out. But that's her. Their mother.

MARGERY: She's jist put their cats out.

LA PRIEL: Oh my goodness, that's all that outfit needs is cats. Can't take care of theirselves.

MARGERY: Ain't no hair on the tails of them cats. You see that?

LA PRIEL: Neither one of them? What do you suppose is the matter with them?

MARGERY: Well, there's many things about cats that aren't quite understood. There was that cat that took the breath of Linnie Traper's baby. You remember when that baby of hers died crib death.

LA PRIEL: Oh Margery, that was quick pneumonia.

MARGERY: There's also the example of the one twenty years ago or so. Now whose baby was that? Selfie Warby's baby, I think. They used to live out in Manderfield, remember? Then they moved into the Holdaway place up by the race track. Well, their baby died of the same thing. And when they looked into it, there was a cat involved there, too.

LA PRIEL: Margery, them's jist old wives tales.

MARGERY: I always thought that cat of yours had something to do with the baby you lost.

LA PRIEL: Now listen here, I lost that baby because it was not whole. That's what they all told me. Doctor Quarrie, Iva Hamilton, all of 'em. There's ways nature has of takin' care of some.

MARGERY: You see, cats are furry. People will trust anything that's furry. But the fur of a cat is only their camouflage. If you've ever seen a cat wet, you'd think different about them.

LA PRIEL: I got to git me some more water.

(Rises and goes to stove.)

MARGERY: Course a cat don't like water. It's their instinct to stay dry.

LA PRIEL: You need any more water?

MARGERY: Because if people seen 'em wet, cats would not be invited into people's houses the way they are. And they would not be given to children as pets.

LA PRIEL: Can't I jist warm this up a bit?

MARGERY: It's really their mouth that gits the breath. Especially the breath of a little baby. You see, people got jist a plain mouth, whereas cats got the triangle mouth. A little pointed here.

(Imitating a cat face.)

LA PRIEL: They're spreadin' out now, Margery. You better pay attention. If you really want to see them . . .

MARGERY: How they steal the breath is related to two things: their feet and their mouths. The feet are so they can walk very quiet on your chest until you breathe into a rhythm. And their mouths are so they can put 'em up close to the face. And then they can take the breath direct from you into them. It's the strangest thing you'll ever experience. Course, most of them, especially babies, don't survive it.

LA PRIEL: There's the one without a ear. Can ya see him? See? He's right out there by them four o'clocks.

(She knocks on the window and gestures him away.)

MARGERY: They're dead before they have a chance. And the cat that caused it is far away by the time it's discovered.

LA PRIEL: Oops, that little one with the strange foot. He ain't got good balance. You can see that?

MARGERY: Because a cat is such a quiet walker, and also because the taking of the baby's breath is such a quiet thing. *(Quietly.)* There is a little humming sound when it happens, they say. And that's all.

LA PRIEL: *(Frozen. Very quietly.)* Now see? You don't hear nothing. That's what they always do. They're hiding. They'll be up under the porch, all around in the bushes. They're hiding.

MARGERY: Well probably that's it then.

LA PRIEL: What?

MARGERY: It's the cats that have give them kids all them deformations.

LA PRIEL: Is that what you call it?

MARGERY: Well, it's what I call it. When you see a bunch of children without all their parts, you might jist as well check out their cats. That's what I call it, all right.

(She moves as if to leave.)

LA PRIEL: Margery. I wouldn't go yet, if I was you.

MARGERY: Why not? I seen 'em.

LA PRIEL: When it's quiet like this, they're jist hiding.

(Blackout.)

ENTR'SCENE ONE

In darkness, the sound of children breathing, some of them with snotty noses. Sound of twigs breaking, brushing, rustling. Then the far-away sound of a child laughing, then calling. The echoing sound of a game being played. That fades after several seconds. The sound of the twigs remains as does a quieter sound of children breathing.

Lights come up. Sound of children breathing in unison. Sound of children breathing a chant, the words unclear. On the third time through, we understand the words:

Last night, night before
Twenty-four robbers at my door.
Who all is hid?
Who all is hid?
Last night, night before
Thirty-four robbers at my door,
Who all is hid?
Who all is hid?

(Sound of Letha chanting the rhyme alone, the other children breathing the chant:)

Last night, night before
Forty-four robbers at my door.
Who all is hid?
Who all is hid?

(During this time, La Priel moves to the stove, picks up the tea kettle, holds it. Puts it back on the stove. Turns on the heat, turns off the heat. Moves to the sink, turns on the water, in an attempt to drown out the noise. Turns off the water. Moves to the back door, peers out. Moves to the kitchenette. Stands frozen.

This action is not seen continuously, but only from time to time. We catch snatches of it. The lights should be cued to the sound.

Then silence and steady illumination. La Priel returns to her chair in the kitchenette. Brushes the crumbs from the table cloth. Leans on the table with her elbows. And lights fade.)

SCENE TWO

The scene is the same. It is later. The lights warm to a sunset. La Priel is in the same position. The sound of someone bounding on the porch. La Priel starts.

LETHA: Ya got any Jello powder?

(Standing at the screen door, her face pressed into it. She is a tall, lanky nine-year-old in ill-fitting shorts, tennis shoes, and elasticized top, which makes her look like a pole. She is energetic, disarming, sometimes intentionally obscene and grotesque. She has only three fingers on her right hand.)

LA PRIEL: Now look here. Ya half scairt me out of my wits.

LETHA: *(Small laugh.)* I know.

LA PRIEL: Well, see you don't do it again. It's rude.

LETHA: Didn't mean to, La Priel. Was a accident.

(Pause. She puts her right hand up on the screen.)

So have ya?

LA PRIEL: Have I what?

LETHA: Got any Jello powder?

LA PRIEL: Yes.

(Letha enters.)

But ya can't eat it in here. Last time ya done that, ya left them little gritty things all over the kitchenette.

LETHA: I'll take it outside, La Priel.

(Crosses to cupboard, stops, points at it.)

Is it up here?

LA PRIEL: Don't point, Letha, please. I'll git it for you.

(Begins to rise.)

LETHA: I'll git it.

(Pats her shoulder. La Priel starts.)

You jist relax, La Priel.

(Opens the cupboard, runs her finger across the boxes lined up on the shelf.)

Ya ain't got black cherry yet. I keep thinkin' you'll be gittin' black cherry.

LA PRIEL: Ya don't need black cherry.

LETHA: Sure I do.

LA PRIEL: You'd jist eat more of it than ya already do. You've got to learn to keep yourself in tow.

LETHA: *(Idly elevates onto her toes.)* I guess I'll have lime.

(Takes the box from the shelf. Tears it open, then sprinkles the powder in her hand and licks it. Pause. Leans against the sink. Pause.)

Jello powder is real relaxing, ya know. At the end of the day.

LA PRIEL: It probly rots yer stomach.

LETHA: No. I'm used to it. Now it's relaxing.

(Noting the cups in front of La Priel.)

Two cups of coffee probly do the same thing.

LA PRIEL: It's Postum.

LETHA: Oh yah. That's a pretty relaxing drink.

LA PRIEL: Fer grown-ups, yes.

LETHA: If you have two cups, it can be relaxing.

LA PRIEL: Jist one. Letha, you git that on the floor and I'm gonna paddle you.

(Begins to clear the dishes.)

LETHA: (Pause.) How come ya got two cups?

LA PRIEL: Fer my sister.

LETHA: Who's your sister?

LA PRIEL: A lady.

LETHA: What's her name?

LA PRIEL: Margery.

LETHA: Where's she live?

LA PRIEL: Other side of town.

LETHA: She look like you?

LA PRIEL: Not much.

LETHA: You like her?

LA PRIEL: Course.

LETHA: I don't have no sisters. Jist four brothers. You got any brothers?

LA PRIEL: No.

LETHA: Yer lucky. I got four. They're all dumb.

LA PRIEL: That's nice.

LETHA: It ain't either! It's awful. Uncle June's dumb too. Dumber than a chicken. He can't even read good. He reads out loud with his fingers pointin' at the words. It's embarrassing.

LA PRIEL: Well, I'm sure that ain't the worst of yer problems.

(Moves Letha out of the way.)

LETHA: Me and Ma is the only smart ones. I got all my brains from her. And that's lucky. Cuz it could of been a lots worst. That's what Ma says.

LA PRIEL: (Thinks on it. Shudders.) Yes. Well, I suppose it could be.

(Moves Letha out of the way.)

How many others ya got over there, did ya say?

LETHA: Kids? Five. Includin' me. I'm the oldest. Then is Waller, then Tice, then Minter an' Mayton. Them last two is twins, but they don't look nothing alike.

LA PRIEL: None of the kids in yer family looks anything alike.

LETHA: I'm the oldest. Guess how old that is. *(Pause.)* Wrong! Nine and leven-twelfths. I be ten on September the twenty-eighth. One month. A teenager starts at ten.

LA PRIEL: *(Startled.)* No. No it don't, Letha.

LETHA: Nine is half-way between girl and teenager. Ten is a teenager.

LA PRIEL: Well, that depends on the person.

LETHA: It depends on me, I'm gonna be a teenager.

LA PRIEL: I wouldn't rush into that if I was you.

LETHA: Better, a lot better than bein' a baby er a kid.

LA PRIEL: Some people don't do so good with it, don't fergit. Bein' a teenager. *(Moves Letha. Begins washing cups and saucers and spoons in the running water.)*

LETHA: *(Pause. Idly looking at a 1920s photograph of a cupid.)* Who's this pitcher of?

LA PRIEL: No one.

LETHA: Is it jist decoration?

LA PRIEL: Yes.

LETHA: Did somebody give it to ya?

LA PRIEL: Yes.

LETHA: Who?

LA PRIEL: My husband.

LETHA: Fer a present?

LA PRIEL: I suppose.

LETHA: Do you like it?

LA PRIEL: Course.

LETHA: It's kinda weird. What's she holdin' them arrows like a triangle for?

LA PRIEL: It's fer Valentine's Day.

LETHA: *(Moves near the hallway.)* Oh. Where's yer bedrooms?

LA PRIEL: Down the hall.

LETHA: Mine's in the fruit room. I'm only one gits their own room. Cept fer the fruit's in there. Where's yer husband live?

LA PRIEL: He don't.

LETHA: Is he dead? Wewww. *(Pause.)* What's his name?

LA PRIEL: Who?

LETHA: Yer husband.

LA PRIEL: Rulon.

LETHA: Is he buried?

LA PRIEL: Yes.

LETHA: Do you sleep in the same bedroom?

LA PRIEL: That's enough, Letha.

LETHA: Weww, that's scary. You sleep in the same room as a dead man. Is it the same bed?

LA PRIEL: I said that's enough, Letha.

LETHA: If it was a big bed, that would be *real* scary. I got a little bed. It's a Army cot. But I'm the only one gets their own room. Where's *yer* kids sleep?

LA PRIEL: *(Washing the two cups again with a kind of nervous ferocity.)* Don't have any.

LETHA: How come?

LA PRIEL: I jist never had any.

LETHA: Why?

LA PRIEL: That ain't polite to ask, Letha.

LETHA: I ain't gonna have none neither. It's too fussy all the time, fightin' around and stuff.

LA PRIEL: Well, you got a long time to think about that.

LETHA: Too much messing around and noise. I might git married though. I might do that.

LA PRIEL: Well, that's a long time off.

LETHA: You got it pretty good, I think, without no kids, and with this many rooms.

LA PRIEL: Yes. Well, I'm used to it. But ya do miss some things.

LETHA: I wouldn't miss nothing. What'd ya miss? *(Pause.)* La Priel, ya already washed them once.

LA PRIEL: I know.

LETHA: Are ya gonna wash 'em all again?

LA PRIEL: No.

LETHA: Why?

LA PRIEL: They're clean.

LETHA: *Everything* is *clean!*

LA PRIEL: *(Forcefully.)* Well, that's one of the things that comes of not havin' so many kids.

LETHA: Yah. *(Pause.)* You got any beers?

LA PRIEL: What?

LETHA: Got any beers?

LA PRIEL: No. A course not.

LETHA: I like beers.

LA PRIEL: Not that kinda talk, now Letha.

LETHA: Uncle June bought a whole case of beers once. So's he could take 'em to the races and make money. He never, though. He jist got picked up. *(Pause.)* Uncle June hat to stay all night in jail once.

LA PRIEL: *(Sighs. Picks up dish towel and begins to wipe dishes.)* Ya don't have to tell everything ya know, Letha.

LETHA: See, Waller stold this gun and he hid it in the truck. Then Uncle June got picked up. And they says . . .

LA PRIEL: He what?

LETHA: Got picked up.

LA PRIEL: No. Before that.

LETHA: Waller stold a gun . . . and hid it in the truck.

LA PRIEL: That's what I thought you said.

LETHA: Yah. And then Uncle June got picked up. And they says, "What's this?" And it was the gun. And Uncle June says, "It's a toy gun," cuz he didn't never see it. But it wasn't, so they took him to jail cuz he lied. *(Pause.)* Well, they *thought* he lied, but he didn't really because Waller stold it. But he hat to stay all night in jail.

LA PRIEL: *(Controlling herself.)* What'd they do to Walter?

LETHA: *(Correcting.)* Waller. Nothin. He's only eight. Uncle June trounced him good, though. He hat to do everything he said for a whole week. It was like everthing he said Waller *hat* to do it. And they would be real hard things, like go in there and carry all them chairs into the living room. Then when he got done, carry 'em all back into the kitchroom again. Uncle June says it was like the Army. If that's what Waller wanted to play, he could jist as leaf play real Army.

LA PRIEL: *(A bit shaken.)* Which one is Waller?

LETHA: Don't have a ear.

LA PRIEL: Oh yes.

LETHA: You seen him?

LA PRIEL: Yes.

LETHA: He's usually around.

LA PRIEL: Well, you jist tell Waller he's not to come on this lot.

LETHA: *Okay!*

LA PRIEL: And I don't want no one else that steals on my lot neither.

LETHA: Well, Waller would be the only one there. But I'll tell him. Sides, I'm oldern him. I can beat him up.

LA PRIEL: Well, I don't like beatin' up neither.

LETHA: Oh yah. Me neither. It's not polite.

LA PRIEL: It certainly ain't.

LETHA: Choppin' the head off snakes is okay though, huh?

LA PRIEL: *(Rattled.)* I think ya better go on outside with that now, Letha.

LETHA: Okay.

(Exits to the porch and mounts the porch railing. La Priel checks the room. All is clean. She resolutely sits down at the table. Looks out the window. Long pause.)

It's pretty good here now, huh?

LA PRIEL: *(Preoccupied.)* What?

LETHA: Doin' this.

LA PRIEL: What?

LETHA: Watchin' it git dark.

LA PRIEL: Oh. Yes.

LETHA: It's a pretty good one, huh?

LA PRIEL: What?

LETHA: Sunset.

LA PRIEL: Oh. Yes.

LETHA: You can see the sunset good from yer windows, I bet.

LA PRIEL: You can see it good from the porch.

LETHA: Oh yah. It's good here, too. I like to watch sunsets. They're relaxing.

LA PRIEL: Yes. I guess so.

LETHA: *(Pause.)* It's the dirt does it.

LA PRIEL: Does what?

LETHA: Makes it colors. We used to live by the smelter. It was great sunsets there. Did you ever live by the smelter?

LA PRIEL: No.

LETHA: We did. It was a lots more dirt. *(Pause.)* But it smelled jist like farts sometimes.

LA PRIEL: Not them kinda *words,* Letha, please.

LETHA: There ain't any other word for it.

LA PRIEL: Yes there is.

(Realizing she could be caught.)

Never mind.

LETHA: *(Pause.)* Have you ever got on a bus at sunset and rode it all night?

LA PRIEL: No. I haven't.

LETHA: I done that. When I was eight. But I hat to sit behind the driver chair cuz this *other* man kept moving his zipper and keeping me awake.

LA PRIEL: *(Eyes closing.)* Letha, please . . .

LETHA: You couldn't see very much, though. Cafés and stuff was mostly all. That's when I went to Pioche. Did you ever go to Pioche?

LA PRIEL: No. Not that I can remember.

LETHA: Well, you would remember if you was there. They got these big bee-tles all over. Specially at the gas station. And they're maybe like two inches er maybe like three inches — acrosst. And I don't know how long. They sorta crawl around and fly into things and stuff. They're maybe like part bird and part bug. Beetles. You can kill 'em easy though. *(Pause.)* But it's awful if you step on one without no shoes on.

LA PRIEL: Yes, Letha. That's enough on that.

LETHA: Yah. *(Pause.)* I seen a cat eat one once.

LA PRIEL: Letha! Listen here. Did you *come* from Pioche?

LETHA: Nah. Jist went there.

LA PRIEL: Where'd ya come from?

LETHA: When?

LA PRIEL: Before this.

LETHA: Right before? Winnemucca. Then before that Panaca. Then before that Wendover. Then before that Elko. Then before that Truckee. No, Caliente. One of them two. Then before that Barstow. I was born in Barstow.

LA PRIEL: *(Sighs.)* I see.

LETHA: What other towns you live in?

LA PRIEL: None. Jist this one.

LETHA: Goll. That's weird.

LA PRIEL: Well listen here. Ya gotta behave in this town. It ain't like them oth-ers ya been in.

LETHA: Can I come in and git a drink of water?

LA PRIEL: If ya behave.

LETHA: *(Enters and begins to drink from the faucet, catches herself, opens the cup-board, gets a glass, drinks. Sets the glass on the counter. Catches herself again. Picks it up, washes it in imitation of La Priel and wipes it. Then puts it away. La Priel looks on with relief. Letha then moves to the table and sits down opposite La Priel. Spreading her hands on the tablecloth.)*
I heard ya playin' the piano fer 'em today.

LA PRIEL: That wasn't me.

LETHA: Who was it?

LA PRIEL: A lesson.

LETHA: You jist learnin' it?

LA PRIEL: Teachin' it.

LETHA: You teach 'em how to play the piano? Ya wanna teach me?

LA PRIEL: *(Looks at her hands.)* It costs money, Letha.

LETHA: How much?

LA PRIEL: Two dollars and fifty cents a lesson.

LETHA: Maybe I might buy one.

LA PRIEL: *(Disturbed.)* Where would you git . . . the money?

LETHA: From Uncle June.

LA PRIEL: This Uncle June. Is he yer real uncle?

LETHA: Yep. Uncle June.

LA PRIEL: Is that his real name?

LETHA: Yep. Uncle June.

LA PRIEL: That ain't a man's name.

LETHA: He's born in June.

LA PRIEL: Oh.

> *(Listing the months for herself.)*
> Uncle July, Uncle August, Uncle September, Uncle October, Uncle November, Uncle December.
> *(She nods.)*
> Uncle January, Uncle February.
> *(She looks sceptical.)*
> Uncle March.
> *(She shrugs.)*
> Uncle April, Uncle May.

LETHA: See, it could of been a lots worst. That's what Ma says.

LA PRIEL: Yes, I guess it could.

LETHA: You know what else? *(Pause.)* Ma's gonna have another kid.

LA PRIEL: *(She starts.)* Ohhhh, she is not, Letha.

LETHA: In April er something.

LA PRIEL: I don't think so.

LETHA: I do.

LA PRIEL: Listen here! Everyone of the kids in yer family has been born with something less than the one before. Yer mother ain't gonna have no more kids. That's jist temptin' fate.

LETHA: She is anyway.

LA PRIEL: Well, I don't believe ya.

LETHA: And it's gonna be a girl. All the rest from now on is gonna be girls.

LA PRIEL: From now on?

LETHA: Is gonna be all girls.

LA PRIEL: Well, ya can't tell them things.

LETHA: Yes ya can if ya look.

LA PRIEL: *(Rattled.)* Five kids is already . . . Ya have to have money fer kids.

LETHA: We got money. Uncle June's got lots of money. When I git money, I'm gonna have nine kids, er less maybe thirteen. And they're all gonna be girls.

LA PRIEL: Letha, go on outside now. *(Rattled pause.)* I can't look at ya lickin' that stuff no more.

LETHA: I don't want no more anyway.

LA PRIEL: Well leave it then.

LETHA: I'll jist put this box back up here.

LA PRIEL: No. Leave it.

LETHA: *(Puts the Jello box on the table.)* Well don't throw it away. Cuz I'll finish it tomorrow.

(Crosses to screen door.)

And don't let anybody else have it. And don't tell Waller ya got Jello powder, else he'll pester ya.

(Exits. Turns back, pressing her face on the screen.)

I'll ask Ma if we can buy me a piano lesson from ya.

(La Priel starts. Letha bounds off the porch. She speaks from a distance.)

La Priel . . .

LA PRIEL: Yes. What.

LETHA: *(Off.)* You really ought to git black cherry sometime.

(La Priel freezes. Sighs. Head in hand. Elbows on the table as the lights fade.)

ENTR'SCENE TWO

In darkness we hear the sound of a rope hitting against the pavement. It could sound like whipping at first. Later it sounds like a jump rope being turned. Lights come up. Sound of a rhyme being chanted by children as they jump.

A, my name is Alice,
My husband's name is Al.
We live in Arkansas,
And our house is full of apples.
How many children do we have?
One, two, three, four, five.
B, my name is Bradley,
My husband's name is Brad.
We live in Bakersfield,
And our house is full of beetles.
How many children do we have?
One, two, three, four, five, six.

C, my name is Carlie,
My husband's name is Carl.
We live in California,
And our house is full of cats.
How many children do we have?
One, two, three, four, five, six, seven.

> *(When the rhymes are finished, we hear only the sound of the rope, brushing on the pavement. It begins to sound more like whipping.)*
>
> *During this time, La Priel goes to the cupboard, opens it, counts the cups, counts the glasses, counts the saucers. She takes each set of items from the cupboard, then counts as the children count. Returns the set and takes another set. Each set has the same number as the children count.*
>
> *Again, we see only snatches of this business. The lights should be cued to the sound.*
>
> *The rope sound stops abruptly. La Priel starts. In silence and steady light she returns the last items to the cupboard. She moves to the back screen, peers out, latches the screen door, checks the kitchen, leaves the room through the hallway entrance. The light in the bedroom goes on with a click, then black-out.)*

SCENE THREE

> *There is the sound of water, a hose running into a metal bucket. Then the lights come up.*
>
> *The scene is the same as before, but it is later. It is dark outside. The room is empty. Night light bleeds in from the windows in the kitchenette. The Jello box is on the table where it was left at the end of Scene II.*
>
> *A light offstage goes on, La Priel's bedroom light. We hear her walk the length of a hall to the bathroom. Another light goes on. We hear drains being checked, the toilet handle being rattled. Then the sound of someone urinating. Sound of toilet flushing.*
>
> *Silence, then the sound of crickets. That sound continues through the entire scene. La Priel enters, dressed in a light blue robe. She tightens both faucets in the kitchen sink. Turns on a light near the back door. Goes to the back screen, peers out. She is startled by a figure she sees on the lawn.*

LA PRIEL: *(Pause. In a loud whisper.)* You got that water on er something?

MRS. HICKS: *(Off.)* Yeah. I got this water going fer jist a minute. Then I'll turn it off.

LA PRIEL: *(Pause.)* What's wrong with yer own?

MRS. HICKS: *(Off.)* Wake the kids up.

LA PRIEL: *(Pause.)* Well, there's rationing, ya know. I ain't spozed to run that tap in the yard today.

MRS. HICKS: *(Off.)* It ain't today now.

LA PRIEL: Oh. *(Long pause.)* Yer fillin' that *bucket* up with water.

MRS. HICKS: *(Off.)* Unh-hunh.

LA PRIEL: *(Pause.)* What you need a bucket of water for?

MRS. HICKS: *(Off.)* Wash my hair.

LA PRIEL: *(Pause.)* Ya got a sink fer that.

MRS. HICKS: *(Off.)* This is better water.

LA PRIEL: It's the *same* water.

MRS. HICKS: I like water that's come through a hose. Fer washin' my hair.

LA PRIEL: Oh. *(Pause.)* Well, don't leave it running. I hate the sound of that dripping.

(Pause. We hear the water shut off. La Priel is startled. She speaks out of fear of the silence.)

I once . . . I once seen a thing out there by the tap. There's long grass out there. It was this thing out there was the face of a monkey. No *body* with it. Face . . .

MRS. HICKS: *(She appears silently on the porch, wearing an old white flannel night-gown, carrying a bucket. She is forty, thin, aged beyond her years. She has a low direct vocal pattern, a slow menacing rhythm. She is both seductive and threatening.)*

Can I take yer bucket fer tonight?

LA PRIEL: *(Startled, not having seen her approach.)* You people have a way of sneaking up on people's porches. Taking them by . . . by surprise.

MRS. HICKS: I bring it back tomorrow.

LA PRIEL: Oh. Yes, well . . . *(Pause.)* Listen here! You ain't pregnant, are ya?

MRS. HICKS: No.

LA PRIEL: Well! See that ya ain't. *(Rattled.)* Because ya got to do something about Letha before that.

MRS. HICKS: Like what?

LA PRIEL: Well . . . she ain't gonna turn out normal!

MRS. HICKS: What can I do about it?

LA PRIEL: Well, my gracious, git rid of that cat, fer one thing. Maybe then there'd be a chance of something growing back. She ain't got all her height yet. Something could grow . . .

MRS. HICKS: Git rid of what cat?

LA PRIEL: Either one. They both look alike. Only people in yer family that look alike is the cats! The one without no hair on its tail.

MRS. HICKS: She died.

LA PRIEL: Then the other one. The one that looks jist like her.

MRS. HICKS: That's the one. She died.

LA PRIEL: I seen 'em both today. Two of us did.

MRS. HICKS: They wasn't our cats. *(Pause.)* They was jist locked in the attic when we come.

LA PRIEL: *(Winces.)* How'd they live?

MRS. HICKS: Off the mice.

LA PRIEL: Oh. *(Long pause.)* Well, how'd she die?

MRS. HICKS: Who?

LA PRIEL: The cat!

MRS. HICKS: I killed it.

LA PRIEL: Oh.

MRS. HICKS: Last week. I put it in a bucket of water.

LA PRIEL: Oh.

MRS. HICKS: The kids got tired of it. They started to git to it. Set fire to it. Tie it up. Them kinda things. I decided it was time I got rid of it.

LA PRIEL: Oh. *(Pause.)* That what ya gonna do with that bucket of water?

MRS. HICKS: Huh?

LA PRIEL: Drowned the other cat?

MRS. HICKS: No.

LA PRIEL: Make Jello, maybe.
   (Small laugh.)

MRS. HICKS: No.

LA PRIEL: Letha like Jello, and Waller . . .

MRS. HICKS: I know.

LA PRIEL: *(Pause. Quietly and intently.)* I seen them cats today.

MRS. HICKS: It might of been today.

LA PRIEL: *(Pause.)* That ya killed one? Oh. Well, it was.

MRS. HICKS: Ya might be right.

LA PRIEL: Yes. Well . . . I am. *(Pause.)* Ya need some newspapers er something?

MRS. HICKS: What for?

LA PRIEL: In case you spill that on your floor. Have to sop it up with something.

MRS. HICKS: I won't spill it.

LA PRIEL: Well, that bucket leaks.

MRS. HICKS: Yeah. I know.

LA PRIEL: Drip buckets rust out at the bottom, ya know.

MRS. HICKS: I know.

LA PRIEL: *(Moves to the screen.)* Didn't see anything out by the water tap, did ya?

MRS. HICKS: No.

LA PRIEL: Well, it's been a long time since I did. I ain't been out there . . . in a while. Melvin coulda took it off by now. *(Pause.)* Nothin floatin' in that bucket?

MRS. HICKS: No.

(She turns away and moves to the edge of the porch.)

LA PRIEL: Listen here! You people ain't got weapons stored in yer house, have ya?

MRS. HICKS: *(Turns back and faces La Priel. Pause.)* No.

LA PRIEL: Er in that truck? That truck looks like it might have weapons er guns in it.

MRS. HICKS: No. 'Fraid not.

LA PRIEL: Well. See to it ya ain't.

MRS. HICKS: I'll do my best. G'night, La Priel.

(Turns away.)

LA PRIEL: What!

MRS. HICKS: *(Turns back to La Priel. Pause.)* G'night.

(Turns away.)

LA PRIEL: Listen here . . .

MRS. HICKS: Yeah.

LA PRIEL: Well, cats. They hate water.

MRS. HICKS: *(Long pause.)* This water ain't fer cats.

(She goes down the porch steps and off, carrying the bucket.)

LA PRIEL: Oh . . .

(She watches her leave. She stands alone, quite frightened. She hums "Sweet Mystery of Life" with a rather forced effect, as if she simply must fill up the silence. She moves quickly to the sink, grabs the edge, and looks down into it as the lights fade.)

ENTR'SCENE THREE

In darkness the sound of crickets which have been audible since the opening of Scene III. The volume grows, and the sound becomes lower in pitch. There is a definite rhythm to the sound. Lights come up.

Sound of one child mumbling a prayer, uncertain about the exact words, trying to commit them to memory:

Now I lay me down to sleep
I pray the Lord my soul to keep.
If I should die before I sleep,
I pray the Lord my soul to keep.

(*Sound of two children mumbling a rhyme as if it were a prayer:*)

One two, throw your shoe.
Three four, close your door.
Five six, throw up sticks.
Seven eight, lay down straight.
Nine ten, big fat hen.

(*Sound of giggles from the two children. The sound of the one child again, trying to get the prayer right.*)

. . . If I should die before I *wake*,
I pray the Lord my soul to *take*.

(*During this time we see La Priel move to the stove. She picks up the tea kettle. Puts it back on the stove. Thinks about a larger pan. Gets an enamel pan from beneath the sink. Fills it with water. Sets the pan of water on the countertop. Gets a saucepan from the stove top and fills it with water. Sets it on the table in the kitchenette.*

As before, this action is seen intermittently. The lights are cued to the sound.

Abrupt silence.

La Priel starts. In the silence and steady illumination, she moves both pans of water to the stove top. Checks the room. Turns out the light near the back door. Exits out hallway. Light goes on in her bedroom. Then blackout.)

SCENE FOUR

The scene is the same. It is morning. Sunlight bleeds through the windows in the kitchenette. The box of Jello is still on the table, the pans of water are on the stove, occupying two of the four burners. La Priel enters, unlatches the screen door, and begins making breakfast.

There is a jaunty air about how she does things, a kind of confidence we have seen only among experienced craftsmen. This is all ritualized business. She alternately hums, whistles, and sings "Sweet Mystery of Life."

She puts water in the tea kettle, puts it on the stove, turns on the heat, scratches something off the knob. Gets bread from the refrigerator, unwraps several layers of paper, plastic, and foil. Counts seven slices, takes out three, begins to wrap the others back up, thinks again, unwraps them, breaks one more slice in half, wraps the rest back up, returns them to the fridge. Puts two slices in the toaster, does not depress the button, checks the water on the stove, gets a cup and two saucers from the cupboard, puts them on the counter. Opens the drawer, gets a spoon and a knife, sets them on the countertop. Checks the water on the stove, checks the bread in the toaster, scratches something off the toaster, wipes off the counter where the bread was unwrapped, brushes the crumbs into the sink, runs the water to wash them down.

Gets a plastic placemat from one of the drawers, puts it on the table. Gets a paper napkin from the holder on the table, folds it, places it on the left side of the place setting. Counts the number of napkins left in the holder. Moves the box of Jello to the counter.

Checks the water, checks the bread in the toaster. Looks out the windows in the kitchenette, looks out the back screen door. Moves to the toaster, presses the button, checks the water, notes the time. Wipes the counter off underneath the remaining slice and a half of bread, puts the crumbs in the sink, runs the water to wash them down. Moves the box of Jello back to the table.

Gets the Postum from the cupboard, counts the bottles left. Puts the bottle on the counter, unscrews the lid. Opens the cupboard door under the sink, takes out a paper sack that contains a bottle of instant coffee, unscrews the lid, takes the teaspoon and fills it heaping, dumps it in the Postum bottle, looks in, adds another level teaspoon. Puts the lid on the coffee bottle, puts the bottle in the sack, puts the sack back under the sink. Gets the butter and mint jelly from the fridge, sets the butter on the counter, puts the jelly on the table, moves Jello box back to stove.

The tea kettle begins to whistle. She turns off the heat, takes the kettle to the counter, pours water in the cup, sets kettle back on the stove. Puts a spoonful of coffee-Postum in the water, stirs.

Toast begins to burn. She watches it, counts to two, then pops it up. She takes the toast from the toaster, scrapes it with the knife into the sink, sets each slice near the butter. Butters each slice, cuts them in two, puts them on the extra saucer, carries knife, toast, and coffee-Postum to the kitchenette, arranges them.

Wipes the crumbs from the counter, turns on the water to wash them down. Moves Jello box to top of fridge. Sits at the table.

The sound of children playing. She freezes. Resolutely she gets control, picks up half piece of toast and spreads it thinly with jelly. Sets it down. Wipes her fingers with the napkin, presses a few crumbs on the table with her fingertips, and touches them to her mouth. Blows the coffee-Postum, samples it, picks up the toast.

Sound of someone bounding on the porch. La Priel starts.

LETHA: *(Cupping her eyes to see in the screen door.)* You eatin' breakfast?

LA PRIEL: Listen here. I wisht you people wouldn't jump up on the porch that way.

LETHA: Scared you again, huh? *(Pause.)* What ya havin' fer breakfast?

LA PRIEL: *(Looking out the window in front of her.)* A little burnt toast.

LETHA: Oh. We had oatmeal.

LA PRIEL: Oh.

(She bites the toast and looks out the window.)

LETHA: I hate it whenever we have oatmeal. I *never* eat it. So I jist had coffee and a cigarette.

LA PRIEL: You did not, Letha.

LETHA: Did so.

LA PRIEL: Children do not drink coffee and smoke cigarettes.

LETHA: I'm not a child. I'm the oldest.

LA PRIEL: You're still a child.

(Spreads another piece of toast with jelly.)

LETHA: What kind of jam is that?

LA PRIEL: Mint jelly.

LETHA: Oh. Do you eat that all the time?

LA PRIEL: Yes.

LETHA: So do we. *(Pause.)* All the time.

LA PRIEL: That's nice.

LETHA: *(Pause.)* Do you really like it?

LA PRIEL: No.

LETHA: Why you eat it?

LA PRIEL: So's I won't eat too much of it.

LETHA: Keep yerself in tow?

> *(She idly elevates to her toes.)*

LA PRIEL: That's right.

LETHA: *(Pause.)* Can I come in?

LA PRIEL: Jist fer a minute. I'm busy.

> *(Letha comes in, sits down opposite La Priel. Pause. La Priel spreads another piece of toast with jelly. Letha watches.)*

LETHA: I seen some bread once that was blackern that, and it wasn't even toast yet. *(Pause.)* It was in a plastic bag. *(Pause.)* I hate plastic bags. Have you ever seen raw liver in a plastic bag?

> *(La Priel freezes, sets down her toast. Looks at Letha.)*

That's about the worst thing I've ever saw.

LA PRIEL: Watch out what you say, Letha, when people are eating.

> *(Out of force of will, she picks up the toast again and bites it.)*

LETHA: Did you eat all that Jello last night?

LA PRIEL: No.

LETHA: Well, maybe I'll have that.

> *(Gets up and heads for the cupboard. Stops and points.)*

Is it back here again?

LA PRIEL: It's on the top of the fridge. I'll git it for you.

LETHA: I can reach that high.

> *(Grabs the Jello box.)*

I'm five foot three and a half. That's tall for my age.

> *(Puts Jello on the table.)*

I think I'll have a little plate like that.

LA PRIEL: They're in the cupboard over the drainer. See that you're careful.

LETHA: *(Gets saucer. Sits down. Pause.)* These are pretty good little plates. I like little plates. I don't like big plates near as well.

LA PRIEL: They're saucers.

LETHA: Yah, I know. We have a lot of saucers.

> *(She pours the Jello powder on the saucer, then, rather daintily, in imitation of La Priel, presses her finger into it and then to her mouth. Pause.)*

This is a good room, huh?

LA PRIEL: I guess so.

LETHA: Them curtains are real good, I think. Do you have curtains in your other rooms?

LA PRIEL: Yes.

LETHA: So do we. We have a lots of curtains in every room.

LA PRIEL: That's nice.

LETHA: Yah. We enjoy 'em. *(Pause.)* I really like a clean kitchroom. *(Pause.)* *This* is a pretty clean kitchroom.

LA PRIEL: Sometimes.

LETHA: Yah. Sometimes it gits dirty. But it's *pretty* clean.

LA PRIEL: I'm gonna have to do the floors soon.

LETHA: Yah. The floors needs it. But the rest is pretty good.

LA PRIEL: Think so.

LETHA: Well, fer reglar things, you know, breakfast and stuff, it's quite good, I think. Course, if you was gonna have a whole bunch of kids er something, it wouldn't be enough chairs.

LA PRIEL: Well I wouldn't worry about that . . .

LETHA: Yah. In ours there's a lots more chairs.

LA PRIEL: You need 'em.

LETHA: If you was ever gonna have a lots of people or something, you could probly borrow some of our chairs probly.

LA PRIEL: I'll keep that in mind.

LETHA: Yah. You probly could. *(Pause.)* These chairs match pretty good, too.

LA PRIEL: I guess so.
(She rises. Goes to the counter and puts another slice of toast in the toaster.)
Do you want this half piece of toast?

LETHA: I guess so.
(La Priel drops the other half in the toaster, depresses the button. Pause.)
You gonna be learnin' people the piano today?

LA PRIEL: Not today.

LETHA: How come?

LA PRIEL: It's Thursday.

LETHA: Oh yeah. *(Pause.)* If I was gonna buy one, I would buy it on Friday.

LA PRIEL: Would ya?

LETHA: Yah. Fridays are more relax. Not all this running around like on Thursdays.

LA PRIEL: *(Pops up the toast, unburned.)* Do you want butter on yours?

LETHA: I guess so.

LA PRIEL: *(Butters the toast, gets another saucer for Letha, brings it all over to the table. Sits. Spreads jelly on her toast.)* Jelly's there if you want that.

LETHA: I like the powder better.

LA PRIEL: This is jelly, not Jello.

LETHA: Oh yeah. I git them two mixed up sometimes. Well, I guess probly I'll jist have some jelly then.

LA PRIEL: *(Help yerself.)* Help yerself.

LETHA: *(Spreads the jelly on, in imitation of La Priel.)* We're goin swimmin' today. Ma's gonna take us swimmin.

LA PRIEL: That's nice.

LETHA: To the rez-avoy. Do you know where that is?

LA PRIEL: Yes. But ya ain't supposed to swim there.

LETHA: Ma's got somethin she wants to dump in the water.

LA PRIEL: That water's for drinking, Letha. See to it she don't dump something awful in there.

LETHA: It's the baby. She ain't gonna have the baby no more. It's in a bucket. And we're gonna let it loose in the water.

LA PRIEL: *(Starts. Sets down her toast.)* Letha. I'm gonna paddle you if you don't learn how to talk.

LETHA: We're leaving as soon as Uncle June gits off the shift. Ma says about 3:30. What time is it now?

LA PRIEL: It's still morning.

(Long pause. La Priel is in a nervous state. She picks up her toast, sets it down, pushes the toast away from her, pulls the coffee toward her, picks up the cup, puts it back down, puts her face in her hand, sighs deeply. Finally, exerting much control, and at the end of her breath, she speaks softly.) Where is it now?

LETHA: Where's what?

LA PRIEL: The . . . bucket.

LETHA: Oh. It's in my room and the fruit's room.

(Bites her toast.)

LA PRIEL: *(Exhaling the last bit of air.)* Letha, I can't watch you eat when you talk that way. Now go on outside.

LETHA: Okay.

(She slides her plate toward La Priel, then snatches the piece of toast from it and flits out the screen door. She stops on the porch and turns back to La Priel, pressing her face against the screen. Whispering.)

And La Priel . . .

LA PRIEL: What.

LETHA: When we go swimming . . .

LA PRIEL: Yes.

LETHA: We ain't wearin' suits.

(She jumps from the porch. La Priel freezes. Inhales slowly, clutches her napkin, looks into her plate. Then blackout.)

SCENE FIVE

There is the sound of wind. The lights come up on the scene, which is the same, La Priel in the same position. The wind sound modulates and becomes the sound of children rushing. They make train buzzing sounds like airplanes or cars. The sound of fast-moving feet. These sounds grow, and the lights burn to white.

La Priel rises, the sound abates, and the lights go to amber. She moves to the screen door, looks out. She strokes her thigh, then moves to the table. She freezes, and the sound recurs. She moves to stack the dishes from breakfast, and for as long as she is in motion, the sound abates.

She entertains the idea that the sound is related to her actions. She freezes intentionally, and the sound recurs. She moves the dishes back and forth on the table. The sound abates. When she stops abruptly, the sound recurs.

She then begins a very meticulous, nearly choreographed ritual of cleaning up the kitchen after toast. It involves very precise business and constant motion, though she does not move fast. The ritual should include much running of water and washing things down the drain. This business should take several minutes. We should always be aware that behind everything she does, underneath everything she does, there is the noise of the children, the threat of the noise of the children. During this ritual, she moves the Jello box five times: from the table, to the countertop, to the stove top, to the fridge top, to the cupboard, and back to the table. We are aware at times of the sound this activity makes, of a rhythm, and the occasional defiance of that rhythm.

When the kitchen is immaculate, she stops to study it. We hear the sound of a truck start up, drive nearer, and then disappear. She listens, stands frozen. Lights burn to white. Sounds of children mingle with those of the truck. When the sound has faded, the lights move to amber.

She moves to the screen door, peers out. Fills the tea kettle with water, sets it on the stove, turns the heat on under it. Stands at the screen door again, intentionally becalming herself. She sighs, then goes to the cupboard and gets a very large glass, the mouth of which is large enough to cover her mouth and nose. She holds the glass and looks out the back door, her face tipped into the glass.

A wind comes up. She sets the glass down on the stove, empties the large pan of water left on the stove since Entr'scene Three, puts the pan away under the sink. Checks the water in the tea kettle. Grabs the broom and exits to the back porch. Sweeps the porch. Wind blows her dress.

She stands looking off the porch. The wind gets stronger. She re-enters and stows the broom. Something crashes in the bedroom. She exits quickly through the hallway door, and we hear the sound of someone closing a window and picking things up, putting them back. The tea kettle begins to whistle. She rushes back in, takes the kettle from the heat, pours the hot water in the large glass, turns off the stove, takes the glass of water to the table.

There is far-away thunder, and the sun is covered by a cloud. The wind is gusty. She sits at the table, again attempting to calm herself. She slowly puts her face into the glass again.

There is a large crack of thunder. She starts. Then moves to the back door, latches the screen, and closes the door. Peers out. The sound of a truck, louder than before. It comes nearer, shifts gears, moves more distant. She freezes. It begins to rain.

She returns to the table and sits back down. Again the intentional becalming. She sits very still except for her right hand, which writhes as if she were smoothing her fingernails.

She drinks some of the water, cupping the glass with both hands. The rain continues. Another clap of thunder. She starts. She rises quickly and goes to the fridge, takes out an egg, puts it in the saucepan on the stove, full of water from the night before. Turns on the heat.

She returns to her chair in the kitchenette. Another clap of thunder. She reaches for the Jello box in response. It is in front of her on the table. She smells it, trying to calm herself. It seems to work. She then sprinkles the powder in her hot water. It is red. It is black cherry. She calmly drinks of it, as if she did not notice the color, and also as if she drank Jello all the time. She sits quietly. She is now, in fact, quite calm. The rain abates.

She rises and goes out the archway to the livingroom, and we hear a piano playing "Sweet Mystery of Life." It is played four different ways: plain, romantic, very fast, very quietly. She re-enters. Turns off the heat under the egg. Gets a large spoon from the drawer. Spoons the egg from the pan of water on the stove. Carries it to the kitchenette. Puts it on the table near the glass and resumes her seat.

All is quiet. We see her thinking. She rejects some ideas. Entertains others. She comes to a decision. We sense resoluteness. She picks up the egg. Holds it in her palm, fingers surrounding it. She looks out. Cracks the egg on the edge of the glass, drops the whole thing in the the glass, shell and all. She looks at her hand. Egg is on it. She looks at the egg in the glass of Jello. She looks up. Wipes her hand on her right breast. She is resolved. She sighs in acknowledgment. Lights fade. She sighs again.

SCENE SIX

> *The scene is the same. It is now dusk. Dying light bleeds through the windows. La Priel is in the same position. She sits frozen looking out. The glass is still before her on the table, as is the Jello box.*
>
> *Mrs. Hicks appears on the back porch. La Priel hears her approach, and so takes the glass to the sink and puts it down inside.*

MRS. HICKS: La Priel?

LA PRIEL: *(Nervous now, but trying to remain calm.)* Yes.

MRS. HICKS: I got yer drip bucket here.

LA PRIEL: *(Moves to the screen door.)* I see.

MRS. HICKS: You want me to put it back out under the tap?

LA PRIEL: I didn't see ya drive up.

MRS. HICKS: We come up the back way. Parked over the other side of the house.

LA PRIEL: *(Growing more nervous.)* Did yer kids come back with ya?

MRS. HICKS: They're at the Dairy Queen.

LA PRIEL: I didn't see 'em.

MRS. HICKS: We left 'em at the Dairy Queen.

LA PRIEL: All five of 'em.

> *(Nodding in the hope of validation.)*

MRS. HICKS: They was hungry.

LA PRIEL: All five are eatin'.

MRS. HICKS: Swimmin makes 'em hungry.

LA PRIEL: Cuz ya took 'em swimmin'.

MRS. HICKS: To the rez-avoy.

LA PRIEL: Ya took 'em all to the rez-avoy and ya left 'em all at the Dairy Queen.

MRS. HICKS: They're gonna walk home.

LA PRIEL: When they git done eatin'.

MRS. HICKS: It's jist a few blocks.

LA PRIEL: Yes. Three. *(Slight pause.)* And the rez-avoy is where ya was.

MRS. HICKS: It's way low.

LA PRIEL: Well, they was a storm today.

MRS. HICKS: Not there.

LA PRIEL: That might help a bit.

MRS. HICKS: It didn't happen there.

LA PRIEL: When it's low you drive down on that gravel part by the weir.

MRS. HICKS: That's what we done.

LA PRIEL: Woman once drove right in the water when it was low like that. Drove herself and a baby right into the water. Didn't git 'em out fer a week.

MRS. HICKS: That ain't what we done.

LA PRIEL: No! *(Pause.)* Well, that's good.

MRS. HICKS: So . . . you want this bucket back out under the tap?

LA PRIEL: That's where it goes.

MRS. HICKS: I jist thought maybe since . . .

LA PRIEL: Unless yer fraid to go out there. Cuz I don't like it out there myself.

MRS. HICKS: No, La Priel.

LA PRIEL: If that's the case, I can have Melvin put it back when he comes.

MRS. HICKS: No. I ain't scared. I jist thought maybe it ain't worth puttin' back. It don't do much good with the way it leaks.

LA PRIEL: Yes. Well. Maybe yer right. I can't remember why it was out there in the first place.

MRS. HICKS: I thought ya done it fer the birds.

LA PRIEL: When ya think of how all that grass grows around it. Might be jist as well not to have it. There's things collect out there.

MRS. HICKS: If the bucket didn't leak, ya could use it fer the birds.

LA PRIEL: Birds?

MRS. HICKS: They always come, you leave out water like that. It's real nice.

LA PRIEL: Oh. Yes. Well. *(Nervous pause.)* Birds, well I'm afraid I'm not much fer birds.

MRS. HICKS: My mother used to always have a pan of water fer birds.

LA PRIEL: But not a bucket . . .

MRS. HICKS: They don't care how deep it is. They jist like water.

LA PRIEL: The birds here is mostly starlings and sparrows.

MRS. HICKS: Well ya got robins, and ya got them black ones with the white and red wings . . .

LA PRIEL: Magpies.

MRS. HICKS: Yeah.

LA PRIEL: Well, I wouldn't want them around. Kids kill 'em. Shoot 'em with bee-bee guns all the time.

MRS. HICKS: Then you'd git other kinds if they was all this water. Humming birds, canaries, black birds, crows . . .

LA PRIEL: But they could come up to that water and die in there. Float around dead in that bucket.

MRS. HICKS: They come up to drink and take a bath, La Priel. They don't come up to die.

LA PRIEL: Oh. Well . . .

MRS. HICKS: When June gits paid, I'll git ya a new bucket. *(Threatening.)* We'll put it out there, see how ya like it.

LA PRIEL: June.

MRS. HICKS: My husband. He's working fer the creamery. He'll be gittin paid every two weeks.

LA PRIEL: Yer kids call him uncle.

MRS. HICKS: That's jist Letha. June ain't her real father. So I told her she could call him uncle. Makes her feel different.

LA PRIEL: Well, it would.

MRS. HICKS: I guess it's jist natural when there's so many.

LA PRIEL: I guess it is.

MRS. HICKS: So. Ya want me to put this bucket back out under the tap er not?

LA PRIEL: No. It's all right. Jist leave it there.

MRS. HICKS: *(Sets the bucket down.)* Well, g'night then.
(Moves to the edge of the porch.)

LA PRIEL: *(Goes out the door.)* Lookit. Letha keeps talkin' about piano lessons.

MRS. HICKS: She said you's a teacher.

LA PRIEL: Well, I don't know how good it would work without all their fingers, ya know.

MRS. HICKS: She says she wants a piano fer her birthday. Course, she don't know nothing about how much they cost.

LA PRIEL: Well, maybe I could teach her something. I don't know how much . . .

MRS. HICKS: We thought maybe we'd git her lessons fer her birthday, stead of the piano.

LA PRIEL: See how she does fore ya git one.

MRS. HICKS: See how she does fore we git one.

LA PRIEL: Well, I could maybe give her a couple and see.

MRS. HICKS: Two fifty each, right?

LA PRIEL: Well I could *give* her some to start out. *(Abruptly.)* She ought to know how to do something if she's gonna be a teenager.

MRS. HICKS: No. I'd want to pay.

LA PRIEL: But if ya couldn't . . .

MRS. HICKS: All the others pay, don't they?

LA PRIEL: Yes. But if you couldn't manage it . . . right yet, ya know.

MRS. HICKS: I'd want to pay ya something.

LA PRIEL: Yes, well. That'd be good too. Whatever it was. *(Slight pause.)* If she's gonna be a teenager, ya got to give her something she can do.

MRS. HICKS: I guess ya do.

LA PRIEL: Ya do!

MRS. HICKS: *(Moves down the steps.)* Well. We'll work somethin' out.

LA PRIEL: Ya don't give 'em something, they can git in trouble, if ya don't.

MRS. HICKS: Maybe Letha could do some work for ya to help make up fer the rest of the money.

LA PRIEL: This little town. Wouldn't seem like they would git in trouble. But they do. All the time. I seen it happen right and left.

MRS. HICKS: I guess yer right.

LA PRIEL: A course I am! I watch 'em.

MRS. HICKS: All's I know is I don't want her gittin' married.

LA PRIEL: Oh no. I guess not . . .

MRS. HICKS: Gittin pregnant er something and then gittin' married.

LA PRIEL: Well, that's a danger.

MRS. HICKS: That's what I done, and I don't want it happenin' to her. I told her I don't care what she does with herself, but she ain't gittin' married.

LA PRIEL: Well, I think you might be right.

MRS. HICKS: Course I am! I made that mistake. So she don't have to. That's what I tell her.

LA PRIEL: That's a way of lookin' at it.

MRS. HICKS: My mother tried to tell me, but I wouldn't listen. Bull headed. I wouldn't listen to nobody. But Letha's gonna listen to me if it's the last thing she does.

LA PRIEL: Listen. Would ya like to sit down? Wait fer the kids.
(*Mrs. Hicks sits on the step. La Priel leans against the railing. They both look out.*) Well, it's really quite nice out here tonight. Jist a little fall. You can almost tell.

MRS. HICKS: Next month, after all.

LA PRIEL: That's right. Be September.

MRS. HICKS: Cooled off real nice from today.

LA PRIEL: Well, it always does that here. We're so high up, it always cools off at night.

MRS. HICKS: Good place to sleep then . . .

LA PRIEL: No matter how hot it gets in the day. Always cools off at night.

MRS. HICKS: (*Pause.*) What's that sound?

LA PRIEL: Them birds? It's medal larks. They come in to them pastures out back. Oh, bout this time, usually. About sunset.

MRS. HICKS: Nice sound.

LA PRIEL: There's water out there. The slough goes through them pastures. Always water there.

MRS. HICKS: Well, birds like to come where there's water.

LA PRIEL: (*Moves to steps and sits down.*) Yes. (*Pause.*) Lookit, I know how come ya needed my bucket. Letha told me.

MRS. HICKS: Well, Letha sometimes says more than she knows.

LA PRIEL: *(Nervous pause. She fidgets.)* I lost a baby once. It was after I seen that thing I was tellin' you about . . . Out by the water tap . . .

MRS. HICKS: I didn't lose a baby.

LA PRIEL: That thing that was a monkey face without the body . . .

MRS. HICKS: *(A story she has invented. Delivered almost as if memorized.)* I had some bottles of bad peaches, a few quarts of tainted beets.

LA PRIEL: A big scare like that can *make* ya miscarry.

MRS. HICKS: Something was wrong with the seal on them bottles.

LA PRIEL: Some kind of real upset like that, you know.

MRS. HICKS: I don't know what it was went wrong. I guess they wasn't at the right temperature er somethin' when I put the lids on 'em.

LA PRIEL: *(Pause.)* I jist went out to change the hose, put it on another part of the lawn. Walked up to that tap and I seen it.

MRS. HICKS: They all went bad. The beets went sour. You could smell 'em. And the peaches was bitter kinda. Mustardlike.

LA PRIEL: Soon as I seen it, I come right inside. Set down in the kitchenette.

MRS. HICKS: Lost the whole mess. Everthing I put up last summer.

LA PRIEL: And it was this kind of warm thing come in my stomach, like when, like, like they was a little piece of sun riding inside there.

MRS. HICKS: Hard to lose everything like that.

LA PRIEL: *(Pause. Having trouble finishing the story. But resolute about trying.)* I kept checking the sky to see if the sun was shining through the window onto my stomach because it was so warm. But there wasn't no sun. It was already evening. By then when it happened. When I seen the thing by the tap, it was evening. Rulon was gone milkin'. Wasn't nobody here. So I set there. I didn't know what to do.

(Genuine frozen panic.)

Something already happened. I was jist waiting around to find out what. So I went in the bathroom and run the water in the tub.

(Waiting for control.)

Soon's I got in the warm water, it happened. *(Pause.)* I got kinda dizzy and sick to the stomach. Then she come.

(She blinks away a few tears. Gets control. Mrs. Hicks lights a cigarette.)

Melvin and all them says it was a cocoanut shell, floatin' in there, with them three holes facin' up. But it didn't matter what they says, it was still in my mind as bein' a monkey face. And wouldn't change, no matter what they said. No matter how hard I try to git it another way in my mind.

(Slight pause.) And I got this thing in my mind that maybe the same thing happened to you. You lost yer baby the same way.

MRS. HICKS: I didn't lose it. I jist let go of it.

LA PRIEL: Well, that's a way to put it, I guess. *(Pause.)* With mine, they kept tellin' me it was probly fer the best, probly had something wrong with her. Sometimes I think about that. What might of been wrong with her.

MRS. HICKS: Well, I couldn't stand to think about that.

LA PRIEL: Oh no. A course ya couldn't. *(Pause.)* Did ya name yours?

MRS. HICKS: Nah. I already used up all the names I like.

LA PRIEL: I named mine. LaRene.

MRS. HICKS: That's quite a different name.

LA PRIEL: I only made up that it was a girl. I couldn't tell. It was only a couple er three months.

MRS. HICKS: I only made up that this one was a boy.

LA PRIEL: They go on living, ya know, after. Sorta in yer mind.

MRS. HICKS: They might. I dunno. I never lost one before.

LA PRIEL: Well, I guess ya didn't. She might of been a real piano player er something. Yours too. He might of been a piano player.

MRS. HICKS: Well, maybe so. But I sorta doubt it.

LA PRIEL: Never can tell.

MRS. HICKS: Nope.

LA PRIEL: Well, that's it. That's how it goes.

MRS. HICKS: I guess it is.

LA PRIEL: *(Pause.)* Well, look here. It's gonna be fall.

MRS. HICKS: Month er so, guess so.

LA PRIEL: I always like fall.

MRS. HICKS: Yeah. I like fall.

(Pause. Sound of children and the sound of a truck. A gust of wind comes up.) Them kids is home.

LA PRIEL: It looks like storm. That'll clear things off again.

LETHA: *(She enters, breathless, with a Dairy Queen ice cream cone, dripping from her elbow. She alternately licks the ice cream and her arm and elbow.)* Ma, Waller jist buried Tice, all 'cept his head, in that hole out there Uncle June dug to bury the trash.

MRS. HICKS: You only been back here forty seconds. Waller couldn't bury Tice in forty seconds.

LETHA: Nope. Waller and Tice come home earlier. He buried the cat like that too. All but the head. They're both buried out there.

MRS. HICKS: *(Noting the ice cream cone.)* You're dripping that thing on my foot.

LETHA: Sorry.

    (Backing up. Looking at La Priel.)

MRS. HICKS: *(Rising, tossing a glance at La Priel.)* I gotta go see to it.

    (She exits with a sigh. Off.)

    Don't you stay there, Letha. Git yourself home now.

    (Letha stares for a moment at La Priel. Letha is something like an animal at this point. They stare at each other for a moment. Then La Priel moves inside the door, looks at Letha through the screen. A beat. Letha jumps quickly out of sight. We hear voices further off.)

    Waller, you git out here with a shovel.

LETHA: *(Off.)* He can't, Ma. The cat bites him if he gits anywheres near to her.

MRS. HICKS: Waller . . .

    (Voices die away. La Priel moves to the table and sits. She pleats the tablecloth, lets go of the pleats, understanding the irony of the moment. As the lights fade.)

END OF PLAY

The Encanto File
by Rosa Lowinger

For Fred

BIOGRAPHY
Rosa Lowinger is an art restorer living in Los Angeles. *The Encanto File* was her first play. She writes on art and architecture for magazines and is finishing a novel.

ORIGINAL PRODUCTION
Rita Divina Cook
Julian . . . . Tom Kopache
Natalie . . . . Dorie Joiner
Directed by . . . . Melia Bensussen

CHARACTERS
RITA: A woman in her early forties. She is Cuban and speaks with a light but distinct accent.
NATALIE: A woman in her thirties.
JULIAN: A man in his forties to fifties.

PLACE
The action occurs in the office of the owner of a small construction firm in Miami. The time is around 6:00 PM, shortly after work. It is December and already dark outside.

THE SETTING
The office is in one of those ubiquitous nondescript, one-story office complexes that line the expressways of Miami. The interior is furnished plainly and the decor is bland. Light colors tend to be overused in the decor; beige for walls, carpets, drop ceilings, and upholstered furniture. This is someone's idea of expensive taste, but it misses for lack of any individuality.

The following items are needed: a desk and chair; a locked closet; exit door and bathroom door; a window facing the parking lot; a photocopying machine; a wet bar or kitchenette; and an office supply storage cabinet. A seating area with a sofa and coffee table are also suggested.

AUTHOR'S NOTE
Improper grammatical usage and inverted syntax are used throughout the script, especially in Rita's dialogue. Her sentence construction often reflects a literal translation from Spanish to English. It should also be noted that Rita's accent, such as it is, can be revealed by punctuating the wrong word in a phrase as well as by pronunciation. The staccato rhythm of Cuban Spanish, which differs from South and Central American dialects, is heard in Rita's English.

THE ENCANTO FILE

Mid-December. Evening.

The remains of a business meeting (coffee cups, documents, cigars, empty bottle of scotch) are on the coffee table.

Rita sits on her desk polishing her nails. She talks to Natalie, who is in the bathroom offstage. Water is heard running offstage.

RITA: You want to know what this is all about? This guy thinks because he's finally looking at money he can jerk us around. The cash register went Ding! in his head and all of a sudden he doesn't have to consult us anymore. Thinks he's free to do whatever the hell he pleases.

(Water is turned off. Rita gestures with the nail-polish brush.)

No matter what he says, I know the facts. This contract's been ready for at least two weeks, and he had to know they were planning to sign today.

(Natalie enters patting her eye with a towel.)

The last estimate to come in was the electrician and that was already six weeks ago. Julie showed me all the numbers before Thanksgiving. I remember perfectly cause it was when he was still talking to me straight. So what I want to know is what for do we have to be in such a big rush? Man's got balls. No. He's got no balls.

(Rita waves hand to dry.)

He was on the phone with Felipe ten times over the last week. He's gonna tell me this comes like a surprise?

NATALIE: Maybe it does.

RITA: Hey, don't tell me . . . I don't mean you, I mean he. Julie is not gonna tell me he just found out. Who does he think he's dealing with? You wanna know the truth? The truth is he sprung it deliberately cause he doesn't have the balls to talk to my face after how he's been acting. And that is all what you have here. A man who's afraid to face up to his own actions.

(Natalie clears the coffee table.)

You know what I mean?

NATALIE: I don't know. Could be.

RITA: What's the matter, you're not interested? I'm not just talking for myself you know. This affects both of us.

NATALIE: The ashes bother my eyes.

RITA: You don't care, just say the word. I can shut up right here.

NATALIE: I'm concentrating on my eye. See, it's irritated.

RITA: I don't see nothing.

NATALIE: *(Walks over to Rita.)* It's just a reaction to the cigars. My eyes are sensitive to the smoke.

RITA: You better go put some more water on it. Or some drops. You got eye drops?

NATALIE: I'll be all right. Let's finish getting ready. He'll be back in fifteen minutes.

RITA: What you need to do is go see a new doctor.

NATALIE: Okay, Rita, thank you.

RITA: I mean a psychiatrist. They say this kind of thing most of the time is just from nerves. Maybe they can give you something to calm you.

NATALIE: It's not nerves. I'm allergic to smoke.

RITA: Yeah, yeah. This whole country is like one big allergy. I never saw so many people who couldn't breathe — itching, coughing, spitting all over the place. You ask me, it's a racket from the doctors. I mean it. If you're suffering and they tell you it's an allergy, what are you gonna do, huh? Because if you're the one in pain you got no choice. I mean, that's what most people think. You go for shots, pills, visits, each time it costs you what, forty dollars?

NATALIE: A specialist costs much more than that.

RITA: So what, fifty, sixty, eighty?

(She shakes her head.)

Eighty dollars for a shot you don't even know if you need it. But you pay it cause you're invested. The doctor has you grabbed by the tail.

NATALIE: Not quite.

RITA: I mean it's just like Julie. He walks in here this morning hyped up like it's the end of the world and we're supposed to jump cause he says so. And what, may I ask, is all of a sudden so important? We've been working six months to get this ready.

NATALIE: What does this have to do with my allergies?

RITA: I'm not talking about your allergies. I'm talking about rushing around cause someone else says so without showing me a good reason.

NATALIE: *(Picks up ashtray full of cigar butts.)* I don't know.

RITA: You don't know what, huh? You don't think it's a little strange Julie just forgets to mention the contract until Felipe's already on his way?

NATALIE: I really don't know.

(Puts ashtray near Rita.) Dump this out, please.

RITA: *(Shakes head and waves hand to dry.)* I don't want to smudge. He wants us to socialize with the client tonight, then I gotta have time to freshen up. *(Natalie rinses her hands.)*

Whole place stinks from these stinking Cuban cigars.

NATALIE: Well, well, well.

RITA: What? I can say whatever the hell I want. You and Julie better don't say nothing cause that's a different story.

NATALIE: *(Begins piling dishes on tray.)* You don't have to worry about me.

RITA: I better not. I mean, you know, I hope you don't feel some kind of problem is there. Julie gets me crazy the way he swings around back and forth. First he's angry, telling it to me like I'm responsible he hasn't been able to do business with the Cubans, then he's kissing Felipe's ass for a few bucks. Really burns me up.

NATALIE: As far as I'm concerned, Felipe's money is as good as anyone else's.

RITA: Julie's complaining all the time but he forgets that before 1960 all that was here was a bunch of old New Yorkers with mink coats in eighty degrees weather. Because the Cubans came, now what you got is an international city.

NATALIE: If Felipe has his way, we'll be calling it Havana.

RITA: Don't be to sure about that, my friend. Believe me, he's plenty happy this is Miami. Back in Cuba he wasn't nobody.

(Turns bottle of scotch upside down.) Look at this. He must have a wooden leg.

NATALIE: What?

RITA: He finished the whole Johnny Walker.

NATALIE: You mean a hollow leg.

RITA: What?

NATALIE: *(Takes tray to sink.)* If someone drinks a lot, you say they have a hollow leg, because it can fill up. Not a wooden leg.

RITA: Whatever. *(Pause.)* A hollow leg, huh? But a wooden head. He's complete crazy, that one. In Cuba they used to call him Felipe el loco. And let me tell you something. I don't care he's a millionaire fifty times over, he's still crazy. Because, I ask you, what does he know about building a department store?

NATALIE: I don't know, what difference does it make?

RITA: What difference does it make? You gotta know styles, different fashions, what people are wearing these days, and that, my friend, takes a person of class which is something you are either born with it or you're not. This El Encanto was a big deal back in Cuba because it was the best department store for its time and place. Even so, anyone with money was coming to Miami to shop. But you're gonna tell me he's gonna compete with the American chains here? Forget it, Charlie. And what about that location? That is complete ridiculous. No one shops in downtown anymore. No one even walks there anymore unless they're looking to get raped or killed.

NATALIE: The whole point is to have it in the center of downtown.

RITA: Yeah, yeah. It's gotta be a big monument like anyone cares. All he wants is to make a big stink for himself like he's some kind of great citizen. He's gonna lose a whole mountain on this one, but what do I care? Long as he's signed the papers, we get paid no matter if he goes into bankruptcy.

NATALIE: *(Turns water off during Rita's speech and searches the desktop.)* Did you move the papers?

RITA: I put 'em in "Contracts Pending."

NATALIE: *(Searches.)* They go in the Encanto file.

RITA: Since when?

NATALIE: That's what Julian said.

RITA: Since when? We always put the contracts in "Pending" until the first payment is made. Julie always said no matter what's signed in black and white, till we see the green, it's pending.

NATALIE: He said it when you were out.

RITA: He did, huh? *(Pause.)* You want to tell me what's going on here?

NATALIE: Nothing. What makes you think anything's —

RITA: I just want to know are there any other changes I need to know about? You seem to know what he wants, maybe you can tell me.

NATALIE: Hey, come on. There are no other changes.

RITA: No, come on nothing. He doesn't tell me anymore what he wants, maybe you got the answers.

NATALIE: He hasn't told me anything, okay? I don't know what's going on. I'm sure he knows what he's doing. Just . . . uh . . . help me with the dishes, will you? We've got to get ready.

RITA: I am not going to stand here washing dishes while Julian screws around with us on this deal.

NATALIE: *(Quickly.)* I think you're getting nervous over nothing. There is nothing to worry about.

RITA: I'm not nervous at all, all right? I'm complete calm. *(Pause.)* I'll tell you. . . . *(Sighs.)* I get plenty tired of this crap. Things always at the last minute.

NATALIE: *(Blinks several times and presses on her eyelid.)* You won't have to worry about it much longer.

RITA: The deal, no, of course not. But Julian will stay the same pain in the ass until I finally do something about it. I didn't say nothing to him this afternoon because it was all too "at the last minute." But, I'll tell you, he's gotta be shown he can't make by himself decisions that concern us too.

NATALIE: You're making too much of this.

RITA: Well, I don't think so. For fifteen years he's been asking me this and that how to get a project going on with the Cubans, but now he's forgetting that I am who's been helping him get this all along. And you, too, of course. But I mean I've been thinking with him about this for a long time so I have a right to some expectations. I come to expect a certain pattern to his behavior, you follow what I'm saying? All along he's "Rita this and that and will you do this for me please, my darling?" But since Thanksgiving, he's acting like a different person, you know what I mean? So, I sense someone is changing the rules. Okay, that's fine. But it's a two-way street.

NATALIE: Uh-huh.

RITA: If someone is treating you fair and nice with some consideration of your feelings, then I say lay down and let 'em walk on top of you. BUT if someone starts pulling stuff, making what does he call it — machinations, you don't know even what's going on anymore, then you gotta start looking out for number one.

(Turns with the water running.)

And the only way to do that is with bargaining power. Like I always told you. You got to have bargaining power.

NATALIE: Rita, the water?

RITA: What about it?

NATALIE: Don't let the water run like that.

RITA: What are you worried about? Does it come out of your salary?

(Turns back to dishes. Pause.)

Here's what I think. You and I get together and show him we can call some of the shots.

NATALIE: Oh, really? What do you plan to tell him?

RITA: Telling him is not gonna do anything. We're gonna talk to him with our actions.

(Sees dish on coffee table. Slowly walks over to it with the water running.)

You show your bargaining power with your actions.

NATALIE: Rita, will you —

RITA: Like say we decide not to show up tonight.

NATALIE: Are you crazy?

RITA: *(Interrupting.)* Why? Tell me why?

NATALIE: It's a ridiculous threat. The whole deal could fall through.

RITA: *(Turns back to the dishes.)* That's not my problem.

NATALIE: Of course it's your problem. It's all our problem. This is much too important to let a squabble with Julian get in the way.

RITA: What do you mean, squabble? Has he said anything to you?

NATALIE: No —

RITA: What did he tell you?

NATALIE: Nothing.

RITA: Then why do you say about that we had a squabble? I didn't say anything like that.

NATALIE: Rita, you're driving me crazy. I'm just referring to what you've been saying about him. Look, I know why I'm here . . .

RITA: Oh, yeah, why is that?

NATALIE: The money. Plain and simple. In case you forgot, I have a daughter to support.

RITA: How can I forget?

NATALIE: Go ahead, say anything you want. But if you had any idea what it takes to raise a child by yourself, you'd know that the financial benefits of this job far outweigh any inconveniences. I have no desire to endanger the whole deal just because —

RITA: *(Deliberately.)* The deal, my friend, goes through no matter what happens tonight.

NATALIE: Oh, you're sure about that?

RITA: Excuse me, I think I know a little more about this than you do.
    (Pause, then firmly.)
    The deal is not gonna fall through. Put the worry out of your head. *(Beat.)* What are you looking at?

NATALIE: You got nail polish on your skirt.

RITA: Where? All over — Ay, dios mio . . . fucking —

NATALIE: Don't rub. It will penetrate the fabric.

RITA: So what am I supposed to do?

NATALIE: Bring it to the cleaners. If you bring the bottle along, they'll know what chemicals are in it and they can take out the stain.

RITA: My cleaners? Right. What they know about cleaning you can write on your thumb. Last week I spilled something on a sweater, looked like it was milk, and they told me that it ate up the wool.

NATALIE: It must have been the enzymes.

RITA: Whatever it was they charged me four bucks anyway.

NATALIE: Four dollars for one sweater?

RITA: Yeah, and they left in it a hole this big *(Indicates size.)* But you know what I did? I said to them, "That's all you can do? Okay, fine. Here's what I think of your excellent service," and I threw it in the trash in front of the whole store. Plastic bag and all.

NATALIE: Did the other customers hear?

RITA: Why else would I do it? Hand me that bottle.

NATALIE: Careful. You'll strip the color.

RITA: Yeah, yeah.

(Rubs at fabric vigorously.) Anyhow, anyway —

NATALIE: That was your bargaining power, right?

RITA: Exactly right. Which is why I say we tell it straight to Julie when he gets here. He wants to play fair with us, fine. If not, he can go by himself to — Aha. Here it comes. Will you look at that? Just a little ring but in a few minutes, fresh and clean. I should go into the cleaning business myself. Not stick around here with wheelers and operators, you don't even know who's bumping you from behind anymore.

NATALIE: I'm sure by tomorrow you'll forget all about this.

RITA: I don't think so. If you ask me, he's up to something and once that contract begins, he doesn't need to cater to us — Ahh, shit. It's still red. Not gonna work.

(Rita goes over to the closet and fumbles with the door, which is locked. Checks the desk drawer.)

I try to be a nice guy and always "wait until tomorrow" or "when he's less tired and busy" but there comes a time when enough is enough. Where's the key?

(Natalie reaches into her pocket.)

Did he take the key?

NATALIE: *(Hesitates, then hands it to her.)* No. I have it. I . . . uh . . . just forgot to put it back.

RITA: *(Opens the closet and looks in.)* What's the suitcase for?

NATALIE: I don't know.

RITA: Who put it there?

NATALIE: *(Makes herself busy.)* I guess Julian did. Probably.

RITA: I've never seen this one before. Is he going on a trip?

NATALIE: I said I don't know. Maybe —

RITA: What?

NATALIE: I don't know, maybe he's staying at Bay Pointe tonight after the party.

RITA: Well, that's just great. I usually know about these things.

(Tries to open suitcase.)

And he locked it. Is he staying with someone else? I don't know, why don't you tell me. Maybe it's you.

NATALIE: Don't be ridiculous.

(Presses on her eyelid.)

RITA: Well, what did he say about it?

NATALIE: Nothing.

(Exits to bathroom.)

RITA: Then how'd you know it was his?

NATALIE: I DON'T know it's his.

(Returns with towel on her eye.) I didn't examine it.

RITA: Did you see him put it there?

NATALIE: Check my eye.

RITA: What?

NATALIE: There must be traces of smoke in the room.

RITA: Turn to the light.

(Looks in Natalie's eye.) Nothing there.

NATALIE: Are you sure?

RITA: It looks perfect. Wait . . . look up. No. It's fine.

(Shakes suitcase.)

That man's gonna give me a few answers when he gets back. That is *for sure*.

(Puts back suitcase. Looks through the closet.)

What do you mean he's staying at Bay Pointe? Did he say that?

NATALIE: I don't know WHAT he's doing.

RITA: I mean, cause I usually stay with him, in case you forgot. It's a little unusual, is all I'm saying. Hmmm, tough, tough. Doesn't matter anyway. This is the only thing I have here.

(Takes out a bright red skirt.)

I'm full with nail polish and I'm not gonna wear this.

NATALIE: Why not?

RITA: Too many fancy dinners, my friend. I'll be busting out from all this socializing.

NATALIE: I thought that's what you liked.

RITA: Not me. Julie. But forget it. I'm not doing him no favors. He can take me like I am or fuck 'im.

NATALIE: I know someone else who would like you in that dress.

RITA: *(Beat.)* Let me tell you something. That's exactly what I don't want. One time with Felipe is good for my whole lifetime, thank you very much.

NATALIE: But not for him apparently. He hardly paid any attention to me.

RITA: Consider yourself lucky.

NATALIE: I don't know about that. *(Beat.)* You can look at it anyway you want.

RITA: Oh, yeah?

NATALIE: Sure. I mean . . . One thing you could say is that given the way Julian has been acting, you might be better off with Felipe. I don't mean just financially, although that's certainly a consideration.

RITA: I don't think so.

NATALIE: He's certainly interested.

RITA: I'm flattered.

NATALIE: You should be. *(Pause.)* Has he made you an offer?

RITA: To work for him? All the time.

NATALIE: That's not what I meant.

RITA: I've been with Julie a long time now, and I'm not looking for someone else. We don't have no issues between us most of the time.

NATALIE: Except for his wife.

RITA: Yeah, well he's got his problems like anyone else. Felipe has a wife too, in case you forgot.

NATALIE: I'm sure she doesn't question what he does.

RITA: I wouldn't either. And that's just the whole thing. Look. You don't know the type like I do.

NATALIE: I just thought you might be happier.

RITA: I appreciate you thinking about me, but no thank you. *(Pause.)* Can I tell you something?

NATALIE: Sure.

RITA: This is confidential between the two of us. I'm not supposed to say, but since you're worried about the deal —

NATALIE: What is it?

RITA: It's been guaranteed to go through a long time. You don't know the whole story involved.

(As she speaks, Rita climbs on a chair to reach the top shelf of the storage cabinet. She removes a box of copy paper situated behind other boxes.)

Here we go. You may not be too happy about this —

NATALIE: What is it?

RITA: *(Opens the box and searches.)* Hmmm.

(Hands the box to Natalie.)

Put this on the desk.

NATALIE: What's this about?

RITA: Just a second.

(Climbs down and leafs through papers in the box and on the desk.)

NATALIE: What are you looking for?

RITA: Hold it a second. I'm trying to think.

(She climbs up again and looks at the side of the other boxes.)

No. No. It wasn't in any of these.

(She climbs down and leafs through desktop calendar.)

We were at Bay Pointe on . . . the . . . here it is . . . the last day of October. I sent the pictures off, let's see, it was probably the first. I put them in here. I know this is the box.

NATALIE: What's going on, Rita!

RITA: Son of a bitch. He's done something with the pictures.

NATALIE: Pictures of what?

RITA: Let me think a minute.

NATALIE: Of us?

RITA: The night you and I stayed at Bay Pointe with Felipe. Julie hooked up a camera.

NATALIE: Where?

RITA: In the bedroom, where do you think?

NATALIE: Are you kidding me?

RITA: Go look in the second bedroom tonight if you don't believe me. Julie put in a camera behind the mirror.

NATALIE: How long have you known about this?

RITA: Look, it wasn't my idea, but I didn't think it was any worse than what we were already doing.

NATALIE: *(Interrupting.)* You mean to tell me this whole deal goes through because we're blackmailing him?

RITA: I told Julie you had a right to know from the start, but he thought you'd get upset.

NATALIE: Of course I'm upset. I'm . . . I . . . what do you expect?

RITA: I know, I know. I'm sorry. But, at least you don't have to worry about tonight. The deal goes through no matter what.

NATALIE: Where are they? I want to see them.

RITA: That's the problem. I can't find them. Check the Encanto file.

NATALIE: They're not there.

RITA: *(Looks over at the closet.)* Yeah, I'll bet. *(Sighs.)* Okay, okay. It's time to stop playing games.

(Takes out the suitcase.)

Let's see what he's hiding in here.

NATALIE: You can't open it. We don't have the combination.

RITA: *(Checks the lock.)* Hmmm.

NATALIE: I don't believe you got me into this! You lied to me!

RITA: How did you know it was a combination?

NATALIE: What do you mean?

RITA: You said, "We don't know the combination." How did you know that?

NATALIE: See for yourself. It's a combination lock. What do you want?

RITA: Five minutes ago you said you didn't examine it.

NATALIE: What are you talking about?

RITA: Look here. The combination lock is hidden under the flap. There's no way to know that unless you examined it or somebody told you.

NATALIE: Get off my case, huh? I'm upset.

RITA: So who's lying to who? You gonna start talking or what?

NATALIE: Will you stop it? You're completely paranoid.

RITA: You think so, huh? You haven't seen paranoid yet.

(Throws the suitcase on the desk.)

You gonna tell me what's in here or I'm gonna blow this whole fucking deal out of the water. I've got my own set of these pictures. All I have to do is let Felipe know that and you got no deal, sweetheart.

NATALIE: I have had it with your threats. I don't know who you think you are or what kind of power you THINK you hold —

RITA: You want to see? You want to see the kind of power I hold over you?

(Takes the scissors off the desk.)

NATALIE: What are you doing? Put those down.

(Rita moves toward her with the scissors.)

RITA! What are you —

RITA: *(Pulls back.)* Had you there. Hah! Te digo yo . . .

(She attempts to pick the lock.)

I can be a very nice person, but if you're crossing with me, I turn into the biggest son of a bitch in the world.

NATALIE: You're going to break it.

RITA: Get away. You had your chance to be straight with me. Now there's the right way, the wrong way, and my way.

(She starts to tear through the side of the suitcase. Julian enters as she does this. He is expensively dressed and conscious of his appearance.)

JULIAN: Rita! Rita what are you — That's a handmade suitcase. Will you — Come on. Give me those scissors!

RITA: You want it? Take it.

(She thrusts the scissors at him with the point out.)

JULIAN: Will you — Jesus Christ! You cut my sleeve! *(Puts scissors down.)* Look at it. You cut my fucking ARM! Goddamn blood all over my cuff.

RITA: Let's see. Well, so there is.

JULIAN: This is a new shirt. Crazy lunatics, tearing up my office. Are we supposed to be going somewhere or what?

RITA: I don't know, Julian. Are you going someplace?

NATALIE: What took you so long?

RITA: *(Picks up suitcase.)* What the fuck's this all about?

JULIAN: I've been arranging some things for our mutual profit, all right? Am I the ENEMY all of a sudden?

(Rita starts to pull back the torn flap of the suitcase.)

Goddamn it, Rita. Leave it alone. I don't believe this! I'm fucking cut!

(Rolls up his sleeve and looks at his arm.)

RITA: We can go to the red cross if you want, get you a transfusion.

JULIAN: Just give me that.

(He takes the suitcase away from her and puts it in the closet.)

Walk into my own office and my staff's tearing up the premises.

NATALIE: I didn't do it, Julian.

RITA: Give me a break!

JULIAN: Christ, there's a fucking hole in my skin! Natalie . . . a bandaid please?

(Natalie goes to get the bandaid.)

(To Rita.) I'm a little put out with you, all right? We're supposed to be someplace in a few minutes and I come in you're ripping stuff up, stabbing me in the arm.

(Takes bandaid from Natalie.)

I gotta get a hold of myself. You'll give me a heart attack. I swear, I'm gonna fucking die before this is over.

NATALIE: *(Coldly.)* Julian, I want to know something. Why are we going to Bay Pointe tonight?

JULIAN: What? It's a little celebration.

NATALIE: Yes, but why —

JULIAN: *(Looks at his watch.)* Shit. He's gonna get there before us. Look, we have to go.

RITA: We've been sitting here doing nothing. Where the hell have you been?

NATALIE: I think you have some explaining to do.

JULIAN: *(To Natalie.)* You're doing me a FAVOR? Listen. Wait in the car. I gotta talk to Rita.

RITA: She can stay. I got no secrets. You got secrets, Julie? You got a problem you can't talk to me straight? You in a rush?

JULIAN: I want to talk to you alone. It's my prerogative. Natalie. The car, please.

NATALIE: *(To Rita.)* I'm sorry. I have to hear it from him.

RITA: Go ahead. See if I care.

NATALIE: Rita told me there are pictures of us with Felipe —

JULIAN: She did that, did she?

RITA: She's not gonna do anything. Besides, she's in them she oughta know. Maybe she wants to put one on her Christmas card — "Good will to all men."

JULIAN: *(Simultaneously with Natalie.)* That's a good one, Rita. you're getting better all the time.

NATALIE: I don't believe it! How could you do that?

JULIAN: There's nothing to worry about.

RITA: No more fairy tales, Julian. It's time to start talking straight. As of now, Nat and I are getting correlated so we each have the total picture what's been going on here.

JULIAN: Say, I'm awfully glad to hear it.

NATALIE: I kept my part of the bargain.

RITA: Oh, you have a bargain together. That's just very nice. Be sure you get your part in writing, my friend.

JULIAN: Okay, that's enough.

RITA: So where'd you put them, Julie?

JULIAN: You haven't figured it out? Nat? You got any ideas? Let's hear some ideas.

RITA: We're not playing no more games.

JULIAN: You got a set. You show her.

RITA: Where is Felipe's set? What did you do with the negatives?

JULIAN: *(Overlapping.)* She was keeping them in her car. You better watch she doesn't get pulled over.

RITA: Let's talk about Felipe's set.

JULIAN: Talk to me, love. I'm waiting for some input.

RITA: Listen Julian. The time has passed for our input. Far as I'm concerned it's time for your output.

JULIAN: That's brilliant. What a turn of a phrase. Let me get my book, I'm writing it down. Shit! *(Sighs.)* Listen, Nat. Look at me? *(Pause.)* You've been working here almost a year now, right? What would you say is the most important lesson you've learned about the business world?

RITA: *(Groans.)* What bullshit —

JULIAN: You started this, now let me handle it.

(To Natalie.)

Things are hardly ever the way they seem. A seemingly straightforward situation can actually be full of twists and turns and secret machinations because that's the way of the world, am I right?

NATALIE: I think it's very simple. Are we, or are we not, blackmailing Felipe with photographs?

JULIAN: Will you let me finish what I have to say? All I'm trying to illustrate is that the reverse is also true. Pictures, photos, whatever — okay. They do exist. But it's not what you think. It seems like a complex situation but it's actually very simple. That is, simple in its own complex way. You see, ah, first of all, technically, we're not blackmailing him. But, yes, the pictures exist. Or rather, they did. I just gave him all the copies and negatives and he burned them up. I saw him do it.

RITA: You gave him the negatives before a payment was made?

JULIAN: Don't get excited. Nothing has changed. Come tomorrow we are all going to be very well off. You know, you astonish me. I . . . I'm wounded, no really, WOUNDED by all these suspicions. I mean . . . have I ever denied you a fair share of the compensation? The books are open. Check all the Encanto figures if you like. Is there some other dissatisfaction you want me to address? I'm open to it. We can discuss this all night if you want. But if we still want this to go through without any problem, we have a client to attend to.

RITA: Rule number one. Never keep the client waiting.

NATALIE: What's he waiting for?

JULIAN: How's that?

NATALIE: We're going to Bay Pointe, right? So are you thinking of taking more pictures of us with him?

JULIAN: Nat, my dear, once he knows the setup, that's no longer a possibility.

NATALIE: So this is purely social.

JULIAN: *(Pause.)* Felipe invited a few people from the mayor's office.

RITA: Oh, that's so nice. How well are we supposed to get to know them?

JULIAN: He just wants a little extra insurance to make sure there are no problems from City Hall.

RITA: You got a lot of nerve, my friend.

JULIAN: Hey, listen, listen. I just found out about it myself. Felipe just, uh, asked me. As a favor.

NATALIE: Oh, Julian you can't be serious. Last time it was all in fun, at least I thought it was. This is something altogether different.

JULIAN: You're right. It is different. For one thing, there will be extra compensation for all of us.

RITA: For you too? For doing what?

JULIAN: Okay, then for you. Fine. For Natalie, whatever you want.

NATALIE: You've got to think I'm crazy. How do I know what he's actually going to do with them? I could wake up one morning and they're all over the Herald.

JULIAN: No one is ever going to see these pictures. And you know why? A little lesson in business, ladies. Because those pictures are an insurance policy. They're only valuable as long as they're hidden. The day Felipe cashes in by publicizing them, they aren't worth a dime to him. They're toilet paper. It's the threat that empowers the materials, not the delivery.

NATALIE: I'm sorry, Julian. I've got a daughter to think about, my whole family lives here —

JULIAN: That's okay with me. I'm not the one who was gonna make money on this. Still . . . *(He pulls a check out of his pocket.)* . . . twenty thousand seems like a lot to lose.

NATALIE: How much exactly?

RITA: Who gives a shit?

NATALIE: Twenty thousand dollars for this?

JULIAN: It must mean a great deal to him.

NATALIE: Are you serious? Okay, okay . . . wait a minute . . . Is that each?

RITA: Ya se jodio esta cosa.

JULIAN: That's the total.

NATALIE: Still that's . . . that's a different story.

JULIAN: Like I was saying.

RITA: Nat, listen, this is bullshit . . .

JULIAN: *(Pushes the check across the table to Natalie.)* Ten thousand in advance as a measure of his good faith. The rest will be delivered in cash as soon as he gets the negatives, which can be tomorrow if you see to it yourself.

NATALIE: This is extra, right? You're not including this as part of my original cut. This is exactly as you say it. An extra ten thousand for a few pictures tonight.

JULIAN: All my cards are on the table.

NATALIE: You're not going to go back on it tomorrow?

JULIAN: Have I ever done that? Come on. Where is the limit to all these accusations? Let's shake on it.

RITA: Forget it, Natalie!

JULIAN: Shhh. I 'm paying for some peace and quiet. Is it a deal or not?

NATALIE: Okay.

JULIAN: *(He shakes her hand.)* Now you better get going. He's gonna be waiting and not very happy about it. Tell him we'll be there in a few minutes.

(Natalie looks at Rita.)

RITA: It flows with the tide cause it don't have a backbone.

(Natalie exits. Julian and Rita stand in silence. He looks out the window as Natalie pulls out. There is a long silence. Julian continues to look out.)

JULIAN: You know . . . It's a good thing that I still love you after all these years. Otherwise I swear I could break your fucking neck.

RITA: Is that right?

JULIAN: I don't know how many times I've said that to myself. "Julie, that woman is too hot tempered for her own good. One day you're gonna have to stop her before she kills you."

RITA: *(Walks right up to his face.)* Look at this. I'm shaking with fear. I'm really scared shit, can't you tell?

(She leans her neck to him.) Go ahead, I'm waiting. Go ahead, I said.

(He walks away from her.)

Yeah, I thought so. So you got something to tell me, my boy? You got balls, so talk to my face. Come on. I'm waiting for some input.

JULIAN: Rita, you tempt me.

RITA: *(She takes the suitcase out of the closet.)* Let's start with your travel plans. Let's see here.

(She pulls back the torn flap.)

JULIAN: Leave it alone.

RITA: *(Starts ripping the flap open further.)* You got a fucking handmade suitcase, Julian? For what? Oh, I see.

(She pulls men's clothes out of the suitcase.)

You going on a trip? Let's see. What do we need for our little vacation?

(She pulls out a shirt and rips it open as she speaks.)

Shirts, of course. That's nice. What else?

JULIAN: Leave it alone! Goddamn it!

RITA: *(She pulls out of reach holding a jacket.)* Very nice. Feels like silk. Must be some place nice you're going. But you know, I don't understand Italian, I'm not so sophisticated like you.

(She rips out the label.)

Why don't you read it for me?

JULIAN: Give me that, Rita. I'm warning you.

(He grabs the jacket away from her and part of the lining rips out.)

(Rita laughs simultaneously with action above.)

Goddamn you!

(He grabs her arm.)

You're in a ripping mood, honey? Now it's my turn!

(He takes the scissors off the desk and catches her hair in the blade.)

RITA: Let go of me. Who do you think you are?

JULIAN: Go ahead, spill your guts out. Let's hear some more. I could cut this right off.

RITA: Stop! Julian —

JULIAN: Make me a relic of my poison-tongued Rita, right?
(He lets go.)

RITA: *(She turns around and shoves him in the chest.)* Goddamn you! Look at this —
(Pulls out a handful of loose hair.)
You hurt me. I'm not gonna forget this —

JULIAN: I hurt you? What about me? I left here an hour ago and everything was working out. We are about to get paid for all our years of hard work together. I get back and all of a sudden you're ripping my stuff, telling Natalie all our secrets.

RITA: Just talk to me straight, Julian. Ever since Thanksgiving you've deliberately forgotten to tell me things. I can't stand these little secrets, these . . . these LOOKS and contract clauses. How am I supposed to trust anything you say?

JULIAN: Ah, you think we should trust each other? Well, that's an original notion. All your talk about loyalty and commitment —
(He walks around to face her.)
Who commands your loyalty? Natalie? You want to include her? So consult me. Let's talk about it. FIRST, not after the fact. Fidelity, constancy, a pact of absolute trust. This is what unites us against our mutual enemies. What are we worth without this foundation? How the hell do we hope to survive against the Felipes of this world?

RITA: I'm so tired of this.

JULIAN: I know you are. That's why — I want you to take it easy for a change. Now, come here.
(He takes off her shoe and rubs her foot.)
You've been working too hard, my love. And I'm appreciative. Want to see my gratitude?

RITA: *(Pulls her foot back.)* No, I don't.

JULIAN: *(He puts her foot against his groin.)* Check it yourself. Mmmm.

RITA: *(Angrily.)* Stop it.
(He kisses her foot.)
I mean it, Julian!

JULIAN: You'll have to force me.

RITA: I'm not playing any games.

JULIAN: Every delicious part of this foot deserves attention.

RITA: *(Laughs.)* Get out of here.

JULIAN: Is that a smile? No, wait. What if I nibble right in there?

RITA: *(Pulls her foot back laughing.)* Don't start that now.

JULIAN: *(Moves his hand up her leg.)* Or better yet —

RITA: *(Slides down onto the floor.)* Okay, you asked for it. Now you gotta finish what you started.

(She pulls him onto her.)

JULIAN: Right this minute?

RITA: Right this minute, my friend.

JULIAN: *(Kisses her, then checks his watch.)* We really have to go.

RITA: Come on. What's your rush?

JULIAN: Felipe does not like to be kept waiting.

(Rita sits up.)

What? What's the matter?

RITA: He signed the contract, didn't he?

JULIAN: Yeah, he did.

RITA: So far as I'm concerned I don't care what he thinks anymore.

JULIAN: Unfortunately, that's not a good attitude to have.

RITA: I don't have any attitude. He doesn't control us anymore. You said it before. Once we get his signature, we have him where we want him. Right? That's what you said, isn't it?

JULIAN: *(Pause.)* It's not so simple.

RITA: What do you mean? Why not?

JULIAN: *(Pause.)* He likes you.

RITA: I don't care what he likes. I care about me and you. That's it.

(Silence.)

What is it?

JULIAN: We had a good idea at the beginning. We knew his history, what he's trying to achieve for himself in this town, the type of women he likes and that you would be sure to get his attention. We stalked him, learned about him, pursued him in every way we knew and with a little photographic insurance we proposed to him in a way that couldn't fail. And because of all our hard work and shrewd planning, finally we're going to see a piece of the real action. You would imagine that we accomplished what we set out to do.

RITA: That's what I say.

JULIAN: But it's not so simple, my love.

RITA: Okay, Julian. What happened to the deal?

JULIAN: Nothing. Nothing. We got the contract. I just miscalculated thinking that's all we'd get. Dealing with Felipe is not as easy as we thought.

RITA: You think it has been easy for me? Then after fifteen years you don't know anything about me. What do you think I feel when he goes on about building a landmark from Havana here, like he's a great man of the people. The only cause he's ever been interested in is his own pocket. And that is fine with me but I don't want to hear this wrapped around in some sentimental bullshit about Cuba. His only interest in any of this is to make publicity for himself and even more money than he already has. You think these are just words, Julian? Don't you hear what I'm saying?

JULIAN: I hear what you're saying. *(Pause.)* Felipe is just better at this game than we are. Some men retaliate with any number of threatening situations when they get pushed against the wall the way we did it to him. Felipe makes offers that are much harder to resist.

RITA: Who cares? He can't touch us. You know I got copies. We got him where we want him not the other way around. Now . . . Come on. Come here. What are you worried about?

JULIAN: *(Pause.)* He's buying me out.

RITA: What?

JULIAN: I did my best, Rita. He's just better at it than I am.

RITA: What are you talking about?

JULIAN: He's giving me a decent price. I'll say that much. Twice what Encanto would have been worth. So it's not so bad after all. Except I . . . uh . . . Well. He suggested . . . He wants me out of the picture. I have to leave town for a little while.

RITA: No way, Julie.

JULIAN: You'll still get your full share of Encanto and I promise, no I swear to you, I'll still manage to see you.

RITA: Julie — Look, now — just hold on there a minute. We have to discuss this further.

JULIAN: There's nothing I can do. It's in the contract.

RITA: Who gives a shit about the contract? Are you gonna let him control us like that? What have we been doing this for? —

JULIAN: I'm sorry, love. A man like me doesn't say no to Felipe.

RITA: A MAN? That's what you call yourself? Some whore with a loaded wallet, can't speak English after twenty years walks in here and buys you out just like that *(Snaps.)* A man! You make me laugh. Eres una puta! A puta is what you are with no balls, just like him!

JULIAN: Enough! Watch your mouth. Everything's gonna be fine. We'll be getting plenty of money anyway and . . . uh . . . it'll be fine, okay?

RITA: *(Grabs the contracts.)* No it won't.

JULIAN: Come on, Rita. don't do anything you'll regret.

RITA: You're the one that's gonna regret what you did!

JULIAN: Come on, come on. Give me those.

RITA: Forget it!

(She starts to tear them, but they're too thick. Julian gets hold of her arm and tries to pull them away. She holds them out. He grabs at them with his other hand. She flings them across the room. He pushes her onto the desk and holds her there.)

JULIAN: We got what we wanted, Rita.

RITA: This is what YOU wanted! I wanted to make something together.

JULIAN: Just listen —

RITA: You are not selling me off.

(She pushes out with her leg and knocks him onto the floor. She sits on him and he struggles to breathe.)

Now you listen to me!

(He groans and gasps for air.)

Don't think you're gonna get my sympathy with that routine. You are not selling me off! You can shove it up your ass, Julian. I am not — You having trouble breathing? That's just too bad. Maybe you and Natalie want to invest in a private doctor.

JULIAN: Off my chest, goddamn — I can't breathe!

RITA: So catch your breath. I got all the time in the world.

JULIAN: Please —

RITA: I'm in no rush. I got no place to be tomorrow cause I am NOT going to work for Felipe.

(He stops coughing.)

I don't care about it, Julian. You are not selling me off. I am not gonna let you give everything we worked for to that hijo de puta for a couple of dollars. The money doesn't mean shit! You got that, Julian? *(Pause.)* Julie? *(She gets off.)* Hey, Julian!

(He sits up still unable to quite catch his breath.)

What is it? Are you all right? Julian?!

JULIAN: Jesus — You trying to — *(Coughs.)* You trying to kill me I swear to God.

RITA: Don't scare me like that. All right? *(Pause.)* You okay? You want some water?

(He nods. She brings him water from the sink. He drinks and motions for her to sit.)

JULIAN: You're a dangerous one, Rita girl.

RITA: Shut up and drink.

(She loosens his collar.)

You lazy frightened fuck. You haven't thought this one through correctly. Now talk to me, tell me how it happened. We'll figure out some solution together. Like we always did. There's got to be a way to change this mess.

JULIAN: What am I gonna do without you?

RITA: No one said you have to be. Nobody owns you. You got a choice here. Jesus, Julian. Okay. Are you okay, are you fine?

(Julian nods.)

You want some more water?

(He shakes his head.)

Okay. Look. I got this figured out. Go ahead and sell him the business. He gave you a good price, huh? So fine. Give your wife finally whatever she wants, and let's just get out of here. We'll go — Anywhere. I don't know, pick a place you want to live. I don't care long as it's out of Miami.

JULIAN: You don't understand the significance of the whole thing. If you listen to me and play this right, it could be the best thing that ever happened to us.

RITA: No. I'm not listening to that anymore.

JULIAN: You can't leave now. He wants you here. He wants you to work for him.

RITA: Out of the question! You are not selling me off!

JULIAN: Of course not, love. No one can make you do anything you don't want. I'm not even suggesting you stay here indefinitely. Just do it temporarily. Think about the possibilities for a moment. Can you believe what kind of access you'll have? There's no telling what you could find out about his operation. If everything you say about him is true, I can bet you he's gonna reveal something that could put him right in the palm of our hands for good.

RITA: How can you seriously ask me to do this?

JULIAN: You know he doesn't play by the rules. There's something there and if anyone can find out, it's you.

(He pulls her toward him.)

Just keep your purpose in mind. Remember who he is, what he stands for, how he's manipulated us all to his advantage. This is the best way to get him back for everything he's ever done to us or anyone else. We can teach him the lesson he'll never forget and get rich at the same time. And I swear to you, we'll go anywhere you want then. Just the two of us.

(He takes a photo out of the suitcase.)

Remember this? You were 25 years old in this picture. Only here for two years when you marched into my office with your broken English and won my heart on the spot. What do you think really matters to me after all? Nothing but you and me. I have no commitment but to see the two of us together —

(Natalie enters.)

free of Felipe and my wife and Natalie or anyone else that would like to see us fail.

(He starts to kiss her.)

But we have to take advantage of opportunities that come our way.

NATALIE: You know, moments like this are so rare, I really hate to interrupt. However, I seem to recall that a few minutes ago this was a three-way deal.

JULIAN: What are you doing here? Why aren't you at Bay Pointe?

NATALIE: I had a change of heart. And lucky for me, I might add.

JULIAN: I don't fucking believe this! Didn't we have an agreement?

RITA: Where have you been all this time?

NATALIE: Sitting in traffic. It's a parking lot on that expressway. But it gave me some time to contemplate my future. And I thought I ought to come back.

JULIAN: Jesus, Natalie. I better call him.

NATALIE: Never mind, I took care of it. I told him that Rita spilled nail polish on her dress while she got ready for tonight, so she was running a bit late. He seemed to like the idea that she was getting ready for him.

JULIAN: And what came over you to make that decision?

NATALIE: *(Pause.)* I thought I should have the contract for tonight in writing.

JULIAN: Is that right?

NATALIE: It's nothing personal, Julie. Business, after all, is business.

I hate to sound suspicious but are there any new arrangements I should be aware of?

RITA: You have nothing to worry about.

NATALIE: That's easy for you to say. It falls into your lap, baby. I wish I knew your secret. And Felipe's too for that matter. You come to this country and make money better than the rest of us who've lived here all our lives. Right. Julie? Now, what about the contract? If it's all the same . . .

JULIAN: No problem.

NATALIE: Rita and I will split tonight. And the sale of the business?

JULIAN: It's all in the Encanto file.

NATALIE: As long as nothing's changed.

RITA: Nothing has changed.

NATALIE: *(Finds a paper and pen and writes silently. She shows the paper to Rita.)* Is that suitable?

RITA: Who cares?

NATALIE: I'm doing this for both of us.

(Rita turns away from her.)

Okay, if you're not interested. We'll only need two copies. *(Beat.)* Does that mean I get the full twenty?

JULIAN: Just make three copies. Rita's still in.

(Natalie copies the page. He signs them.)

NATALIE: *(To Rita.)* Here you go.

(Rita doesn't take it.)

It's up to you. I'm putting it on the desk.

JULIAN: Well, Nat, looks like you've learned a thing or two.

NATALIE: Like Rita always says, just looking out for number one.

JULIAN: *(Laughs.)* So, are we ready to go?

NATALIE: Shotgun!

(To Rita.)

You know that expression? Nah, probably not.

JULIAN: *(To Rita.)* Come on.

NATALIE: Wait. You have to change your dress. Felipe will be suspicious.

JULIAN: Hurry up. We'll wait for you.

RITA: No, no. Um . . . You go ahead.

JULIAN: You sure? We can wait. *(Looks at his watch.)* But not too long. We have to get this party rolling.

RITA: It's better if you go.

JULIAN: Are you sure?

RITA: Yes.

JULIAN: Don't be long, okay?

RITA: Good-bye, Julian.

NATALIE: *(She pulls Julian towards the door.)* Come on.

(Julian and Natalie exit. Rita closes the door behind them. She leans on it for a moment. Natalie and Julian are heard outside.)

NATALIE: For the other ten you could convince me I was having fun.

(Julian's response is muffled. Natalie laughs. Rita sees the check on the desk. She picks it up and takes a lighter out of a drawer. Two car doors are slammed in rapid succession. She lights the check. A car is heard pulling out. She drops

the check in the trash and throws in the contracts. She picks up her handbag and starts to open the door.)
(Lights out.)

END OF PLAY

Freakish Times
by Lesli-Jo Morizono

ABOUT THE PLAYWRIGHT

Lesli-Jo Morizono has had staged readings at Tribeca Performing Arts Center, Cherry Lane Alternative, Women's Project & Productions, and New York Theater Workshop. In 1993 her play, *In the Valley of the Human Spirit,* was selected for the Eugene O'Neill National Playwrights Conference. She received a master of fine arts in Dramatic Writing from New York University Tisch School of the Arts and is a member of The Dramatists Guild.

ORIGINAL PRODUCTION

Freakish Times was originally produced at Women's Project Theatre, May 21–22, 2000. It was directed by Cecelia Antoinette with the following cast:

Young Woman . . . . Christine Toy Johnson
Old Woman . . . . Micki Grant

CHARACTERS

Young Woman, twenties.
Old Woman, fifties or older.

TIME

Sometime in the future, after the apocalypse.

SETTING

A graveyard.

FREAKISH TIMES

Overcast sky hangs over a graveyard. Old Woman wanders through the yard with her nose in the air. She sniffs the air making loud hog-like sounds. She grows excited as she follows her nose, walking quickly with confident steps. She stops in front of an open grave and smiles. She leans over and reaches into the grave and holds up an arm and sniffs it. The body attached to the arm sits up. Old Woman recoils with surprise but recovers quickly.

YOUNG WOMAN: What year is it?

OLD WOMAN: The — the twenty-fifth year after the plague. Were you napping, young girl, or have you come back from the dead?

YOUNG WOMAN: I — I'm not quite sure. Is it night or day?

OLD WOMAN: It is both.

(Old Woman smells Young Woman.)

OLD WOMAN: Mmmm. You have no odor, you must be an undead. What a lucky day. How old might you be?

YOUNG WOMAN: I don't remember.

OLD WOMAN: Do you remember the plague?

YOUNG WOMAN: What is this plague that you speak of?

(Old Woman smiles and opens her picnic basket. She removes a blanket and spreads it on the ground. She makes herself comfortable on it and takes out food and various jars.)

OLD WOMAN: An evil time when the devil's blanket fell upon the earth and covered it whole. The year I was born the land became charred. We had no place to live except in the ocean. I grew up inside a whale's belly, and the year blood flowed between my legs the devil grew bored and took his blanket back. I walked on land for the first time. Babies became children before I learned how to use my legs properly, and when I was able to walk without fear the plague came. Everywhere one saw only dead bodies. They say it was once called the black plague and came to a city called Euro hundreds of years ago, but we called it the red plague because the infected were covered with festering red sores that made the body hot as if a fire burned inside them. There was nothing we could do for them except listen to their screams. Eat this.

(She holds out a piece of bread.)

YOUNG WOMAN: Thank you. I am glad I do not remember this red plague.

OLD WOMAN: What do you remember?

YOUNG WOMAN: Well . . .

OLD WOMAN: Do you remember a man named Trump?

YOUNG WOMAN: Should I?

OLD WOMAN: He was a formidable being, powerful enough to thwart the devil. *(She pulls out of the basket a book and holds it up. It is a book by Donald Trump.)*

OLD WOMAN: When we walked on land we found hundreds, thousands of these books. His books and tins of Spam were the only things that the devil did not devour. Do you know of him? Perhaps he lived in your time.

YOUNG WOMAN: I — I don't remember.

(Old Woman sprinkles salt on sticks of celery and gives it to Young Woman.)

OLD WOMAN: Make sure you chew the root but not too fine.

YOUNG WOMAN: I don't know you, yet you share your food. It is a good sign that perhaps this new life of mine will be blessed.

OLD WOMAN: Wait until you see what we're having later. Give me your hands. *(Old Woman holds up Young Woman's hands.)*

OLD WOMAN: Your flesh is ample yet firm. Death has preserved you well. What is this? One, two, three, four, five! You are missing two fingers. What happened to them?

(Old Woman holds up Young Woman's hands.)

YOUNG WOMAN: I don't know what you mean. How many fingers do you have?

OLD WOMAN: Seven, of course. Perhaps you were in an accident or your birth was cursed. What can you remember?

(Slight pause.)

YOUNG WOMAN: I remember . . . finding shade inside a mountain . . . a smile, yes, I remember a young buck's smile. Pain . . . a great deal of pain and blood. I remember being split into two . . . and an emptiness as if my insides had been scooped out . . . weariness, overwhelming weariness that's what I remember most.

OLD WOMAN: Could this be a new plague or some unknown disease? Show me your teeth.

(Young Woman opens her mouth.)

OLD WOMAN: You have all your teeth and they look young and strong. The dead always remember how they died, why can't you? Once I found a young man, so juicy and tender, who had walked into the ocean and realized he had forgotten how to swim. That's what walking on land will do. Another time I found a pack of young ones whose mother left them to hunt for food and didn't return. They were all bones and no meat. Most of the dead are victims of the plague. No one will touch them. Your body is ample and your skin is without marks or sores, so perhaps you did not die of disease.

YOUNG WOMAN: I remember hearing a cry, a wail, high and shrill yet so sad and low. Even thinking of it now . . .

(She shivers as she covers her ears. Old Woman washes Young Woman's face and body, caressing her gently.)

YOUNG WOMAN: You feed me and now you wash me. I am not used to such good fortune.

OLD WOMAN: Your skin is soft and your meat lean, I will chew gently.

YOUNG WOMAN: I remember . . . I remember a touch, yes, the way you're touching my body, I have felt this before.

OLD WOMAN: Your belly is loose. I think I know how you died. You spawned a baby.

YOUNG WOMAN: *(Surprised.)* But I have no memory of this. Surely one would never forget such a thing.

OLD WOMAN: It is quite common to forget one's young. I never knew my mother. When you live in a whale's belly, it is easy to get separated and lost.

YOUNG WOMAN: Do you have any memories of your mother?

OLD WOMAN: The others say she died after giving birth to me. I like to think that she was a good female. Fair and kind who would have loved me no matter how different I am. I was told that my mother lived in the twenty-first century, after the great war and before the devil's blanket. The land was growing hotter and night became day. People roamed the land in search of shade and food until finally only the ocean was left. My mother must have been a wise female to convince a whale to share his belly.

YOUNG WOMAN: Was it difficult to live inside a whale?

OLD WOMAN: One can get used to anything, especially if one knows nothing else.

(Old Woman spreads grease on Young Woman's face and neck.)

YOUNG WOMAN: What is that awful smell?

OLD WOMAN: Your skin needs oil.

YOUNG WOMAN: Why are you so kind to me?

OLD WOMAN: You ask foolish questions.

YOUNG WOMAN: No, you are proof that this life will be different. Perhaps I will even see the moon.

OLD WOMAN: The moon exists only in stories, now hush before I change my mind. I curse this hunger in my belly. Living on land allows one to spawn many eggs. There is only so much spam to go around.

YOUNG WOMAN: I have smelled this before. It is — fish oil!

OLD WOMAN: Only the best for this feast.

YOUNG WOMAN: Will I be going to your feast?

OLD WOMAN: I will make you the guest of honor. Eat more bread. Color is coming back into your face. The others say that before the great war there was a celebration where people ate for days. It was a celebration to give thanks for all they had been given and they were given a lot although they did not think so. Berries and bread were eaten, but the main attraction was a bird, a large one that was roasted. They say it was an ugly-looking bird that walked on two legs. I would have liked to have seen this bird. The others say he made a sound like this . . . *(Wails.)*

(Young Woman grows uneasy.)

YOUNG WOMAN: Stop it!

OLD WOMAN: Do not be cross, young one, it makes the intestines sour.

(Old Woman massages her again.)

YOUNG WOMAN: What will be eaten at your feast?

OLD WOMAN: Whatever one can find.

(Young Woman stands up almost losing her balance. She walks around testing her legs. Old Woman sniffs the air.)

OLD WOMAN: What are you doing? Come back to me.

YOUNG WOMAN: Your food has given me strength.

OLD WOMAN: Sit down. You must not move too quickly. Bruised meat is tough.

YOUNG WOMAN: The earth agrees with my feet. I must have walked on land before. How long has it been since you first walked?

OLD WOMAN: There are too many lines on my face to count. Now come to me.

YOUNG WOMAN: Answer my question and then I will lie in your arms.

OLD WOMAN: Soon after blood flowed from my legs we walked on land, now I am as dry as the bread you greedily ate.

YOUNG WOMAN: Perhaps I am not too late.

OLD WOMAN: For what?

YOUNG WOMAN: To find my young.

OLD WOMAN: That is impossible. How can you look when you don't remember anything?

YOUNG WOMAN: I remember her cry.

OLD WOMAN: You remember nothing.

YOUNG WOMAN: The bird sounds you made remind me of my girl, yes, you see I remember, I gave birth to a girl. She was the strangest-looking girl I had ever seen. I gave birth to her at a time of great chaos. It was as if the earth had turned upside down. Each day that passed more people died. Money was useless, water and shade were the only things of value. People fought to stand in the ocean and when that wasn't enough we had to go under water. I swam with fishes and birds and when my contractions started, they helped me find shelter in a cave that smelled of fish oil and that's where I gave birth. Before I passed I saw her. I touched her face. I heard her wail. I want to know if she survived.

OLD WOMAN: That land is cool now but it is impossible for a young to survive alone, especially if there were no others to teach her.

YOUNG WOMAN: She was so unusual, perhaps she survived.

OLD WOMAN: Impossible.

YOUNG WOMAN: But you survived without your mother.

OLD WOMAN: I had the others. Death has made you foolish. Now stop your chatter and come to me. Let my hands soothe you.

YOUNG WOMAN: It is too cruel to live your next life with the same bad memories of before. I curse the gods who pulled me from the ground.

OLD WOMAN: Let me help you ease your pain.

(Old Woman holds out her arms, but Young Woman remains still.)

YOUNG WOMAN: Do you enjoy eating the dead?

OLD WOMAN: The land produces only dead people.

YOUNG WOMAN: How many will I feed?

OLD WOMAN: My pack has ten. Your toes and fingers will be feed for the young.

YOUNG WOMAN: How will I be cooked?

OLD WOMAN: Wrapped in sheets of fish fat and seaweed and baked in the land for two days.

YOUNG WOMAN: Will you be the one to cook me?

OLD WOMAN: I will not leave your side. On the day you are served, the others will gather and sing and dance to our gods. Then we will laugh and talk as we feast pretending that our food is not of our dead but that of other creatures. We will drink sea water and say it is sweet and soothing. We will eat your flesh and remark how the meat falls from the bones enticing us to eat more. And when our bellies are full and the table is bare, the others will tell stories of life before the devil's blanket covered the land. A time when people had no need to eat their dead. Come to me.

(Old Woman holds out her hands.)

YOUNG WOMAN: First you must make that bird sound again.

(Old Woman wails. Slowly Young Woman walks over to her, they embrace. Old Woman slowly rocks her in her arms.)

YOUNG WOMAN: She is better off dead. One cannot live with a shadow over one's face.

OLD WOMAN: What do you mean?

YOUNG WOMAN: She was hideous-looking, a freak with no chance of surviving. Even if there were others to help she would have been an outcast. Death is the only kindness she could have known.

OLD WOMAN: Hideous in what way?

YOUNG WOMAN: One needs all the senses to survive.

OLD WOMAN: You are the blind one now.

YOUNG WOMAN: Where there should have been eyes was only skin. No eye sockets or anything remotely resembling eyes, only skin, smooth and blank. A nose, a mouth, and nothing else. It was as if the gods had suddenly lost interest and stopped work on her. She was a freak, no doubt about it. A freak for freakish times.

OLD WOMAN: How do you know this? You died giving birth to her.

YOUNG WOMAN: I saw her briefly before I passed. It was the sight of her that caused my heart to stop.

OLD WOMAN: You speak of the impossible.

YOUNG WOMAN: She is dead, and when I enter the other world perhaps this time your gods will favor me and allow me to meet her.

OLD WOMAN: This is a cruel trick. I am old not stupid.

YOUNG WOMAN: I am ready to be roasted. Take me, old woman, I am all yours. Only promise me that you will eat my heart. And when you chew, chew it well at least a hundred times or more. Although it is filled with pain, I give my heart to you.

(*Young Woman holds out her hands to Old Woman who stares at her. Slight pause.*)

YOUNG WOMAN: What is wrong with you? Have you changed your mind about me? Perhaps I am too skinny for you. I assure you there is enough to feed your pack. Look at my hips, see its width? The flesh on my chest and back will satisfy the most hungry. Speak old woman. Do not tell me that you have lost your appetite.

OLD WOMAN: I hunger for you more than ever.

YOUNG WOMAN: Then what is it?

(*Old Woman removes her veil and turns her face to the audience. She has no eyes. Young Woman looks stunned. She looks at Old Woman with disbelief, then recognition, and finally joy.*)

YOUNG WOMAN: The gods have heard me.

(*Blackout.*)

END OF PLAY

The Only Woman General
by Lavonne Mueller

Special thanks to Bryna Wortman

BIOGRAPHY

Lavonne Mueller's play *Letters to a Daughter From Prison*, about Nehru and his daughter, Indira, was produced at the Women's Project's First International Festival of the Arts in New York City and went on to tour in India. Her play *Violent Peace* was produced in New York City at the Women's Project and later was produced in London and was the "Critics Choice" in *Time Out* magazine. Her play *Little Victories* was produced by the Women's Project in New York City and was later produced in Tokyo by Theatre Classic Productions and directed by Riho Mitachi. Her play *The Only Woman General* was produced by the Women's Project in New York City and starred Colleen Dewhurst and later went on to the Edinburgh Festival where it was "Pick of the Fringe" by the Scotland critics. She was awarded the Roger Stevens Playwriting Award which she received at the Kennedy Center in Washington, DC, in 1992. She is a Woodrow Wilson Scholar, a Lila Wallace–*Reader's Digest* Writing Fellow, and has received a Guggenheim Grant, a Rockefeller Grant, three National Endowment for the Arts Grants, a Fulbright to Argentina, an Asian Culture Council Grant to Calcutta, and a U.S. Friendship Commission Grant to Japan. Her plays have been published by Dramatist Play Service, Samuel French, Applause Books, Performing Arts Journal, Theatre Communication Group, Heinemann Books, and Baker's Plays. Her textbook, *Creative Writing,* published by Doubleday and The National Textbook Company is used by students around the world. She has taught at Columbia University for five years. As a Woodrow Wilson Visiting Scholar, she has helped colleges around the United States set up writing programs. She has been an Arts America speaker for the USIS (United States Information Service) in India, Finland, Rumania, Japan, the former Yugoslavia, and Norway. She was recently a Fulbright Fellow to Jordan and also received a National Endowment for the Humanities Grant to do research in Paris during the summer of 1995. She has been a writing fellow at the Edward Albee Foundation, the Djerassi Foundation, Hawthorden Castle, and Funduncio Valperasio in Spain. She has edited three books of monologues for Heinemann: *Baseball Monologues, Elvis Monologues,* and *Monologues From the Road.* Her play *American Dreamers* was selected for the book *Best American Short Plays*, Applause Books, 1995–96. Her play *The Confession of Many Strangers* was produced at The White Barn Theatre and has been published in *Best American Short Plays 1998* as well as Oxford Press. Her play *Carrying the Light* opened in Tokyo on November 15, 2000.

ORIGINAL PRODUCTION

The Only Woman General was first presented at the Women's Project, American Place Theatre in New York City, directed by Bryna Wortman. The cast included:

The Only Woman General . . . . Colleen Dewhurst

All the male characters . . . . John P. Connolly

The play later went on to the Edinburgh Festival where it was "Pick of the Fringe" by the Scottish critics.

CHARACTERS

OLIVE WIGGINS: U.S. Army Officer.

SANDY DAWN: Daughter of Olive Wiggins, in the U.S. Army, age twenty. One actor plays all the male roles.

INTRODUCTORY STATEMENT

Colleen Dewhurst *was* the *Only Woman General.* She was everything I hoped to capture in the play — she was bold yet softly feminine, a beautiful warrior who adjusts to her duties in isolation. But my purpose in the play was to show that no matter how successful women are in the military, they will never rise in rank. Perhaps they can only rise *literally.* Thus I have Olive Wiggins circling the earth as the ultimate supreme high commander. What better way for the U.S. military to deal with a woman general?

THE ONLY WOMAN GENERAL

Set: As the lights go up, Wiggins is in a space capsule seated on a steamer deck chair. A life preserver is on the side of the chair. The life preserver reads: "U.S. Cruise Ship One."

Solid panels of buttons, knobs, and dials are on the walls of the capsule. There is an area around the space capsule for Wiggins' memory scenes.

At Rise: Wiggins is sleeping. After a beat, an alarm rings. Wiggins slowly reaches out to a knob on the wall and turns it off. She yawns, straightens up, and tries to get awake. She lifts up an Army mess kit by a string tied to the chair and puts the kit on her lap. She takes two large capsules from a packet on the wall panel. She drops one capsule in the tin cup and one on the plate. She swirls the cup, stirs with a tin spoon, inhales with a "memory" of coffee, and drinks (spoon still in the side of the cup). Then she stabs the capsule on the plate with her fork (it's a pill of thick paste). She chews the capsule and tries to savor . . . swallows, leans back. She takes a toothpick from her pocket and gingerly picks at her teeth.

VOICE: Cruise Ship 1 . . . Cruise Ship 1 . . . Roger me? *(Pause.)* Do you roger me?

WIGGINS: When am I going home? I miss my daughter.

VOICE: Had breakfast?

(Silent pause as Wiggins glowers.)

VOICE: I don't have to tell you how important a good breakfast is to start off the day.

WIGGINS: Why am I here, Disk 84?

VOICE: Is the deck chair comfortable?

WIGGINS: Like a cowcatcher on a gook train.

VOICE: It was designed by the State Department.

WIGGINS: Why does State have to get involved?

VOICE: When you say "out of the country" . . . they're involved. *(Pause.)* Is your Bible secure?

WIGGINS: I had to remove twenty pages for cigarette papers.

VOICE: Are you taking your blood pressure regularly?

WIGGINS: Every day.

VOICE: And it's normal?

WIGGINS: Normal.

(She puts her legs in the air to do simulated marching.)

WIGGINS: 84 . . . 84 . . . when do I go back!

VOICE: You're *combat,* Wiggins.

WIGGINS: At Fort Bragg Infantry School, we learned that 160 soldiers are in a combat unit.

VOICE: You're combat minus unit.

(A beat as the Voice receives data that Wiggins is simulating marching.)

VOICE: Wiggins!

(Wiggins stops her simulated marching.)

WIGGINS: I've gone over my past . . . trying to find some reason for this duty.

VOICE: Don't look back.

WIGGINS: I have plenty of time to think.

VOICE: It's dangerous. The thousand-yard stare.

WIGGINS: I drift. I can't stop myself.

VOICE: French soldiers got lost in the past. In Indochina. Their memories were their conversation. Walter Reed Hospital calls it La Cafard. The spiritual disease. *(Pause.)* Transmit data, Wiggins!

WIGGINS: *(Reading gauges on her capsule wall:)* Light fraction . . . payload H-T-G . . .

(She pauses, then looks up dreamily and speaks:)

WIGGINS: I began as a warrant officer . . .

VOICE: Cease drifting. You're regular Army.

WIGGINS: R-A all the way! I deserve to know my orders.

VOICE: That's classified.

WIGGINS: I'm a full-bird Colonel. Senior officers know their M-O-S.

VOICE: You must wait for clearance from G-2.

WIGGINS: I wasn't issued a P-39 C-ration can opener. I've been floating through space without a regulation bulletin board. What am I doing here?

VOICE: You're under orders of the United States vis-à-vis the military. Not the military vis-à-vis the United States. *(Pause.)* Continue . . .

(Silence.)

VOICE: Wiggins . . . the "light fraction."

WIGGINS: OK . . . OK . . . light fraction. *(Reading a gauge:)* Payload H-T-G-R. *(A beat.)*

You know, 84, it's weird up here. The stars are reversed. The Big Dipper's inside out.

VOICE: Yes . . . yes . . . I know. And the moon's vertical. *(Pause.)* Continue.

WIGGINS: *(Reading a gauge:)* Seismic signal — balanced deuterium.

(She stops, listens, then leans her head against the side of the capsule.)

WIGGINS: I hear faint little static from earth . . . like a baby crying.

VOICE: This Ancient Mariner Syndrome was common in the Winter War of Finland. And Trieste — during the evacuation when Tito wanted to take over in '53.

WIGGINS: Sometimes I just ache to talk to strangers.

VOICE: Only your daughter has phone clearance. *(A beat.)* The gauges!

(She looks at the gauges, hesitates, fidgets, then picks up her mess kit and rattles the spoon back and forth inside the tin dish like a rioting prisoner.)

VOICE: You ate.

WIGGINS: I'm not asking for a side of beef. Just a couple strips of bacon.

VOICE: We don't want to nitrate ourself, now, do we?

WIGGINS: That's conjecture.

VOICE: Bacon was tested out at Livermore laboratory. By Teller himself.

WIGGINS: I'm talking food, 84, not bombs. *(Pause.)* Ahhh the old days to mix a batch of dough in my shell casing. To broil a steak on the steel plate of my claymore mine. Back home in Paw Paw, Illinois, me and my daughter use to grill outside . . . loins of ocelot . . . red flannel hash. Why my little Sandy Dawn could throw salt in the stew from a yard away.

VOICE: Transmit gauge readings.

WIGGINS: I was only fifteen when I enlisted for Korea . . . lied about my age . . .

VOICE: Wiggins!

WIGGINS: . . . I was stationed in the little town of Yong Dung Po . . . Yong Dung Po . . . I'm drifting, 84 . . . I'm drif . . .ting . . .

(Eight bells are heard.)

VOICE: Eight bells, Wiggins. Stay . . . stay in space . . .

(The lights go down slowly on the space capsule.)

(Wiggins unzips out of her space suit.)

(The light goes up on the memory area. Wiggins goes slowly from her steamer chair and walks to a supply case in the memory area. She stands next to a case which has one shelf of C-rations. Remaining shelves are empty.)

WIGGINS: I was Eighth Army supply corporal in the little town of Yong Dung Po. There wasn't too many supplies in Yong Dungo Po. No people, either. It was me . . . six cans of C-ration ham and lima beans and so top secret that G.E. posted a sign over my hut saying: "Do not try to locate yourself."

(She takes the six cans off the shelf and lines them up single file on the ground in front of her.)

(She stares at the cans, then idly knocks each one over with her foot. Then she stares at her feet.)

WIGGINS: *(Musing to herself.)* What if I make a boot with soles that leave the footprints of Korean peasants instead of U.S. soldiers.

(She takes some yellow chalk from her pocket and draws bare feet on the bottom of her boots.)

(She stands and walks around staring at her feet.)

The army was so grateful for my boot invention that they gave me a field promotion to warrant officer.

(Light up on soldier who watches the footprints only.)

WIGGINS: *(Staring at her feet as she walks.)* These peasant footprints are great. I can walk behind enemy lines any time I want to.

(She continues walking. The soldier now follows the footsteps, looking down at the footprints and never at Wiggins. The soldier now makes a grab for her and they both fall to the ground.)

SOLDIER: I got me a Goonie! I'm rear-echelon, and I got me a Goonie!

WIGGINS: Idiot! I'm Warrant Officer Wiggins.

(They both slowly get up from the ground.)

SOLDIER: Them prints . . . is . . . offa you?

WIGGINS: Grunt, keep yer hair above the collar. It pisses off the Lifers.

SOLDIER: *(Reading from paper:)* Yer Wiggins, Olive? Army, 8th? Officer, Supply? Company, Charlie? Battalion, Ground one? Regiment, 9th? Division, 6th? Corps, 4th? Infantry, 9th? Squadron, weapons? Group, Assault, 3rd? Brigade, 12th? Forces, Special, U.S., 3rd . . .

WIGGINS: Get that saluting hand out of your pocket.

SOLDIER: *(Salutes her.)* You just made Second Lieutenant. I got sent to give you these promotion orders — on quarto sheets.

WIGGINS: *(She takes the promotion orders.)* Move out, Grunt. Double time! Your military life expectancy is 0.8 seconds.

SOLDIER: *(He salutes her and then hurriedly exits, skipping in the Korean peasant prints on the floor. Counting his military life expectancy seconds as he skip-exits in the Korean peasant prints.)*

One . . . two . . . three . . . four . . . *(Lights goes down on soldier.)*

WIGGINS: I'm a Second Looey!

(She stands tall and does a little military foot work to another spot in the memory area.)

WIGGINS: After Supply, I was assigned a project involving the training of dogs in the small town of Cat Tai. But not your ordinary hounds. Combat dogs who got promoted just like any soldier. *(Pause.)* I was outranked by no less than fifteen old, gray, cranky, arthritic mutts. Quartermaster promoted me to field-grade Captain so those mongrels would obey me.

(Sound of barking dogs.)

(Wiggins picks up an army stool and motions it toward the dogs like a lion trainer as she speaks:)

WIGGINS: Get off my shoes . . . go on . . . get off . . .

(She puts the stool down and props one leg on it in an authoritative manner.)

WIGGINS: *(To dogs.)* Ok you curs . . . roll outta them pup tents! I said . . . fall out for reveille! *(A beat.)* You, too, Colonel. *(A beat.)* I wanna see a long line of dog rears. All of you! Wall-u! Wall-u! Ain't no easy walk to the Yalu! *(A copter sound is heard. Wiggins pauses, smiles, then looks up.)*

WIGGINS: *(To Copter:)* You've been flying over me and these curs every day for the last month.

(Lights go up on the pilot on another level of the stage. He waves to Olive. She waves back.)

WIGGINS: *(Looking at plane:)* Welllll . . . well . . . ground level flying. Tilting . . . flicking over those branches of trees. Ahhhhh . . . you're definitely making a pass . . . jazzing your throttles . . . taking a bead on me.

(Pause. To copter, coyly:) Did you happen to drop a little periscope head? And an old fuselage? I'd love to return it . . .

(Wiggins is distracted by a dog and pushes him away.)

WIGGINS: *(To dog.)* Mush! And stay out of the warming tent!

(Wiggins now goes back to looking up at the copter.)

(The pilot waves again to Olive and then he takes out a small mirror and signals a message to her.)

WIGGINS: *(Reading the mirror-signal message.)* "worst coffee . . . here . . . it's made . . . of . . . parched corn . . . from Manchuria."

(Olive shakes her head yes very clearly for him to see.)

WIGGINS: *(Reading his mirror-signal message:)* . . . "once . . . I . . . only ate . . . one grape . . . in five . . . days."

(Olive is impressed.)

WIGGINS: *(Mouthing the words large for the pilot to see:)* Hoooooow brave.

(Wiggins takes a compact from her fatigues using the mirror to signal the pilot as she says aloud the message:)

You know . . . flying over a girl . . . so late . . . at night . . . what will your . . . mother say?

(The pilot signals back as Wiggins reads his message:)

If . . . you're . . . the wrong . . . kind of girl . . . flying over at noon . . . would be . . . just as bad.

(Olive now fluffs out her hair to him and then lies on the ground in a seductive position. The pilot makes some loud copter sounds of appreciation:)

WIGGINS: *(To plane:)* Oh . . . what's the use. It's unrequited love. A tingling flush from a wash of blades. A sensuous low rotor pitch now and then. *(She suddenly becomes hopeful . . . and puts the field phone next to her on the ground so that the pilot can see it.)*

WIGGINS: *(Mouthing large words for the pilot to see:)* Call me!
(She points to the field phone.)
(Lights goes down on the pilot. Noise from the copter slowly dies.)
(Olive stares at the field phone for a few seconds hopefully. Then she thinks she hears something and eagerly picks up the field phone.)

WIGGINS: Hello . . . hello . . .
(Silence. She sadly puts down the field phone. She shakes the silent field phone and listens. Nothing.)
(Wiggins now begins to do some marching drills, all the time keeping an eye on the field phone.)

WIGGINS: By the left flank . . . march. By the right flank . . . march. Detail halt. Pre — sent, arms! Eyes left, eyes right.
(She stops abruptly and rushes to the field phone.)

WIGGINS: *(Into phone:)* Hello . . . hello . . .
(She puts down the silent field phone.)

WIGGINS: *(Out to audience:)* After six months of nothing but dogs, a senator in New York got wind of the risks involved and put through a bill that made it illegal to use helpless animals in the Killing Zone.
(Ship bells are heard. The space capsule lights up beckoning Olive to return. Olive looks at the capsule. The phone rings.)

WIGGINS: *(Looking at the capsule and then at the phone:)* Did it get back to the Pentagon that I was fooling around with some pilot on dog duty?
(Phone rings.)

WIGGINS: *(Looking at capsule.)* Couldn't be . . . they promoted me to Major.
(Phone rings.)

WIGGINS: *(Covers up her ears.)* Oh, no.
(Phone rings.)

WIGGINS: Not phone duty. That's one memory I can do without.
(Phone rings.)

WIGGINS: *(To phone:)* OK. OK. *(A beat.)* I was sent to a special school in Anchorage to train in snowshoes and dynamite. I learned how to assemble a collapsed kayak in five minutes, then was cleared to head up a rumor hotline in Washington.
(She walks to another memory area which has a phone and an army cot.)

WIGGINS: I was stationed inside a room in the windowless maze of the

Pentagon. I worked one phone — day and night and slept on a holding cot with rope-mesh springs and buffered by sandbags.

(She starts to lie down. Just as her head hits the cot, the phone rings. She looks at her watch.)

WIGGINS: 3 AM!

WIGGINS: *(Answering phone:)* Rumor.

VOICE OVER PHONE: I hear there's a government overthrow in Zimbabwe.

WIGGINS: The President's motorcycle escorts deserted to the guerrillas.

(Wiggins hangs up and lies down.)

WIGGINS: What am I? Some obstetrician getting up at three in the morning every time a new government's born?

(She settles in her cot and tries to sleep.)

(Phone rings.)

WIGGINS: *(Answering phone:)* Rumor.

VOICE OVER PHONE: How many hordes in a Chinese platoon?

WIGGINS: That's not a rumor. *(She hangs up curtly.)*

(Phone rings.)

WIGGINS: Rumor.

VOICE OVER PHONE: I hear it costs a Commie 27 cents to kill an American.

WIGGINS: Correct.

VOICE OVER PHONE: It costs us $10,000 to kill a Commie?

WIGGINS: We're proud of our superior arsenal.

(Wiggins hangs up.)

(Phone rings.)

WIGGINS: *(Answering:)* Rumor.

VOICE OVER PHONE: I hear a yellow baby was born talking. In Saigon.

WIGGINS: I got stenographic denial notes from Walter Reed Hospital. Right here in front of me.

(Wiggins hangs up.)

(Lights goes up on an army officer.)

OFFICER: Wiggins . . . a-ten-shut!

(Wiggins stands at attention.)

OFFICER: For dismantling the Baby Rumor . . . and diverting a serious international crisis, Headquarters Eighth Army bestows on you . . . The Medal of Solitary Valor . . . said medal to be hereafter known as the Wiggins Cross, factotum.

(The officer pins a minute cross on Wiggins' uniform.)

(The officer salutes Wiggins. She returns his salute. The officer exits.)

(A beat as Wiggins is seen proudly shining her miniature cross.)

(Antiwar chants are heard coming over the speaker.)

WIGGINS: *(Hunkering down and keeping a hand on her Wiggins cross:)* I feel bad about the Vietnam War. It never had the military sex appeal like a lot of others. *(Pause.)* But it was good for my career to get shipped there . . . I crossed the international date line, lost a day, got 24 hours younger. *(A beat.)*

WIGGINS: *(Standing.)* I was assigned a Medical Detachment in double-canopy jungle in Viet Nam. I worked as a Public Relation attaché in a Quonset full of ailing Vietnamese . . . women, children . . . and men. All in black pajamas. *(Pause.)* Being official hostess in that medical Quonset, well, I saw a hell of a lot of pajamas.

(Light goes up on an oriental male wearing a black pajama top and a papasan hat on his hand. He stands with his back to the audience — facing Olive. He is holding flowers.)

WIGGINS: *(Staring at the oriental male:)* It's hard to tell what a body looks like under black pajamas. When they took off their tops so I could inspect them

(Oriental male takes the top off.) . . . well . . . some of those dink men were pretty decent-looking.

(A beat as she stares at the oriental male admiringly.)

WIGGINS: *(To oriental male:)* What pectoral muscles!

(The oriental male shoves some flowers at her.)

WIGGINS: *(She touches the flowers.)* Jungle orchids! *(Pause.)* I can give you a New York quotation on those . . . I'd say . . . 'bout $38 bucks for the lot.

(The oriental male continues to shove the flowers at her forcefully.)

WIGGINS: Ahhhh . . . they're for me. *(Pause.)* You dance? *(She shuffles her feet to explain.)*

(He shuffles his feet to answer yes.)

WIGGINS: Sidle up to me, handsome. Float on my Saigon waterfront. Dance in my fan-tan saloon . . . yer hot ricey breath on my cheek . . .

(Cruise ship lights up.)

CAPSULE VOICE: Cruise Ship 1 calling . . .

(Wiggins looks at the capsule for a fleeting second, then she takes the oriental male's hand and urges him to follow her in a dance. They do an awkward dance as she speaks the following:)

WIGGINS: One . . . two, one . . . two . . . a nice pincer movement in the direction of those swab sticks. Sway by the gauze. Dip here by the jar of gun mounts and parallel assault line . . . and deploy to the left, deploy to the right, . . . a little strafing together and ground zero . . .

(The oriental male slowly backs up to exit.)

CAPSULE VOICE: Olive Wiggins . . . Olive Wiggins . . .

WIGGINS: *(To oriental male:)* Are you gonna drop me — just like that! I cleared up your jungle rot.

(She stares after him.)

(Lights goes down on oriental male.)

(Capsule buzzes.)

WIGGINS: *(To capsule:)* I didn't take any liberties with the "pretty Chink Chest" if that's what you think.

(Pause.) I did the job! *(Pause.)* A tough job, too.

(Capsule buzzes.)

WIGGINS: *(To capsule:)* I helped the natives understand instructions on boxes and jars of medication.

(A beat.)

Anyway, there was me and hundreds of sick natives of the Chung Government. I put my hand on top of a kid because she was bawling. To comfort her. Now, if you go to Nam, you don't ever want to pat anybody on the head. The Vietnamese consider the head sacred — for God only. That's how I lost the tip of my index finger. A yellow kid bites like a parrot. But I made Lieutenant Colonel because of it.

(A beat as Wiggins looks carefully at the audience.)

WIGGINS: Say what you want about the Medical Corps . . . and I'm not knocking Medics . . . but every Career Infantry Officer like myself knows . . . artillery is the final epidemic.

(A beat.)

Around this time, I was assigned Commander of a POW Camp of captured Viet Cong. I can't say taking care of the enemy is my idea of a great military experience, but I had to follow orders. 500 VC . . . feeding them . . . keeping them clean. We captured these VC's after the Tet Offensive and stuck them in a huge wire cage five blocks long. I did roll call every morning . . . yelling to get them pigeons to fall in for a decent formation. Yah, pigeons! Charlie used mangy birds as couriers. Some sergeant caught 500 pigeons with VC maps strapped to their scrawny legs. Messenger pigeons have always been deployed in battle . . . starting with the siege of Mutina in 43 BC.

(Wiggins stands in front of the POW bird cage rattling a stick between the bars.)

Look, I know all about you guys. I did plenty of pigeon racing. Back home in Paw Paw, Illinois. Some of you will try to dive at me. Others are gonna turn vertical and butterfly down with a personal load of manure. Don't. Just coo out your name . . . . rank . . . serial number.

(To audience:) Looking at them birds all day, I got this idea of crossing a parrot with a pigeon. My new *pidg-ot* would be able to speak its message and save on paper. Just as I was ready to unleash 500 sexy lady parrots into the POW cage, the Geneva Convention came down on me . . . stating that pigeon POWs have to be billeted in enemy terrain similar to their natural habitat, i.e., cathedral roofs, treasury building eaves, or fire escapes. The Nam jungle didn't have too much of that, so I had to repatriate the little creeps.

(She takes out a cigar, lights it, takes a deep smoke.)

WIGGINS: A good Guatemalan Cheroot. Like Bradley and Ike smoked.

(Light up on General Stack.)

GENERAL STACK: Got some palm wine I can sign for, Wiggins?

(Pause as Olive takes a long smoke.)

WIGGINS: General Henry Stack . . . known as Dollar Sign . . . came in-country to brief us. The General always carried a green army sock full of grenades that he called wee-pons. A corporal stood behind him with a fly switch.

GENERAL STACK: Got a little de-facto bordertown I can sign for, Wiggins?

WIGGINS: The corporal could turn that fly switch every way possible, twirling it like a majorette. *(A beat.)* That corporal also had the habit of calling out "enemy killed" when the General lobbed a grenade . . . even when the General didn't lob one. *(A beat.)* Sir. Why not go all out and carpet-bomb this area. *(To the audience:)* With General Stack, it was always better to be 100 percent more hawkish than he was.

GENERAL STACK: Remember your Sun Tzu. Overpower the enemy's spirit. Right now I'm composing propaganda pamphlets that will blast away every sneaky slant brain they drop on. *(A beat.)* Got those pipe threaders I can sign for, Wiggins?

WIGGINS: I called General Henry Stack "Dollar Sign" because his initials on a piece of paper looked like a dollar sign. *(A beat.)* Sir. The Senate voted down any additional Army pipe threaders.

GENERAL STACK: Wiggins, politician should stay the hell out of our business. Lincoln was right when he insisted Washington DC be protected. He was wrong when he told McClellan how to do it. *(A beat.)* Got them white neck scarves I can sign for?

WIGGINS: General Stack ordered officers to wear white silk scarves as part of our uniform. Because of the dust and dirt, the men took to having their scarves washed twice a day. *(A beat.)* Sir. Master Sergeant Thundermeyer is complaining about the laundry overload.

GENERAL STACK: Wiggins, stay away from two kinds of people . . . master sergeants and chaplains. Master sergeant is gonna short-sheet ya . . . chaplain is gonna bury you. *(He laughs loudly.)* Got a dink deck of cards I can sign for?

WIGGINS: *(To audience:)* Dollar Sign lost a lot of money playing oriental poker with cards that had pictures of different flowers on them instead of numbers. He always had trouble distinguishing between soapweed and flathead peonies.

(A whine of mortars.)

WIGGINS: Sir . . . the men and I . . . we thought you oughta know that those are mortars coming at our tent right now . . . mortars with base plates the size of tanks.

GENERAL STACK: Wee . . . pons! Incoming!

(Wiggins and Stack hit the ground. The stage goes dim.)

WIGGINS: Luckily, the mortar dudded. But in all the confusion, our only candle went out. *(Beat.)* So . . . there we were . . . Stack, me, three guys . . . all crowded together in this dark tent. *(Beat.)* Then . . . the men started pulling out promotion papers on themselves and shoving them in front of Dollar Sign. I figured . . . what the hell, I might as well do it, too. *(Takes a paper from her pocket and slips it under Stack's hand.)* Drop your initials on this, sir. *(Stack signs.)*

(The light goes up on the stage.)

GENERAL STACK: *(Shakes the promotion paper in his hand that Wiggins gave him.)* What's this! Your bullhide sandals I signed for?

WIGGINS: My promotion papers, Sir. I'm a full-bird Colonel now.

GENERAL STACK: Wiggins, don't ever punish senior staff for their failures. It stops creative movement. It encourages safety. The crucifixion of defeated generals by the Carthaginians lost them the Punic Wars.

(Light out on General Stack.)

WIGGINS: I went back home to Paw Paw, Illinois, on extended leave. Met a cute second Looey . . . Earl . . . got married . . . had a baby — my precious Sandy Dawn. I kept my professional name . . . Wiggins . . . that was a daring thing for women to do in those days. *(A beat.)* When he was off duty, Earl took to wearing a T-shirt like Reagan wore on TV — the one saying "I'm a Contra, too" . . . and one day Earl got shot by a distant cousin of Castro living in Joliet.

VOICE OVER A BULLHORN: This is the U.S. Army. *(Pause.)* Peace Corps members. Women, too. Leave El Salvador . . . quietly. Revolution cannot be solved by pottery. You are aiding Castro with terra-cotta jugs.

WIGGINS: I had to take little Sandy Dawn outta school in Paw Paw and leave her with my mother who lived quite a few klicks away in Nevada. The Army parachuted me into the mountains of El Salvador with a briefcase handcuffed to my wrist. *(Pause.)* I never found out what was in the brief-case . . . maybe a "white paper" from State. If State used less paper and more arsenal . . . I won't get into State here. Anyway . . . the very instant I landed in El Salvador . . .

(She turns her back and holds her hand out to the side.)

WIGGINS: . . . at that very instant I touched down . . . General Romero was overthrown and some provisional Secretary from the Casa Presidencial shot the briefcase off my wrist.

(Gunshot is heard.)

(Wiggins slowly turns to face the audience, still hunched over.)

WIGGINS: The Provisional Secretary flew the briefcase out of Ilopango Air Base before I knew what hit me. That plane zipped over me so low I cold see the rivets on the cowling.

(Pause. She stands straight.)

WIGGINS: It was raining on my first day in El Salvador. Why does it always rain in a revolution? My hair frizzed up like fur on an old field blanket.

(Lights go up on Commandante. He carries a stack of official papers.)

COMMANDANTE: Buenos dias, Amigo.

WIGGINS: *(Taking a long look at the Commandante and tries to smooth back her frizzed hair.)* My . . . my . . . I just can't resist a man wearing spurs . . . especially when he's barefooted. *(Pause.)* What's your name, Commandante? *(Pause.)* You know . . . nameo? Naaaaame. *(She beats her chest.)*

COMMANDANTE: Ahhhh. Nombre.

(A beat.)

Captain Don Luis Abelardo Juan Escobar Hernandez Rafael Manuel Lopez Oswaldo Inocente Maximo, Jesus.

WIGGINS: Jesus?

COMMANDANTE: Si!

WIGGINS: Jesus, can I give you a lift in my jeep?

COMMANDANTE: Si.

WIGGINS: *(Watching the Commandante sit:)* Ahhhhhh, you sit a jeep with a hard gait. *(She smiles.)* That's a very nice ricochet bruise on your cheek. *(Pointing to his hands.)* Are those Abercombie and Fitch shooting mittens? *(He smiles a yes. She looks around.)* It's kinda difficult, Jesus, to find my way around. I mean . . . the mountains here don't have names . . . nombres.

COMMANDANTE: *(He smiles at her.)*

WIGGINS: I guess that would be like "nombring" every grain of sand on a beach.

COMMANDANTE: *(He smiles at her happily.)*

WIGGINS: Do you have a situation map? *(Pause.)* Map . . . Maaaaap . . . Map-o . . . *(Finally, she gestures widely around her to the mountains.)* Muchas tortillas.

COMMANDANTE: Ahhhhhh.

(He wads up a piece of paper that represents a map of El Salvador. He hands the wadded paper to her.)

WIGGINS: *(She looks at the wadded paper and smiles pointing:)* Here we are. *(A beat.)* More mountains, Jesus.

(He happily wads up more paper. They smile. He tosses her wadded paper mountains and she tosses them back.)

WIGGINS: Now . . . you hold the maps while I drive.

(The Commandante picks up an armful of wadded papers and holds them as Wiggins drives. The Commandante sits as a passenger.)

WIGGINS: *(As she is driving:)* It's so romantic here . . . the barking of apes . . . the scream of pumas . . . the ghosts of conquistadores . . . oh, look, cute little vampire bats — the size of sparrows. Some day, when the revolution's over, we'll eat our lunch on the grass and throw them little papaya crumbs.

(A beat as Wiggins drives.)

WIGGINS: Now . . . where are we?

COMMANDANTE: *(He holds up one wadded piece of paper, smiling.)*

WIGGINS: *(Looking at wad of paper.)* We passed it.

COMMANDANTE: Si.

(He tosses it out and holds up another wadded piece of paper.)

WIGGINS: *(Looking at wad of paper:)* We're coming to it.

COMMANDANTE: Si.

WIGGINS: I really like . . . being in a jeep with you, Jesus.

COMMANDANTE: *(He smiles at her making a guttural sound.)*

WIGGINS: You're the first real "puppet commandante" I've ever met.

COMMANDANTE: Gringa . . . mio gringa . . .

WIGGINS: These mountains are sooooo steep . . .

(Crash sound. Lights dim. Papers fly in the air from the Commandante. Light goes down on Commandante.)

WIGGINS: *(Turns to face the audience:)* I came to this pass in the road . . . a

Virgin Mary was on one side and a U.S. major on the other. I took my left hand from the wheel to cross myself . . . at the same time took my right hand from the wheel to return a salute . . . the jeep swerved . . . and the Commandante went flying out and over the precipice. Spurs and all. *(Pause.)* I could of got slapped with a Human-Rights Violation . . . with State and a lot of phony liberals on my back. Except I found out that Jesus was the very one who shot the briefcase off my wrist.

(Light up on the newspaper man.)

NEWSPAPER MAN: *(He takes a flash picture of Wiggins. Then he types. He speaks as he types:)* Stars and Stripes Army News. March, 1984. For the vehicular assassination of Jesus, the U.S. Pentagon and the Directorio Commisionado Guardias has awarded Colonel Olive Wiggins a second clasp on the Wiggins Cross.

WIGGINS: *(Looking at reporter:)* So . . . that proves the Pentagon didn't find out I was duped by another pretty chest.

NEWSPAPERMAN: *(Typing and reading:)* Wiggins, a war widow from Paw Paw, Illinois, has a daughter and is currently serving a tour of duty in the border village of El Poy, El Salvador — a little town off the map between a volcano and the Flora Blanca Stadium where Cortez landed. Wiggins . . . whose father served in World War II . . .

(The light goes down on the newspaperman.)

WIGGINS: I wanted to be a soldier since I was seven. I grew up with the creak of web gear, spit of burp guns, the even roll of machine guns, whirr whirr of motor shells. Daddy used to tie a thick wool scarf around my head so his army helmet would fit on me. I'd do reconnoitering in our backyard keeping wild pigs and cassowary birds off the beans. I'd even wear that helmet to the Paw Paw post office where Abe Lincoln once sent a letter to his mother and where the envelope's displayed with Abe's tongue-print on the flap.

(A beat.)

For all my birthday parties, daddy put his cigar on little paper wheels for a cannon centerpiece.

(A beat.)

In Paw Paw, we had missionaries with Zen statues in their yard right alongside toadfax and skunk cabbage. Them missionaries claimed a big portion of the interior of Paw Paw for karma. They converted our town's dirt-poor Baptists with a lot of chanting and dishes of salmon with the tail in its mouth. One missionary wife was a doctor and for those too poor to go to the Paw Paw clinic, she treated people in her white pith helmet for ailments from stone bruises to madness with ribbon worms, scarab beetles, eight-eye potatoes, and movement of the stars. For free. Daddy took me once to one of their pagoda meetings cause he said we could learn to get a good bead on a foreigner that way. One time those missionaries cooked a whole chicken in a pot, the bird's head hanging over to the side. It was like spin the bottle. They twirled it all around and wherever the head pointed, that's who had to eat it all up. Daddy ate everything but the eyes.

(A beat.)

People in Paw Paw still talk about how when World War II started, daddy swam out on Lake Michigan trying to sink what looked like an enemy warship with his bayonet.

(Musing over hearing her father's name.)

Daddy. *(Pause.)* Oh, daddy, it gets so lonesome over here.

(Light up on Old Dad Wiggins.)

(Memory within a memory.)

WIGGINS: *(Squinting. Not yet in the memory within a memory.)* Is that you . . . daddy?

DAD WIGGINS: I don't much like to fish in this here river. Too many corpses is caught in the weirs.

WIGGINS: *(Now age seven. She hunches down.)* Grand-daddy Wiggins always fished here.

DAD WIGGINS: Grand-daddy Wiggins got hisself blowed up in World War I. They carried him off screamin' French. He weren't never in no France. His blood poured out so quick it didn't even run — just sorta formed a big jelly.

WIGGINS: *(Age seven.)* Why, daddy?

DAD WIGGINS: 'Cause a person don't sneeze once for a lifetime. Or eat one loaf of bread big 'nough for a lifetime. And I don't get me a kill to make me never want to kill again. *(Pause.)* Git that hair outa yer eyes.

WIGGINS: *(Age seven.)* Am I . . . pretty, Daddy?

DAD WIGGINS: Ask a toad that . . . and he's gonna tell you how nice goggle-eyes is. *(Pause.)* Now warsh yer face.

WIGGINS: *(Age seven.)* Look . . . you can see the sky in the water. *(Pause.)* Can I throw a stone in, Daddy?

DAD WIGGINS: Give me that, daughter. *(Pause.)* See this here stone? It's a bullet taking a nap. *(Pause.)* Put it down . . . and don't take it up again till you can use it right. *(Pause.)* Now . . . let's bend down here . . . that's it . . . we'll cup our hands in the water . . . and drink the stars together.

(End of memory within a memory.)
(A short blast of faint machine gun fire is heard.)
(Wiggins slowly stands. She looks in the direction where the gunfire came from. Then she stoops, picks up the stone and throws it in the direction of gunfire. After a beat.)

WIGGINS: You can get lonely in these communist-backed mountains. Especially since all the El Salvador soldiers are in the United States being trained at Fort Bragg. *(She takes out a picture from her pocket.)* I think about Sandy Dawn all the time. She's growing so fast. So sweet in her little wrestling shorts. *(Puts picture away. Silent beat as she looks around at all the mountains.)* If you think about it, a mountain is no big deal. No different from . . . well, any flat ground. Except, instead of being soil "across" . . . it's soil "up." Thinking vertically like that got me to write music.

RADIO ANNOUNCER: And now . . . somewhere behind guerrilla lines . . . U.S. Eighth Army Special Services and the Excuela Militar . . . .bring you . . . The Singing Colonel. Colonel Olive . . . Olive for Peace, Wiggins.
(The announcer hands Wiggins a guitar.)
(A spot goes on Wiggins. She sings a combination blues and rock.)
(Wiggins picks at the guitar. We hear additional instruments accompanying her in the background.)

WIGGINS: *(Singing:)*
When the pacifists make love
the room's gotta be safer
than a trench
and dumb as ammunition rust . . . ah . . . ah. . . ah . . .
inside a rosebush
not ambush
When the pacifists make love
their bones are yellow
not khaki
they hit . . . hit on each other
under quilts of chicken feathers,
chicken feathers . . . ah . . . ah . . . oh, av . . . ove . . .
canary love . . . canary love . . .
SO
give me
give me
give me
hard hard berms

silk sorties are divine,

put a Berretta in my hair

be mine

be mine,

trenches

berms

sorties

put a Berretta in my hair

be mine,

be mine.

WIGGINS: That original song got me a third clasp on my Wiggins Cross and thousands of letters and dollars for the Pentagon.

(A beat.)

I was the Army's Super Star.

(Light up on training film director.)

TRAINING FILM DIRECTOR: *(Using a clapper.)* Training Film 648. Mountain Sniping, Colonel O. Wiggins . . .

WIGGINS: *(Moves into a movie-frame position.)* Those of you watching this training film . . . whoever you are . . . wherever you are . . . lissen up.

(A beat.)

War is like love. That's the hardest thing for you grunts to learn. War is explained like romance. When a civilian talks to me about theory, he don't understand nothing about war because war is not theory. Even if he's gonna say that war is science, still you gotta describe it from the standpoint of imagination, fantasy, from things that we can only learn little by little. There's a kinda infinity to love . . . a girth . . . a terror. Like guy pandas and their unsuccessful mating habits when they can't tell where to put their dingus. Like moving into battle positions when the dead aren't cleared away and spending the night among hundreds of corpses — some ours, some theirs — sleeping with all them wounds, joys, hopes, desires, one after the other stiffening before your eyes. Martial rapture is more useful to a country than its high schools or Kmarts. A thousand years ago, China felt war was savage — their mandarins didn't let their elite join the military. They felt any old limp dick was good enough for their army. And look where it got them? Peace is selfishness. Battle is pure — the bark without the dog — plumes — thighs of forked lightning. So just remember, you grunts come in here virgins. Military passion takes years of practice. You're virgins studying whores.

(Lights up on Chaplain.)

CHAPLAIN: *(Chants.) Kyrie eleison.*

WIGGINS: *Kyrie eleison.*

CHAPLAIN: *Christe eleison.*

(Wiggins steps out of the movie-frame position.)

WIGGINS: *Christe Eleison.*

CHAPLAIN: *Oremus.*

WIGGINS: Morning, Father.

CHAPLAIN: Confession, Wiggins, in the prone position.

(They fall on their stomachs in prone position. The Chaplain puts a small sliding grille between them on the floor.)

WIGGINS: Father, I see a lot of death. The wounded give the yip of a dying dog. Death is not quiet.

CHAPLAIN: Don't fall unconscious right away if you're shot, Wiggins.

WIGGINS: Father, it's hard to tell the winning from the losing here. Nothing looks so much like defeat as . . . victory.

CHAPLAIN: Keep the enemy from taking the only thing you have left.

WIGGINS: I shoot a lot, Father. But I can't tell if it's good or not. Mud and dirt fly up around the target and before it all settles down so I can see again, I don't know if a rebel's dead or just ducked down.

CHAPLAIN: Stay awake till your last bloody breath. You have the right to say adios to life.

WIGGINS: Father, please pray for my daughter Sandy Dawn . . . she's living with her grandmother in Nevada while I'm over here.

CHAPLAIN: Yes . . . yes . . . now say a good act of contrition. I won't salute, Wiggins. In El Salvador — rank meets by a common genuflect.

VOICE: Come in . . . Cruise Ship 1.

(Wiggins and the Chaplain genuflect. The Chaplain exits, firing.)

VOICE: Wiggins . . . answer . . .

(Wiggins goes to another area of the stage to a hotel phone booth. She talks into the phone:)

WIGGINS: Sandy Dawn? It's mommy. No, I'm not back in Paw Paw. I'm in a phone booth at the Intercontinental Hotel in Managua. Hear the maria-chi music? *(Holds out phone.)* How's grandma? She's got intestinal flukes? Oh, that's nothing, honey . . . What's it like here? Oh, very pretty . . . pepper trees, slit trenches, blue-throated lizards, bomb craters . . . right now, I can see men clearing land mines with machetes and digging cute little post holes for barracks. It's just like our home in Paw Paw, Illinois, except here they have teak hammocks and papayas instead of porch swings

and dandelions . . . I know, honey. I miss you, too. Yah . . . yah . . .
mommy's gotta run now. Now you be good. Love ya.

(Wiggins hangs up.)

WIGGINS: After El Salvador . . . I was put on R & R . . .

VOICE: Make contact. Make contact.

WIGGINS: I guess the Army thought I deserved a rest after a touch of scrub-
typhus and night blindness. I wrote a lot of letters to my Sandy Dawn . . .

VOICE: Acknowledge. Acknowledge.

WIGGINS: On the jungle beach of Santiago de Calvo, I sanded little coffins for
dead soldiers whose legs were blown off.

VOICE: Respond. Respond!

WIGGINS: Little white coffins, white as lava beds.

VOICE: Respond. Respond.

WIGGINS: El Salvador's just the runt of the litter in Central America, if you
think about it.

VOICE: Wiggins, make contact. Make contact.

WIGGINS: McDonald wrappers in Cyrillic script are washed up on the beaches
here every day.

VOICE: Respond. Respond.

WIGGINS: Slugs, eels, frigate birds, water snakes everywhere. Being so close to
all that, the Army put me on half rations.

VOICE: Wiggins . . .

WIGGINS: Little Sandy Dawn is growing so fast.

VOICE: Acknowledge, Wiggins. Acknowledge.

WIGGINS: *(Pause.)* OK, 84, I hear you.

VOICE: This is Disk 85. You talked yourself through Disk 84.

*(Wiggins walks slowly to the space capsule. She zips inside her space suit and
sits in the steamer chair.)*

WIGGINS: Anything new?

VOICE: You're classified, Wiggins.

WIGGINS: I got it?

VOICE: Special rushed clearance.

WIGGINS: When do I go home? I miss Sandy Dawn . . .

VOICE: She's doing fine. Joined the Army, you know.

WIGGINS: It's hard for me to believe my baby's that old already. Time flies up
here.

VOICE: There is no time up here, Wiggins.

WIGGINS: That may well be. But a girl still needs her mother.

VOICE: We're working out the details as best we can.

WIGGINS: What details?

VOICE: To be quite honest with you . . . I can be honest with you, can't I?

WIGGINS: Yes, 85.

VOICE: Other countries throw their Plutonium 239 in the sea. Not us. Not the U-S-of A. We think of the future.

We think of our children — your child — America's finest.

WIGGINS: When am I going home?

VOICE: *(Pause.)* Plutonium 239 needs to be isolated from the environment for more than 250,000 years. Since no container has been invented that can store it that long, we did the only thing possible. We loaded Cruise Ship 1 with plutonium and sent you in orbit.

(A beat.)

WIGGINS: Am I correct in saying . . . my tour of duty is . . . 250,000 years?

VOICE: That's correct.

(A beat.)

WIGGINS: I want a transfer.

VOICE: People on earth feel safe with a woman like you in command of Plutonium.

WIGGINS: I'm top echelon. I can request a transfer.

VOICE: But you've been specially trained — for the outpost. *(Pause.)* Waiting for lost patrols . . . training dogs.

WIGGINS: . . . . rumor control . . . sniping.

VOICE: Solitary valor.

(A beat.)

VOICE: Wiggins . . . reach under Gauge 23. You'll find a small moveable panel.

(She does this.)

VOICE: Have you found the panel?

WIGGINS: Yes,

VOICE: Open it.

(Wiggins opens it and takes out a star.)

WIGGINS: It's . . . it's . . . .

VOICE: A star. *(A pause.)* Congratulations . . . General Wiggins.

WIGGINS: Gen . . . eral?

VOICE: Supreme Commander of Infinity. You don't go higher than that — not in this Army.

WIGGINS: Su . . . preme . . . Com . . . mander.

VOICE: When a military officer accepts a post from the executive branch of the government, the President notifies the Pentagon.

WIGGINS: The President of the United States?

VOICE: Correct. *(Pause.)* The Pentagon then acknowledges said command in full dress parade.

WIGGINS: Full dress parade.

VOICE: Correct.

WIGGINS: They . . . never thought I'd go this far.

VOICE: The *far* war, General Wiggins.

WIGGINS: In . . . finity.

(A beat.)

VOICE: Do you accept command?

WIGGINS: Solitary valor.

VOICE: Correct.

WIGGINS: When would the news be released?

VOICE: Within the hour.

WIGGINS: Earth would know within the hour.

VOICE: Correct.

WIGGINS: I accept.

VOICE: We've beamed one star on your capsule license plate.

WIGGINS: I . . . I've got to call Sandy Dawn.

VOICE: If leaving the capsule for any reason up there, regulations require that you cover said star and only display it when present.

(Light up on Sandy Dawn, age 20, in full battle fatigues with a cell phone in her pocket. We see Sandy Dawn crawling. We hear gunfire. Sandy Dawn exchanges fire. Then her phone rings.)

(Lights out on Olive Wiggins in the capsule.)

SANDY DAWN: *(Takes cell phone out of her pocket and answers:)* Corporal Sandy Dawn Wiggins. *(A beat.)* Mom! I don't have time to talk now. Yah . . . Yah . . . I know I haven't called. I'm in a war, Mom. This is Desert Storm. For godsakes, give me a break. *(A beat.)* You got promoted to what? Well, that's great . . . I guess. You know how I feel about officers. Mom, officers are all dorks. Idiots! . . . Not you. *(A beat.)* Yah . . . yah . . . I don't swim near lava reefs. I don't have time to swim. Sure . . . sure . . . Mom, how can I eat right? It's sheep eyes and date paste . . . I'm all right. Nobody's going to rape me. In this country, women don't dress like men the way I do. *(She fires at the enemy.)* It's okay . . . just a sniper. Hey, I found you a kinda neat recipe, Mom. For Asit pudding. You make it with coarse sugar. They serve it here at the Dasman Palace. I'll warn you it takes a couple of years to make . . . they don't have a Christian preoccupation with time here like we do. Mom . . . I'm busy. I got to work two hours late and I have my body count to catch up on. I took the Fahaheel

Expressway on the way here and I had to keep driving east all the time even when I wanted to go west . . . you gotta face Mecca, even when you're driving. Mom, it's dangerous standing here talking to you like this. An Iraqi could sneak up on me . . . of course I can protect myself. Even before boot camp I sweated it out with ten exercise tapes from Blockbuster Video . . . you're the one who always told me that women are just as good combat soldiers as men . . . yah . . . yah . .. I know you never wanted me to be infantry . . . I've heard all that before, Mom. But it's my life. Didn't I take your last name, not Daddy's? What else do you want? I'm noncom Wiggins and your daughter is never going to be an officer. So face it. I have a right to do what I want to. *(She exchanges fire.)* Mom, fighting with the Kuwait Army isn't weird. Kuwait Arabs are our allies. They're not what you call "pagan cross-dressing savages." They're helping us fight the Iraqi. So in some way you can think of them as a kind of terminal Americans. Mom, we're both fighting the same enemy. Doesn't that mean something to you even though I'm ready to admit I don't like their white carrots or their purple money for one thing. *(A beat.)* A lot of the Arab grunts think I'm a little Arab-ish myself. Cause of my name. Sandy. Dawn. Get it? *(A beat.)* Mom, so what if Arab soldiers got a lot of wives. In the Kingdom, everybody does Mom, calm down.

Will you calm down. When Alice Ann went in the convent last Easter, you thought that was great. What's the difference? Yah . . . yah . . . but there's respect in a harem, too. *(A beat as she throws some grenades.)* Did you know that Arab guys make the coffee? So tell that to all our fancy liberated women slaving away on Mr. Coffee for their bosses in offices that haven't ever seen a fig in their lives. Mom, I'm fine. It's not like all this is entirely foreign to me. After all, I heard one of them Arab calls once from the roof of a Best Western Motel in Kansas City during some kind of multicultural festival . . . I've seen *Lawrence of Arabia* fifteen times . . . There are no kangaroo rats in my bedroll. No, my face doesn't swell up from the gulf heat. Where did you get the idea I'm wearing tacky Kohl eyeliner? Mom, I gotta hang up. It's dangerous here talking on the phone. There's a war going on, you know . . . yes, I do get to rest. Some of us go to this really awesome street near the Kuwait Holiday Inn and it has neon signs in Arabic all over advertising Pepsi and Twinkies and that makes me feel at home even though sometimes I really miss a 7-Eleven so much. Now, I'm perfectly safe. Don't worry. I always cover my arms and I never look in public mirrors in shops and display rooms. I'm gonna hang up now . . . Mom, I told you a hundred times, it's my life. Besides, you got a lot to do yourself up there without interfering in my life. Love you. *(Sandy Dawn hangs up.)*

(Lights out on Sandy Dawn. Lights up on Wiggins in the capsule.)

(Silent beat as Wiggins stares at the phone.)

VOICE: Is your daughter excited about your promotion?

WIGGINS: Oh, yes.

(She puts on her star.)

VOICE: It's been a historic day for you, Cruise Ship 1. Brigadier General . . . giving your daughter the news in Desert Storm.

WIGGINS: I'd . . . stand at Parade Rest . . . if I could stand.

VOICE: As you were, General Wiggins. *(Pause.)* 1800 hours. Sign-off time. Farewell . . . till tomorrow . . . *(Faint.)* Mon General . . . Mon General . . . till tomorrow.

(Lights go down softly on Wiggins, who sits tall in her chair as Supreme Commander of Infinity.)

(Curtain.)

END OF PLAY

Betty's Garage
by Carmen Rivera

To my mother — for her strength and love

BIOGRAPHY

Carmen Rivera holds an MA in Playwriting and Latin American Theatre from New York University. Her play *The Next Stop (La Proxima Parada)* opened at Repertorio Espanol in the spring of 1999 and was also produced by INTAR in 1997. *La Gringa* — in which she has played the title role — has also been in rep at Repertorio Espanol for three years. It is part of the New Voices Series that received an Obie Award in 1996 and was presented at the Brooklyn Academy of Music (BAM) as a part of their Spanish Voices Series. Both plays are currently in rep at Repertorio Espanol. Her play *La Lupe: My Life, My Destiny* was produced in the spring of 2001 at the Puerto Rican Traveling Theatre (PRTT) and *Julia de Burgos: Child of Water* was produced in the spring of 1999 at the PRTT. *To Catch the Lightning* was produced at the PRTT in the spring of 1997 and was nominated for an ACE Award for Best Production. She also received the Legacy Award for Achievement in Playwriting awarded by the PRTT.

Other plays by her are *The Power of Words; Betty's Garage; Plastic Flowers; La Pesadilla (The Nightmare); American; Under the Mango Tree; The Nurse; A State of Bliss;* and *Delia's Race.* Her work has appeared at Latino Experimental Fantastic Theatre (LEFT — Founding Member); SOHO Rep; Ballet Hispanico of New York; The Women's Project; National Public Radio; INTAR; La Mama ETC; The Point; La TEA; Theatre for a New City; The Nuyorican Poet's Café; The Henry Street Settlement; The Julia de Burgos Cafe Teatro; Taller Puertorriqueno in Philadelphia; Aaron Davis Hall; Dixon Place; El Puente; City Lights Youth Theatre/Lower East Side Tenement Museum; Theatre 22; the American Alliance for Theatre and Education Conference; Just Add Water Festival at New York Theatre Workshop and at Theatre Festivals in Moscow and Chile. Carmen is also included in *Women Who Write Plays: Interviews with American Dramatists* published by Smith and Kraus. *Delia's Race* is included in an anthology, *Unveiling AIDS . . . ,* to be released in 2002. Her one-act play *Julia* has toured the New York City Public Schools and is included in *Nuestro New York,* an anthology of Puerto Rican Theatre published by Penguin USA. She is a Teaching Artist with Manhattan Theatre Club, Teachers and Writers; City Lights Youth Theatre, New Professional Theatre Arts Connection and Manhattan Class Company. She also teaches playwriting at the City College Of New York City.

ORIGINAL PRODUCTION

Betty's Garage was first produced by the Latino Experimental Fantastic Theatre (LEFT.) in Spring 1996 at La Mama ETC.

Directed by . . . . .Gloria Zelaya
Betty . . . . .Cecilia Arana
Alma . . . . .Milena Dávila
Sol Ileana Guibert
Milagros (Mickey) . . . . .Nicole Flores
George . . . . .Felix Solis
Crystal/Radio Announcer . . . . .Nicole Flores

Betty's Garage was then produced at the Women's Project in Spring 1998

Directed by . . . . .Gloria Zelaya
Betty . . . . .Cecilia Arana
Alma . . . . .Lourdes Martin
Sol Eva López
Milagros (Mickey.) . . . . .Athena Colón
George . . . . .Louis Moreno
Crystal/Radio Announcer . . . . .Athena Colón

Betty's Garage was then produced by (LEFT) at INTAR in Spring 1999

Directed by . . . . .Gloria Zelaya
Betty . . . . .Cecilia Arana
Alma . . . . .Leslie Jones
Sol Victoria Malvagno
Milagros (Mickey.) . . . . .Athena Colón
George . . . . .Louis Moreno
Crystal/Radio Announcer . . . . .Tina Lee Garces

CHARACTERS

BETTY: A young woman in her thirties.
GEORGE: Her husband.
ALMA: A young woman in her forties.
SOL: A young woman in her forties.
MICKEY: A young girl; twelve years old — Sol's daughter.
CRYSTAL: radio announcer — A ten-year-old girl's voice.

AUTHOR'S NOTE

Several years ago I was sent to a temporary residence, in New York City, to facilitate a conflict resolution workshop through drama. This residence was for women and children and the ethnic background of the clients was primarily African-American and Latino. One day a blond woman and her daughter from Tennessee signed up for the class. I found that quite strange — but stranger things have happened in this world, so I just continued with my workshop. On the bus going home, I met a woman from the facility who confided to me in Spanish that this new woman from Tennessee was fleeing her husband, a sheriff in her town, who was trying to kill her. This woman and her daughter had been on the run for over six months. I couldn't imagine the kind of stress she had been suffering. As I got to know her — I never brought up her "refugee" status — I discovered she possessed incredible strength and was determined to give her daughter a better life. One day she was gone, and I mustered the courage to ask the counselor about her. She reluctantly told me about an "underground railroad" for abused women and her facility was one of the emergency stops. This woman said to me, "You're a writer, write about what's happening to our women." This underground railroad currently extends the continental United States.

I never forgot that experience. Imagine if the abuse against women continues unchecked; imagine a world that has declared martial law against women; imagine a world where being a woman becomes a crime . . . this reality may not be as far away as we think. *Betty's Garage* is a futuristic, surreal story of the women and men who work in the underground railroad and their desire to make the world a safer place for all its people.

BETTY'S GARAGE

Scene: It is midnight. Lights go down on the song "Don't Ever Touch Me Again" by Dionne Farris. The sounds of helicopters flying overhead are heard.

VOICE-OVER: *(A little girl's voice is heard.)* Good morning, everybody — this is Crystal with today's news. Today has been the heaviest day of fighting. The casualty number is up seventy-five percent. Twenty women alone were found dead by the riverbank and emergency rooms at the city hospitals are overflowing with injuries. We have just received word that school has been cancelled to allow the schools to function as temporary shelters. Starting tomorrow the banks will be closed — the post office and all federal offices will also be closed. There is no indication when they will re-open. Please remember that the curfew has been moved up to 4:30 PM — so don't get caught on the street . . . Any sign of a ceasefire has now disappeared. All peace talks have been cancelled . . . That's all the news for today folks — thank you for joining me — have a nice day everybody. *(Lights up. Betty and George enter dressed in mechanic overalls.)*

BETTY: I think this is going to be a good place for us.

GEORGE: It's okay, isn't it?

(George looks around the garage.)

Yeah. It's a little far, but it'll work out. Better than being too close to the police.

BETTY: *(She starts laying out some tools and oily rags.)* You know I'll be all right by myself.

GEORGE: I know but, um . . . I don't mind staying with you, and my brother Ray can get us the car.

BETTY: He's never picked up the car before. Did you explain everything to him?

GEORGE: Of course I did. Don't worry he knows what to do.

BETTY: Okay . . . We need some more tires. I'm sure these can't fit all of the clothes of the refugees.

GEORGE: Didn't you tell them to pack light?

BETTY: Of course I did. That's the first thing I tell them.

GEORGE: I was just asking . . . Did you give them the password?

BETTY: Yes. *(Pause.)* Okay and we just wait for Ray.

GEORGE: Yup . . .

BETTY: Are you sure he knows how to exchange the car and avoid being followed and . . .

GEORGE: Betty!

BETTY: Because you could help him — I don't mind staying by myself — I've been working alone since the beginning of this operation.

GEORGE: I'm not leaving you alone and that's it.

BETTY: Fine.

GEORGE: My brother would never let us down.

BETTY: I know that, George.

(Betty finds a bottle cap in a tire.)

GEORGE: Give me that.

(He grabs it from her.)

BETTY: George, it's just a bottle cap . . .

GEORGE: This is why I'm not leaving you alone. We shouldn't even be here alone ourselves. There should be somebody else with us — someone that will protect us.

BETTY: The more people that know about us the more dangerous it is.

GEORGE: The government has a lot of people working against us — we can't keep doing this alone.

BETTY: We're not alone. I have you.

GEORGE: If I wasn't able to get my brother to help us — then I'd be exchanging the car and you'd be here alone.

BETTY: George, we knew it was going to be dangerous.

GEORGE: What's the point of doing it, if you're going to get killed?

BETTY: I'm not going to let anything happen to us.

GEORGE: You can't control that and you know it — I can't get that image of you burning out of my mind.

BETTY: But I was fine, George.

GEORGE: When Ray called and told me the candy store where you were at was on fire — I didn't know what to do . . .

BETTY: I got out in time.

GEORGE: What if you hadn't?

BETTY: But I did . . .

GEORGE: I'm having all these nightmares of you burning in this room, and I'm trying to reach out to you but I can't — you're all I have — I can't lose you . . . I love you and you and Ray are my only family.

BETTY: George, I'm in the same position when you go out and bring the women to the checkout points. I love you so much, I can't let myself think about what might happen. In my mind I know that that might be the last time that I'll see you . . . but in my heart I pray that you'll come back to me safe and sound.

GEORGE: But it's easier for me to get away, I'm a man — the military doesn't stop the men.

BETTY: So you just want me to stop doing this?

GEORGE: How long do you plan on doing this?

BETTY: For as long as I have to.

GEORGE: Is that going to be two years — ten years — twenty years?

BETTY: For as long as women and children need me.

GEORGE: I feel like we can't begin our life . . .

(George is looking through a toolbox.)

Where's the phone?

BETTY: Here!

(She gives phone to George. He is very agitated but Betty is calm.)

George this is part of our life.

GEORGE: We can't have one the way we're living.

(Pause.)

BETTY: I know . . . but I can't stop doing this. Every night in my dreams, I see my father strangling my mother . . . I'll stop doing this work when the nightmares stop.

(Phone rings.)

BETTY: Hello. No Betty here. Wrong number.

(Betty hangs up. Phone rings again.)

Yeah . . . Ray, what's up? It's Ray. George? Yeah, he's here.

(She gives phone to George.)

GEORGE: What? What's wrong? It wasn't there . . . Are you sure you didn't miss it? . . . Damnit, okay listen, Ray, keep driving — stay on highway 12 and don't stop until I call you. Ray you gotta go — NO don't come back, you're not going to help us — I don't want anybody to know where Betty is. Ray . . . Ray — keep driving . . . keep going until I call you.

(Hangs up phone.)

BETTY: What happened?

GEORGE: Ray goes to exchange the car with the same guy we've been working with for years and he's not there.

(George begins checking his watch obsessively.)

BETTY: Maybe the guy was scared when he didn't see you?

GEORGE: No, I arranged everything.

BETTY: What are we going to do? The refugees are going to be here any minute.

GEORGE: I know.

BETTY: Go get a car!

GEORGE: Um . . . okay . . .

(George is hesitating.)

BETTY: Come on, Hotwire King, get going!!

GEORGE: Um, um, I don't want to leave you alone.

BETTY: George, we've just been through this.

GEORGE: I know . . .

(George doesn't leave.)

BETTY: George, the refugees are going to be here soon.

GEORGE: I know . . .I 'm just . . . um . . .

BETTY: Why are you checking your watch so much?

GEORGE: Just trying to make sure that we don't fall behind schedule.

BETTY: We're already late.

ALMA/VOICE: Black bird singing in the dead of night.

BETTY: Oh God, she's here.

GEORGE: Take these broken wings

ALMA: and learn to fly.

(Alma enters.)

GEORGE: Hi.

ALMA: There's no car outside.

GEORGE: I know I gotta go get one.

ALMA: Why?

GEORGE: Complications . . . I didn't want to leave Betty alone. I was waiting
   for you.

ALMA: I apologize, I'm never late. There's something going on in the city. The
   military trucks are everywhere and they're spot-checking everyone. I was
   spot-checked. I had to drive to another neighborhood to get here.

BETTY: George, who is she?

GEORGE: Alma. Alma, this is Betty. Okay, I gotta get a car.

BETTY: Wait a second, George. Who is she?

GEORGE: She's going to um . . . stay with you.

BETTY: Protect me?!

GEORGE: I gotta go, Betty.

BETTY: George . . .

GEORGE: Protect us . . . I brought her here for us — not just for you.

BETTY: So you get me a bodyguard?

GEORGE: I'm worried okay.

BETTY: We don't need one.

GEORGE: Betty, the situation is getting worse. It's better to be safe.

ALMA: Oh, excuse me, we're falling behind schedule.

GEORGE: Aren't you glad she's here — now that I have to leave you alone?

BETTY: What a popular operation this is — you, me, the bodyguard, the refugees — how do we know that she's not a spy?

GEORGE: I got her through the network.

BETTY: Can we trust her?

GEORGE: I wouldn't have brought her here if I didn't trust her.

ALMA: From what I understand the previous refugees at the candy store were spies.

BETTY: She was a woman who got scared.

ALMA: No she wasn't, she was a spy.

BETTY: Great! I'm just supposed to trust her?

GEORGE: Yes. I trust her with your life.

BETTY: You don't trust me?

GEORGE: It's not an issue of trust.

BETTY: You trust Ray to be alone.

GEORGE: Don't give me that woman lib stuff! I got a woman to protect you.

GEORGE: I thought it was to protect us.

ALMA: I hate to break this up — but we need a car.

GEORGE: Can you just work with her and we can talk about it when I get back . . . Betty . . . please . . .

BETTY: Fine.

ALMA: George — you gotta get the car, we're running late.

GEORGE: I'll see you later.

(Betty and George kiss. George exits. Alma starts to unpack her bag, she takes out a bible. There's a long and uncomfortable pause.)

ALMA: Tires are good — we could put the clothes in them.

BETTY: I know, that's why we have them . . . Listen, I've had this operation running pretty good for some time now — I know what to do —

ALMA: Hey, I'm only here to protect you.

BETTY: So, were you followed?

ALMA: No, I wasn't.

BETTY: Are you sure? Didn't you say you were spot-checked?

ALMA: Look, I've been doing this for a while — they didn't follow me.

BETTY: Have you ever met an abused woman before?

ALMA: I helped my mother escape . . . (Alma unpacks a gun.)

BETTY: What are you doing?

ALMA: Getting ready?

BETTY: I don't work with guns.

ALMA: How do you expect me to protect you?

BETTY: Without the gun.

ALMA: Again, I've been doing this for a while AND . . . Your refugees are late.

BETTY: You said there's a lot of chaos in the city.

ALMA: Yeah. How many are there?

BETTY: Two — a mother and a daughter . . . I should call the drop-off point and let them know we're running behind schedule.

ALMA: You should.

(There's an uncomfortable pause.)

(Crossfade. A young girl, Mickey, enters with her mother, Sol. Sol has sunglasses on and she walks with a cane. They stop in front of a garage. They have three bags with them. Mickey also has a backpack. Sol is dressed very nicely. She has dark glasses on and a scarf on her head.)

SOL: Are you sure this is it?

MICKEY: That's what she said.

SOL: It's so isolated. We've been walking for miles.

(Mickey knocks on the door.)

MICKEY: Blackbird singing in the dead of night . . .

VOICE: — ALMA: Take these broken wings . . .

MICKEY: And learn to fly.

ALMA: Get in. Hurry, we're behind schedule.

(Alma lets them in. Betty is still on the phone.)

BETTY: They're here . . . listen we'll be at the drop-off point as soon as possible as soon as the pickup gets here. You're late.

SOL: I'm sorry I . . .

BETTY: I'm Betty, this is Alma . . .

SOL: Sol, Mickey.

BETTY: We don't have a lot of time.

ALMA: You have too many bags.

SOL: I tried to pack the necessities.

BETTY: Alma I have it. I said one bag apiece. If we're too heavy, we're too slow; if we're too slow we're caught. Then that's it.

MICKEY: Mami, I don't need my artwork.

(She takes off her backpack.)

SOL: Yes, you do. This bag is extra . . . summer clothes. I don't need it.

BETTY: Alma take it. We can give it to someone who needs it. Sometimes people come here without anything on their backs.

SOL: Okay.

ALMA: I'll put this away . . .

(Alma exits with the bag. The phone rings.)

BETTY: Hello. No Betty here. Wrong number.

(The phone rings again.)

George, are you okay? You got a car?! Perfect. Yes I already spoke to the drop-off point and he's waiting for them. Okay, please hurry. What? Oh how long is that going to take . . . are you far away? This isn't good George . . . okay just hurry. And be careful.

(Betty hangs up.)

This is unbelievable!

ALMA: What happened?

BETTY: A bomb scare at the bridge. Traffic isn't allowed to cross.

ALMA: Is he all right?

BETTY: Yeah.

(Alma is constantly watching the door and her watch.)

SOL: We just wait then.

BETTY: Yes.

SOL: Who's George?

BETTY: He's going to pick up and take you to the next connection.

SOL: I need to sit down.

BETTY: Here's a chair.

MICKEY: I'll get it.

(Mickey gets her mother a chair. Sol sits down with difficulty. Mickey takes her mother's hand and holds it. Sol doesn't take off her glasses. Betty checks her watch. She paces, but she is calm.)

SOL: It's okay baby, we're gonna be okay.

MICKEY: I know, Mami.

SOL: I know . . .

BETTY: Is walking a problem for you?

SOL: Not really.

BETTY: Are you sure? Because at the next stop we can get you a wheelchair.

SOL: I'm okay, really.

MICKEY: Mami, tell her about your hip.

SOL: I'm OKAY! I mean it Mickey. Just keep it quiet.

BETTY: Are you in pain?

SOL: A little.

BETTY: I'll call ahead to get a wheelchair.

SOL: I'm not a damn cripple.

ALMA: We have to do this tonight.

BETTY: I know that, Alma!

SOL: I'm sorry we we're late.

BETTY: It doesn't matter does it, now George is late.

MICKEY: Where does he take us?

ALMA: To a connection point.

MICKEY: Where's that?

ALMA: You'll find out.

MICKEY: Is it far?

ALMA: You'll . . .

BETTY: Excuse me, sweetie, you're going to find out very soon. Just be patient.

SOL: Did you go to the bathroom?

MICKEY: Mom.

SOL: Did you?

MICKEY: Yes, three times.

SOL: You should go again.

MICKEY: Mami, I don't have to.

SOL: I think you should.

MICKEY: Mami, come on.

SOL: Mickey, go again!!

MICKEY: Where's the bathroom?

ALMA: In the back, on the right.

MICKEY: Thanks.

> *(Mickey exits exasperated.)*

SOL: I don't want my daughter to hear this.

ALMA: What are you trying to hide from her?

BETTY: Alma . . .

SOL: She's my daughter and . . .

BETTY: There's very little you can hide from children.

SOL: I need to know we're going to be safe. She's all I have and if anything happens . . .

BETTY: You'll be a lot safer than you are now.

SOL: Will he be able to find us?

BETTY: No.

SOL: Are you sure?

BETTY: Nobody has ever found the people we've helped. Unless they wanted to be found.

> *(Mickey re-enters.)*

SOL: Are you okay?

MICKEY: Yes mom, I told you that before. I can't squeeze any more out.

SOL: Don't be disrespectful!

MICKEY: I'm sorry.

> *(The phone rings.)*

BETTY: Hello. No Betty here. Wrong number.

(She hangs up and the phone rings again.)

BETTY: George, are you okay? That's impossible. How could they know? We just got here . . . oh my God are you sure? How do you know they're following you? They WERE following you, but you lost them. Are you sure? . . . Traffic is allowed over the bridge now . . . George, please be careful. Okay. We won't move until we know for sure. Bye.

(Betty hangs up.)

ALMA: Are you sure he lost them?

BETTY: If George said he lost them, he lost them.

SOL: Oh God, who's following him?

BETTY: Nobody.

SOL: I think somebody was following him. My husband joined one of those fringe organizations!

BETTY: Sol, it's okay.

SOL: He's going to find us. They're going to help him find us. I know it.

BETTY: George knows how to handle himself and he would never endanger anybody . . . Don't worry.

SOL: I just want this George to get here!

(Mickey takes out her artwork.)

ALMA: You can't do that now.

(Betty is very annoyed with Alma's cold behavior.)

BETTY: We have to be ready to leave when he comes.

SOL: Mickey, put it away.

MICKEY: Sorry.

BETTY: It's okay, sweetie.

SOL: I can't just sit here and wait like this.

ALMA: We can't move until George gets here.

(Uncomfortable pause.)

MICKEY: Are we going to a nice place?

BETTY: It's safe.

MICKEY: Is it near a park? I love the park.

SOL: Why don't you just tell us where we're going?

BETTY: You will see soon enough.

SOL: You keep saying you'll see, you'll see, well I think we should know now.

ALMA: Betty already told you that you will see when you get there.

BETTY: Alma, please!

SOL: Why won't you answer any of our questions?

BETTY: Sol, when we made the agreement, we asked you not to ask any questions.

SOL: My child's life and my life are at stake here. I think we're entitled to some answers.

ALMA: And you'll get all of your answers when you get to your destination.

BETTY: Alma, enough!

SOL: Just tell me where that is.

BETTY: We don't know.

ALMA: Betty stop . . .

SOL: You don't know?!

BETTY: No.

SOL: There's probably somebody out there looking for us to kill us and you don't know where we're going to be taken. And you're going to save our lives?!

ALMA: Betty, don't answer anything further.

SOL: This isn't protection. We're just sitting ducks here.

BETTY: Alma, I'll deal with this.

ALMA: No, I was sent to do a job, and I'll do it.

BETTY: You do your job, and I'll do mine.

SOL: Somebody's job better be about answering MY questions.

BETTY: There are certain things we can't tell you. And there are certain things we don't even know — it's safer that way.

SOL: What if something happens to us? This is all wrong, this was a mistake . . . I put my daughter and my life in your hands and I don't think you know what you're doing.

ALMA: Listen, we're trying to save your life.

BETTY: Alma, Jesus . . . she's scared, they all get cold feet.

ALMA: Well she better warm up real fast.

SOL: I change my mind.

MICKEY/BETTY: What?!

ALMA: You can't do that!

SOL: Yes I can, let's go Mickey.
(Sol gets up with difficulty.)

MICKEY: Where?

SOL: Home.

MICKEY: No, I'm not going back there again.

SOL: Mickey we have to go home, right now.

MICKEY: I hate it there, please, Mami, don't make me go back.
(Alma blocks the door, hiding a gun behind her back.)

ALMA: I'm sorry, I cannot let you leave.

MICKEY: Mami, please NO! We're already here.

BETTY: Alma this is not necessary.

(Alma continues blocking the door.)

ALMA: They can't leave and that's that.

BETTY: Alma, she's still here.

ALMA: Betty, she has to understand that she can't just cancel the plan because she feels like it.

SOL: And why not?

ALMA: Because you know too much.

SOL: What do I know? NOTHING!

BETTY: Sol, you need to calm down.

SOL: It is too much to ask that you answer one damn question?

ALMA: You know what you need to know.

BETTY: Alma, would you please — let me handle this.

SOL: I need to know that we're going to have a life.

BETTY: You're going to have a much better one.

SOL: I wish I could believe that. At least in my own house I know what kind of life I have. Mickey, let's go.

MICKEY: Do you know what he's gonna do to us when he sees us with these bags?

SOL: Mickey, do you think it's fair that we have to leave instead of him? He should be the one that leaves.

ALMA: Come on they never leave.

SOL: Well, I'm not gonna be driven out of my own house.

ALMA: I'm not leaving the door. You're not leaving here.

BETTY: Alma, come over here. ALMA!

(Alma and Betty go downstage right away from Sol and Mickey. Alma is no longer blocking the door.)

ALMA: Betty, if she leaves, she'll tell people where we are — she could be a spy.

BETTY: She's not leaving.

SOL: Spy . . . look I don't know what the big deal is, we just don't do it, that's all. This guy George, who ever he is, is lost somewhere, so just call him and tell him to forget it. There's nothing lost.

BETTY: Of course there's something lost. First there's your life; then your daughter's. Do you think you're the only one who needs this place? There are other people out there who don't think twice about leaving.

SOL: I thought I wanted to leave BUT . . . I know I can work it out.

MICKEY: You tried before, mami, you try all the time and he never changes.

SOL: I'll try harder this time.

BETTY: Sol you can never make anyone change, only HE can want to change . . . If he sees the bags he'll want to know where you've been.

SOL: I won't tell him anything.

BETTY: What you know about this place is enough to jeopardize the whole operation. And you'll put the other people's lives in danger.

SOL: That's impossible, if everything is a secret and nobody knows where anything is, there's no danger.

BETTY: You know where we are. *(Pause.)* Alma, get away from the door, she's not leaving.

ALMA: Betty, don't trust her.

BETTY: Alma, get away from the door . . . this is what I take care of — so stay out of my way.

(Alma gets away from the door and hides the gun.)

If you go through that door, think about why you wear those glasses and with every step you take think about how you got that cane.

(Pause. Sol hesitates.)

SOL: You don't have to tell me. Mickey, let's go.

MICKEY: I'm not leaving.

SOL: Mickey, I need you.

MICKEY: I'm sick of the crying and the screaming and the blood everywhere.

(Mickey runs upstage — away from the door.)

SOL: You get your bags right now.

MICKEY: No.

SOL: Sweetheart, come on.

MICKEY: Don't call me that! That's what he calls you when he wants to be nice. That's what he calls you after the fights. He called you sweetheart all day today. And you go make him that stupid dinner.

SOL: Mickey don't speak to me like that.

MICKEY: Here, sweetheart, thank you, sweetheart, I made your favorite dinner, sweetheart. You're even wearing that dumb locket he gave you. Mami, he didn't even go see you in the hospital. I wish I could throw up that food you cooked. That's why we were late. *(To Betty.)* Because she made him dinner.

SOL: That's enough, Milagros.

MICKEY: Why can't you tell him that's enough!? I hate looking at you . . . you should see yourself. I don't even know what color your eyes are, they're always bloodshot or black and blue or covered by sunglasses. Why don't you look at yourself in the mirror? Look at yourself in the mirror so you could see what I have to see everyday. Go ahead, look!!

(Sol takes off her glasses slowly; her eye is bruised. She faces the audience downstage center.)

Take the glasses off.

(Sol does so.)

I hate looking at your face!

(Sol breaks down, Betty approaches her.)

BETTY: Do you like what you see?

(Sol shakes her head no.)

Then we wait.

SOL: He never touched her. Never, he's a good father.

BETTY: Don't you think what he's done to you has affected her?

SOL: But he, he needs me.

BETTY: She needs you, you need you.

(Pause.)

GEORGE: *(Offstage.)* Blackbird singing in the dead of night.

ALMA: He's here.

BETTY: *(Very angry — to Alma.)* Alma, I know. Sol, your pick-up is here.

(Mickey approaches her mother.)

MICKEY: I'm not going back.

SOL: I know . . .

(They hug.)

I'm scared.

MICKEY: Me too. But I don't care where we go as long as it's far away from here.

GEORGE: *(Offstage.)* Blackbird singing in the dead of night . . .

ALMA: Betty let's go.

(Betty signals to wait.)

SOL: I love you.

MICKEY: I love you too, Mami.

(George enters.)

GEORGE: Blackbird singing in the dead of night. Am I singing to myself?

ALMA: Talk to Betty — she's doing it her way.

BETTY: Excuse me! They're ready, Sol, Mickey.

SOL: Is he George?

GEORGE: That's me.

(George gets their bags. Mickey keeps her backpack.)

See you later.

(He kisses Betty good-bye.)

BETTY: Bye.

SOL: You're not coming with us?

(To Betty.)

BETTY: No.

(Sol hesitates.)

It's okay. He knows what to do.

SOL: . . . Thank you.

(Sol takes off the locket and gives it to Betty.)

Maybe you could sell this and help somebody with it.

BETTY: Thank you. That would be wonderful, but you could be traced. You keep it and remember where you've been and where you don't want to be. Don't ever look back.

SOL: Thank you.

ALMA: You better go, you're really behind schedule.

MICKEY: Thank you.

BETTY: Call me after the pick-up.

GEORGE: Definitely . . . I'm sorry about Alma and —

BETTY: Don't be . . . I'm going to leave with Alma . . . you need to leave. I'll be expecting you at home.

GEORGE: Blackbirds have flown.

(George, Sol, and Mickey exit.)

ALMA: Close, I didn't think she would leave.

BETTY: Don't you dare ever do that again!

ALMA: I'm doing my job.

BETTY: Don't ever give me attitude in front of the refugees — don't every talk back to me and DON'T ever take out a gun. I can't believe you did that.

ALMA: They didn't see the gun . . .

BETTY: I knew it was there.

ALMA: You should never let anyone change their mind once we begin.

BETTY: I wasn't going to let her change her mind.

ALMA: George sent me here to protect you. I'm sorry you don't like how I do it — but I am good at what I do. We can't take any chances. Especially after what happened at the candy store.

BETTY: If we're going to work together — you can NOT take out a gun ever.

(The phone rings.)

BETTY: Hello. No Betty here. Wrong number.

(Betty hangs up. They wait together. The phone does not ring again.)

ALMA: They found us. Let's go. We have two minutes to evacuate.

(Lights fade.)

VOICE-OVER: *(Radio report.)* Sorry to interrupt our regular programming — this is Crystal with some late-breaking news. There have been a mysterious series of bombings today, two churches, a school, the bridge leading out of town, and a garage on the outskirts of town. Reports are that the government is taking more aggressive steps to crack down on resistance groups who damage any chance for an end to the civil war that has been plaguing families for centuries. Although the resistance groups are growing in numbers, the government remains hopeful that they will be eradicated. This is Crystal — have a good evening. Now back to our regular programming.

(Lights continue to fade as the song "Blackbird Singing in the Dead of Night" by Dionne Farris comes on.)

END OF PLAY

the life before/
reconstruction/
reconstructing whiteness
by Alva Rogers

This play is dedicated to my beloved daughter, India

BIOGRAPHY

Alva Rogers is a 1995 recipient of a Dance Theater Workshop/New York Dance and Performance Bessie Award. A graduate of Brown University (MFA in Creative Writing) and NYU's Tisch School of the Arts (MFA in Musical Theater Writing), her plays, compositions, and installations have been performed in theaters and festivals nationwide including The Public Theater, Spoleto, and Trinity Rep in 1998. She is currently writing a screenplay and her play *the doll plays* is scheduled for production in the 2001–2002 season at the Actor's Express Theater in Atlanta. She is a member of the Women's Project's Playwright's Lab, The Dramatist Guild, and ASCAP.

ORIGINAL PRODUCTION

the life before/reconstruction/reconstructing whiteness was presented as part of Tandem Acts VII: Tales of the Weird & Wondrous, new work from the Playwrights Lab & Directors Forum May 21–22, 2000 at the Women's Project Theater. The production was directed by Julia Whitworth. The cast was as follows:

una . . . . Lizzie Davis
mother . . . . Stacy Robinson
anju kei arita
midwife number one . . . . Gabra Zackman
midwife number two . . . . Elena Welty

CHARACTERS

UNA: A light-brown-skinned African-American woman in her mid to late twenties.

ANJU: Eurasian in her twenties.

MOTHER: A twenty-something African-American/ageless.

MIDWIFE NUMBER ONE: A tall Caucasian woman/authoritarian.

MIDWIFE NUMBER TWO: Also a tall Caucasian woman/a novice.

PRODUCTION NOTES

the life before/reconstruction/reconstructing whiteness can be staged alone or with *belly* and *bellies at rest/ in motion/and other problems of inertia* for an evening of three shorts. In that event, the actress who portrays mary in *belly* should portray midwife two and the actress who portrays the jewish woman in *bellies at rest . . .* should portray midwife one.

The Asian actress who portrays the white woman in *bellies at rest* should portray anju, and the actress who portrays miss cake could portray una's mother.

TIME

The next millennium.

PLACE

A birthing chamber.

INTRODUCTORY STATEMENT

I heard an interview with a white supremacist on my local public radio station, during which he expressed his fear of the diminution of "pure white people" in the United States by the next millennium as well as his desire to prevent that from happening. His reason for the cause was the "proliferation" of people of color resulting from miscegenation. So, I asked myself the following question: what institutional process could be implemented to stop or prevent miscegenation and return the white race to a so-called state of purity. I knew the answer to that question would be the premise for the play that I would write.

A few days later, my toddler asserted that she wanted to dictate a story to me. She told the story in two parts and titled part one *the life* and part two *the life before*. I realized that she had written a poetic and encapsulated telling of the blending of people of color and *those without color* (white people), as well as a glimpse of what the next Reconstruction period in our history could look like. It was as if our subconscious minds had a meeting in the middle of one starry night.

the life

suddenly
the rain begins to appear
and
suddenly
she wipes the rain from her eyes
and the baby
poops
on her face
and she runs and runs to get home
to meet her
father and baby
and everything was died
the house was died
the father was died
the baby was died
everything was died
then she put on the blue umbrella
and the yellow umbrella on top of it
then the princess saves her
and then
blue rain came
to save the red rain
then it rained and rained
and the magical umbrella
and it took everything away
the end

— *india rogers-shepp*
8 february 2000

the life before

water appears
then the raindrops
then the candy
falls
and
drops into her mouth
they all mix into the same color
and then
this is the end
of my life story

— *india rogers-shepp*
8 february 2000

THE LIFE BEFORE/
RECONSTRUCTION/
RECONSTRUCTING WHITENESS

PROLOGUE
In darkness, a woman speaks.

WOMAN/MOTHER: the rain appears
  (The rain is heard.)
  and . . .
  *(Lights up on mother/woman. Her wet face appears like a halo in the
  darkness.)*
  she wipes the rain from her eyes
  and the baby
  eliminates
  on her face
  and
  she runs and runs to get home
  to meet her father and baby
  and
  everything is dead:
  the house is dead
  the father is dead
  the baby is dead
  everything is dead
  then
  eden
  a different kind of eden
  there are no apples and no trees
  ignorance is bliss here
  no sky
  no sea blue-green sea
  no moon or stars to dream upon
  no sun to keep us warm
  according to the book
  once upon a time

there was another eden
a man and a woman lived there
according to the book
it was above ground
it was an above-ground garden
according to the book
(Lights out.)

SCENE ONE

Darkness. A woman screams and tosses and turns in bed.

WOMAN/UNA: no moon or stars to dream upon

no sun to keep us warm

(Lights up separately on midwife number one and midwife number two.)

WOMAN/UNA: no moon or stars to dream upon . . .

(The pregnant woman tosses and turns intermittently and remains in a dream state.)

MIDWIVES: You are in the present.

WOMAN/UNA: . . . no sun . . .

MIDWIFE NUMBER TWO: Tell me about her.

MIDWIFE NUMBER ONE: One Una twenty ninety-nine was the first Una born in the year two thousand ninety-nine . . . Her mother was a disquiet one.

MIDWIFE NUMBER TWO: What happened?

MIDWIFE NUMBER ONE: She was eliminated.

MIDWIFE NUMBER TWO: Does she know?

MIDWIFE NUMBER ONE: No.

MIDWIFE NUMBER TWO: She is so light.

She does not look pure.

MIDWIFE NUMBER ONE: Her parents were born before the time of reconstruction.

WOMAN/UNA: the dreams have returned

i open my eyes to wish them away

but they are ever present . . .

WOMAN/UNA: no moon or stars . . .

MIDWIFE NUMBER TWO: And her's is pure!

MIDWIFE NUMBER ONE: Pure!

WOMAN/UNA: . . . to dream on

no sun to keep me warm . . .

MIDWIFE NUMBER ONE: *(To One Una 2099.)* Your dreams.

UNA: my dreams have returned
I open my eyes to wish them away
but they are ever present
MIDWIFE NUMBER ONE: What inhabits your dreams?
UNA: my mother
MIDWIFE NUMBER ONE: Your mother?
UNA: yes
MIDWIFE NUMBER ONE: Does she speak?
(Lights out.)

SCENE TWO
Una's bed appears in a stream of light. She is asleep. Lights up on mother.
Una opens her eyes.

WOMAN/MOTHER: the book
remember
the book
UNA: the book
i have no access to books.
WOMAN/MOTHER: books hold history
stories of the life before
which is why they are no longer
in this time of reconstruction
where you are
ignorance is bliss there
where you are
UNA: who who are you?
(The woman caresses her face.)
WOMAN/MOTHER: i am your mother
UNA: One Una twenty ninety-nine was raised in the eastern worker camps.
One Una twenty ninety-nine's parents ran away to the west to follow
another path
WOMAN/MOTHER: another path?
UNA: Yes.
WOMAN/MOTHER: is that what they told you?
UNA: Is it true?
WOMAN/MOTHER: yes and no
UNA: If you are my mother, why did you leave me?

WOMAN/MOTHER: when i was a girl
 like you
 the world was different
 and the same
 the purest ones continued to rule the world
 the numbers of the people of color had quadrupled
 since the last millennium
 in that year
 pure rulers
 (those without color
 as they were known then.)
 who ruled the world
 were paying their
 daughters to lie in the birthing bed
 as you lie in yours
 it was their view
 that their race was dying
 as people of all colors brown red yellow
 even those without color
 began loving each other
 marrying each other
 having babies
 and mixing into one color
 and so
 it was decided
 that a division would be made
 all people without color
 would live
 above
 with the sun moon and stars
 and
 all the colored people
 would live
 below
 without sky
 without wind
 no moon or stars to dream upon
 no sun to keep them warm
UNA: Mother, where are you now?

MOTHER: i am in eden
    the above ground eden
    where i have returned
    to my purest state
    of heart spirit and soul
    the book says
    we are all children
    above the clouds
    and i am sad to know
    the tears we shed
    for those we miss below
    fall as raindrops
    that you will never know
UNA: Mother after the division?
MOTHER: the parents of an entire generation
    of children of color
    are eliminated
    therefore
    eliminating all knowledge with them
    of the life before reconstruction
    eliminating
    all knowledge
    of people of all colors brown red yellow
    and those without color
    loving each other
    marrying each other
    having babies
    and mixing into one color
UNA: And Father?
MOTHER: your father
    was eliminated
    after a glorious downpour
UNA: Mother
    (She reaches for her mother.)
MOTHER: name your baby Kiran and you will see me again
UNA: Kiran?
MOTHER: Yes Kiran ray of light
UNA: Mother
    (She reaches for her mother desperately.)

MOTHER: before my elimination
an exterminator said
(Lights up on midwife number two.)
MIDWIFE NUMBER ONE: Elimination is necessary to preserve your race.
To preserve and make
your color and all colors pure again. To —
(Mother interrupts her.)
MOTHER: no
you speak not the truth
you do not want to make
brown, red, yellow pure again
you want to
re-create
rebuild
no
you want to
reconstruct
people
without color
you want to
reconstruct
reconstruct whiteness
(Lights out.)

SCENE THREE
*Darkness. Una tosses and turns, in her birthing bed, screaming and babbling
incoherently.*

UNA: no moon or stars to dream upon
no sun to keep us warm
(Lights up separately on midwife number one and midwife number two.)
UNA: no moon or stars to dream upon
*(The pregnant woman tosses and turns intermittently and remains in a dream
state.)*
MIDWIVES: You are in the present.
WOMAN: no sun
UNA: my dreams have returned
i open my eyes to wish them away
but they are ever present

MIDWIFE NUMBER ONE: Does your mother still, inhabit your dreams?

UNA: my mother.

MIDWIFE NUMBER ONE: Your mother?

MIDWIFE NUMBER TWO: Does she speak?

UNA: *(She screams.)* Mother!

> *(Her water breaks. A glorious rain/downpour is heard. Una begins to yell, as if riding a wave in eighty-second intervals. Lights up on mother. Only Una can hear her. Una screams.)*

MOTHER: the rain appears
she wipes the rain from her eyes
and the baby

UNA: ELIMINATES

> *(Una screams.)*

MOTHER: on her face
and she runs and runs and runs to get home

MIDWIFE NUMBER ONE: Delivery time can be anytime between now and ten hours from now.

UNA: The dreams have returned
i open my eyes to wish them away
> *(She opens her eyes.)*

MIDWIFE NUMBER TWO: *(To midwife number one.)* Time for aggressive dream intervention?

MIDWIFE NUMBER ONE: Yes.

> *(Una screams.)*
> *(Lights out.)*

SCENE FOUR

> *Lights up on midwives number one and two separately and there is an asian woman lying on a birthing bed adjacent to una's. Una is still in labor, but her contractions have lessened.*

MIDWIFE NUMBER ONE: Now that your contractions have receded, we brought you a companion to dispel your loneliness. To keep you from dreaming.

MIDWIFE NUMBER TWO: A companion will eliminate your need to connect with your interior life.

MIDWIFE NUMBER ONE: For in the time of reconstruction, there is no time for remembering. Only time to reconstruct. Your DNA has shown that you are having a pure brown offspring. So, you will be returned to the down below. We will return to you, at the time just before delivery.

(Lights out on the midwives.)

WOMAN/ANJU: *(To Una.)* I am Twelve Anju Twenty One Hundred of the Asian quadrangle from down below.

(Una continues to ride the painful waves of her contractions, and she squeals and screams intermittently.)

UNA: One Una Twenty Ninety-Nine.

ANJU: My baby is pure . . . is yours?

(Una screams.)

UNA: Your parents? Where do they live?

ANJU: Parents?

UNA: Yes.

ANJU: they ran away to the west to follow another path

UNA: Another path?

ANJU: Yes.

But, what about your baby? Is your baby pure?

UNA: Who raised you?

ANJU: Twelve Anju Twenty One Hundred was raised in the southwestern worker camps

UNA: Have you ever felt the sun, seen the moon and stars, felt the wind and rain?

ANJU: I have heard that birthing makes one delirious and incoherent
Don't worry, my friend, it will soon pass.

(A very loud and shrill bell rings.)

ANJU: What is that? I heard that bell twice, in the three weeks that I have been here.

UNA: Never mind that.

ANJU: But is your baby pure?

UNA: Yes.

ANJU: I am so relieved. Then I may see you again, and your child. I like you.

UNA: *(Screams.)* My baby is coming . . .

ANJU: MIDWIVES HELP!

UNA: SSSSSHHHHHHHH!

Don't!

I want to tell you something
before they come.
We may be separated
may not see each other

for a while.
when our mothers
were girls
like us
the world was different
and the same
(Labor pains.)
pure rulers
(those without color
as they were known then.)
paid their daughters to lie in the birthing bed
as you lie in yours
it was known
that their race was dying
(Labor pains.)
our parents
were eliminated
eliminating all knowledge with them
of the life before reconstruction
eliminating
all knowledge when
people of all colors brown red yellow
even those without color
began loving each other
marrying each other
having babies
and mixing into one color

ANJU: I do not know if what you speak is factual.
I think you have baby delirium.
It will soon pass, my friend.
(Una screams the most intense scream. Lights up on midwives number one and two separately.)
UNA: MY BABY! PLEASE!
MIDWIVES: PUSH!
(Una pushes.)
UNA: *(To Anju.)* Name your baby Kiran, and you will see me again.
MIDWIVES: PUSH!
ANJU: What does that mean?
(Una pushes.)
UNA: Ray of light.

MIDWIVES: PUSH!
>	(*Una pushes and screams.*)
>	(*Lights out.*)

SCENE FIVE
>	*The next day Anju holds her baby in her birthing bed. Lights up on midwives number one and number two separately.*

MIDWIFE NUMBER ONE: A pure one?

MIDWIFE NUMBER TWO: Yes, a glorious pure one.
>	(*A very shrill bell rings. Anju covers her infant's ears and screams until the bell stops ringing.*)

ANJU: (*To the midwives.*) What is the meaning of that bell?

MIDWIFE NUMBER TWO: Not to worry about the bells. Yours will live. Your girl is pure.

UNA'S VOICE: Name your child Kiran, ray of light

MIDWIFE NUMBER ONE: Every time the bell rings, it means that an unpure child has been born. Mother and child has been eliminated in the elimination chamber.

ANJU: UNA?
>	(*To the midwives.*) WAS THAT UNA'S BELL?

MIDWIVES: Hers was not pure.

MIDWIFE NUMBER TWO: The father of her offspring was without color.

MIDWIVES: She broke the law.
>	(*Lights out on the midwives.*)

ANJU: (*To her sleeping infant.*) I shall name you

UNA: Kiran . . .

ANJU: (*To her infant.*) Kiran . . .
>	(*She places the sleeping infant in bed next to her, lies down, and closes her eyes. Lights up on Una's mother.*)

MOTHER: the rain appears
>	and
>	(*Una enters, carrying her baby.*)
>	she wipes the rain from her eyes
>	and the baby eliminates
>	on her face
>	and she runs and runs to get home

(Una and her mother embrace and then freeze. Anju sits up and sees Una, but Una does not see her.)

ANJU: *(To Kiran.)* . . . then she put on the blue umbrella.

and the yellow umbrella on top of it
then the princess saves her
and then
blue rain came
to save the red rain
then it rained and rained
and the magical umbrella
took everything away

UNA: water appears

then the raindrops
then the candy falls
and
drops into her mouth
they all mix into the same color
and then
this is the end
of my life story
(Lights out.)

END OF PLAY

Look What You Made Me Do

by Lynda Sturner

CHARACTERS

GRACE: A well-groomed and well-dressed woman. Can be played by a woman in her twenties, thirties, forties, fifties, or sixties. Grace uses a memo machine. It is a small hand-sized machine called a VOICE IT. Grace uses the audience to represent the circle of women at the woman's shelter.

TIME
The present.

PLACE
A woman's shelter.

LOOK WHAT YOU MADE ME DO

Grace, well-groomed and well-dressed, enters and talks to a circle of women. The audience is used as the circle of women.

GRACE: I don't belong here, really. I thought I could just sit in and you know listen. But OK if we all have to take a turn . . . I can do that . . . sure . . . uhm . . . guess you don't usually see people like me in places like this. I'm probably wasting everybody's time. Oh it's wonderful what you do here . . . taking women in . . . hiding them and all . . . terrific service . . . safe and : . . excuse me a minute, please.
(Graces takes out a small memo machine — VOICE IT — and turns it on. It beeps.)
Asparagus, sweet potatoes.
(Grace releases button.)
My shopping list.
(Grace remembers where she is.)
Safe. You're Angela right, and you're Kisha and Robin, no, no Robby. See I remember your names. I heard you speak at the benefit luncheon at the Marriott Hotel last month . . . where Elizabeth Taylor was supposed to moderate but . . . well I forget the reason . . . anyway Rosie filled in . . . She's funny . . . but I mean when you pay two hundred dollars and you're seated at the back of the room behind 1200 women . . . but I didn't come here to complain about that they served fish . . . or that you couldn't even get a second glass of wine . . . not that the first one was that great but you know wine is wine is . . . wine.
(Grace presses memo machine.)
Cauliflower.
(Grace releases button.)
I should go home. I can't stop thinking about your stories. Oh God, I'm doing just what Brian hates. Does this drive you crazy too . . . that I never finish a thought? He says listening to me is like Chinese water torture. But I finish thoughts all the time . . . in my head. I start to say something to him and then I see this trapped look on his face . . . like oh shit it's got an opinion again so I forget what I started to say and talk about vegetables. Vegetables are always safe. I'll say for instance . . . the Supreme Court made a big mistake and I think ahhh . . . are those mushrooms

done the way you like them dear? Not enough garlic oh I'm sorry. But I say lots of interesting things when he's not around. I do. When I'm alone thoughts flow, I'm clear, precise. I talk to this machine. I tell it things. If there's an editorial I disagree with or a conversation I wish I had, I just push the button and off I go and when I listen back, I even like myself sometimes.

(Grace holds up the machine.)

This is my new machine.

(Grace touches the machine lovingly and protectively and switches it on.)

Broccoli, celery, brussels sprouts.

(Releases button.)

I should go.

(Grace caresses the machine.)

Look, it's not as if he beats me. He doesn't do that. Brian's a screamer. Does that count? . . . And he throws things but at the walls not at me. I mean I understand when I've been wrong, like when I forget to fill the car up with gas or don't put rice in the salt shaker and it doesn't pour but sometimes he's angry and I don't know what I've done. Like that night we were having breast of chicken with orange glaze . . . he's muttering under his breath . . . "stupid cow." Excuse me I say and he goes, "chicken again, godamm fucking chicken again!" and throws his plate against the wall. I had made him fruit cup and some of the glass from the salad bowl which he also threw landed in the fruit, then he freaked cause there was no dessert. Look what you made me do, he says. He's broken all of my grandmother's dishes. I can't talk about these things with my friends. I don't know before I was married we always bitched about men but now it's like we've all taken a vow of silence . . . married silence . . . shhhh. But it's not as if he hits me.

(Graces turns on the machine.)

Carrots, peas, artichokes . . . shhhh . . . shhh . . . shhh

(Grace turns off the machine.)

I keep thinking about your story Angela. How it started out as a game with your husband. You were the puppy and he was the master and then he kept . . . wouldn't let you out of the cage and now you're into hiking and for the first time in your life every step you take belongs to you. Every step you take belongs . . . All of your stories . . . when I heard them it was like when I first saw *Rent,* that musical, I wanted to jump on stage and be them. *(Sings La Vie Boheme . . .)*

(Grace turns on the machine.)

I killed Brian with my veggie prep knife this morning. *(Laughs.)*
(Grace turns off machine.)
Just kidding. Oh God that felt good. *(Laughs.)* Can I say it again?
(Grace turns on machine.)
I killed Brian. *(Laughs.)* Brian's dead . . . dead dead dead dead dead dead
dead dead *(Laughs.)*
(Grace replays dead dead dead dead dead dead while she talks.)
He broke my memo machine. All I did was ask him to listen to it. Hear
me talk when I wasn't afraid to finish a sentence. Please I said to Brian,
just listen, but he took it and smashed it into the side of the kitchen
counter.
(Grace holds up the memo machine.)
This is my new one. Bought it today before I came here. My new machine.
(Grace holds the machine to her heart.)
I'm not going home. Cause it wasn't like I'd forgotten to fill the car up
with gas or overcooked the pasta or run out of orange juice . . . he . . .
can I stay here?
(Curtain.)

END OF PLAY

but there are fires
by Caridad Svich

As always, this is for my parents

BIOGRAPHY

Caridad Svich is a playwright-songwriter-translator and editor. Credits include her play *Alchemy of Desire/Dead-Man's Blues* at the Cincinnati Playhouse in the Park (winner of the Rosenthal New Play Prize). Most recently, her play *The Archaeology of Dreams* was workshopped at Portland Stage Company's Little Festival of the Unexpected, *Fugitive Pieces* premiered at Kitchen Dog Theater in Dallas, Texas, and *Iphigenia Crash Land Falls on the Neon Shell That Was Once Her Heart (a rave fable)* was work-shopped by Actors Touring Company/UK at the Euripides' Festival in Monodendri, Greece. Her play *Any Place But Here* will receive its European premiere at Theater Malpertuis in Belgium, and she is developing *The Booth Variations,* a multimedia solo project, with performer Todd Cerveris and director Nick Philippou.

She held an NEA/TCG Residency at the Mark Taper Forum Theatre for two years, and was resident playwright at Intar Theatre in New York for four years. She has been guest artist at the Traverse Theatre in Edinburgh, the Royal Court Theatre, and has taught playwriting at Paines Plough Theatre in London, the Yale School of Drama, Ohio State University, and the US-Cuba Writers' Conference in Havana. She was the Thurber House Playwright-in-Residence for the year 2001. Her work has also been seen at the Women's Project, Cleveland Public Theatre, Repertorio Espanol, the Juilliard School of Drama, Ensemble Studio Theatre, Hackney Empire Studio Theatre/UK, and Northern Light Theatre in Canada.

She is co-editor of *Conducting a Life: Reflections on the Theatre of María Irene Fornés* (Smith and Kraus), and *Out of the Fringe: Contemporary Latina/o Theatre and Performance* (TCG). Her translations of five plays and thirteen poems by Federico Garcia Lorca are published in *Federico Garcia Lorca: Impossible Theater* (Smith and Kraus). Play Publications: *Gleaning/Rebusca in Shattering the Myth* (Arte Publico Press), *Scar* in *Latinas on Stage* (Third Woman Press), *Brazo Gitano* in *Ollantay Theater Journal,* and *Any Place But Here* (TCG's Plays in Process). Her critical writing has appeared in *PAJ, Contemporary Theatre Review, Performance Research,* and *American Theatre.* She is a member of New Dramatists.

PRODUCTION HISTORY

but there are fires was originally developed at the Intar Hispanic Playwrights-in-Residence Laboratory in New York, where it received a reading and a workshop directed by the author. The play received its world premiere at the Women's Project (Julia Miles, Artistic Director), in New York, on March 19, 1991. It was directed by Susana Tubert; the set design was by Mark Fitzgibbons;

the costume design was by Barbara Beccio; the lighting design was by Franklin Meissner, Jr.; the sound design was by Bruce Ellman and the stage manager was Jill Cordle. The cast was as follows:

Jeff Metzner . . . . Cliff Weissman
Gina Metzner . . . . Dorrie Joiner
Todd Neely . . . . Patrick McNellis

Special thanks to Irene Fornés, Julia Miles, and Nancy Rineer

CHARACTERS

JEFF METZNER: An earnest, good-looking young man in his early thirties. Not too bright, but making an effort to comprehend himself and his world.

GINA METZNER: His wife. A sensual young woman in her early thirties. Pragmatic, tough. But has her dreams.

TODD NEELY: His friend. An amoral, fast-talking man in his early to mid-thirties. Genuinely charming, a little lost.

TIME AND PLACE

The present. A small town in western Pennsylvania.

SETTING

The stage is divided into two areas, each as distilled and elemental as a Japanese woodcut. One area represents Jeff and Gina's place: a long, narrow platform that functions as a bed; a square table and two chairs; a rectangular block on which sits a hot plate and a coffee pot; a small window frame suspended in the air. The other area represents a playground/park. Suggested simply.

BUT THERE ARE FIRES

SCENE ONE

Gina is looking out the window. Jeff is reading the newspaper. Todd is seen in a slant of light in the background. Silence. Jeff reaches for his customary cup of coffee, but it's not there.

JEFF: Gina? Gina!

GINA: Yes, I'm here.

JEFF: Where's my coffee? You know I can't read the paper without my coffee.

GINA: In a sec.

JEFF: *(Indicating newspaper.)* You should read this. There's this guy, they arrested some guy . . . He was calling women. Asking them to have . . . you know . . . with total strangers. Unbelievable, huh?

GINA: Yes.

(Light change.)

SCENE TWO

The park. Jeff throws a football to Todd.

JEFF: I can't hide anything from her, and yet she can hide anything from me. Why is that?

TODD: You don't know her as well.

JEFF: Yes, but I've known her a long time. I'm the one who saw her first. You'd think that by now . . .

TODD: Maybe you're slow.

JEFF: I'm beginning to think that. I'm beginning to think I'm not as quick as I used to be. Man, when I was eight I was a squirrel. I could climb up any tree at the sound of a car coming, and now . . . I'm lucky if I can cross the street on time.

TODD: She aged you.

JEFF: I got married and lost my reflexes.

TODD: Everything goes.

JEFF: You're telling me. Who would have thought I'd seek the comfort of boxer shorts late at night? I'm serious. I dream about them. I think "if I had a pair of boxers, I'd be set." You know what I'm saying?

TODD: Those jockeys start to dig into your thigh.

JEFF: Yeah, and you don't want to be thinking 'bout your incoming belly and flab right around the edges . . .

TODD: It's a tough thing.

JEFF: I'm feeling it.

(Pause.)

TODD: You got her a gift yet?

JEFF: No. The day's not until Saturday. I've been thinking about a slip, something along those lines. But then I think, maybe go safe, get flowers or chocolate.

TODD: Take her out.

JEFF: Eat out, you mean? It takes her two hours just to go through a menu. I'd have to preorder or else we'd never get out of there.

TODD: You could try fast food.

JEFF: That's not very romantic, is it?

TODD: Could be a throwback to high school: burger, fries, milkshake . . .

JEFF: High school was no good for both of us. No. Fast food is definitely out. It's too easy. She'd think I wasn't thinking of her or something.

TODD: There's always the movies.

JEFF: Yeah.

TODD: Now, there's a dark spot, huh? Cop a feel, pull down your pants, and no one's the wiser.

JEFF: She'd like that. Of course, the question is, finding the right flick or she'll go bananas. Last time we went I dragged her to see this flick, she spent more time looking at the guy up on the screen than at me.

TODD: That's no good.

JEFF: What are you supposed to do after the movies? Talk about how high the guy's cheekbones were?

TODD: . . . Martin Sheen.

JEFF: What?

TODD: Go see something with Martin Sheen. A nonthreatening type, you know. A little action, some politics . . . nothing you'd fall asleep on. And believe me, she ain't going to look at him. Or better yet, Steve McQueen. Now, there's a guy, huh?

JEFF: He's dead.

TODD: He was something.

JEFF: He was good.

TODD: What's that one about poker . . . ?

JEFF: *The Cincinnati Kid.*

TODD: Yeah. Never saw that.

JEFF: It's good.

TODD: That's what I hear. Dead, though. Real shame, cause he was a guy. He was a real guy.

JEFF: Did his own stunts.

TODD: I believe it. I believe it. But Martin Sheen ain't bad. You can take her to one of his.

JEFF: I'll see what's playing.

TODD: That's the spirit, that's the spirit. Now, how 'bout the gift? You still got to get her a gift. You only got until Saturday.

JEFF: . . . Bruno's. I bet Bruno has a good deal going.

TODD: A fur? You're going to get her a fur? Man, she'll eat you alive.

JEFF: You think it's a bad idea?

TODD: It's what they all want. Hell. A fur . . . She feel okay about dead animals?

JEFF: We eat meat.

TODD: Then you're set. Boy, I wish I could take a snapshot when she sees it. The look on her face . . . She is going to fucking die.

JEFF: Bruno's a good guy, right? He wouldn't stiff me?

TODD: No. He's one of the old kind. Old time business type. He'll sell you ten if he has to. I wouldn't worry about him. You just better live up to it, or she's going to be bolting out the door.

JEFF: I'll live up to it.

TODD: . . . A fur. Man, that's exciting.

JEFF: You want one?

TODD: Are you crazy? All that dead hair and shit? No. It's the idea of it. That's all. Buddy, I think you did the right thing. No question.

JEFF: I'll see how much I have in the bank.

TODD: Bruno will give you a fair shake.

JEFF: Yeah, but I still need the money.

TODD: Plastic.

JEFF: My plastic's shot. I put one more thing on that thing and I'm screaming.

TODD: So what? It's American.

JEFF: Yeah, but I can't live it.

TODD: So, cut them up, see where it gets you. Poorhouse, that's where. Credit card companies have millions of dollars. They can afford us. Eight hundred dollars? They shit that in an hour. And we're sweating it off, making the payments . . . Screw them. Buy your wife a fur. They're not going to come after you. Who are they? The fucking FBI?

JEFF: I guess.

TODD: You guess? No wonder your reflexes are shot.

JEFF: I want to do right. By her. And my wallet.

TODD: They don't cooperate, buddy. It's one or the other. Haven't you figured that out yet? *(Pause.)* Give me a light, will you?

JEFF: Are you going to smoke?

TODD: You're going to lecture me? Just give me the light.

JEFF: It's your lungs.

TODD: And my heart and my ass. Look, I don't want nobody worshipping my body. It's not a temple. When I'm wasting, let a bulldozer come over me and tear me down.

JEFF: Gina smokes.

TODD: So I got to put up with your shit?

JEFF: It makes her tense like I can't feel her shoulders she's so wound up. I was thinking "hide the cigarettes," but what good would that do? They got thirty fucking brands all stacked up in the market. It's the smell in her mouth. I can't kiss her. Makes me feel contaminated.

TODD: It's good I don't have to kiss you.

JEFF: That'll be the day.

TODD: In my dreams.

(Pause.)

JEFF: Hey, she'll like the fur, right?

TODD: I think it's a terrific idea.

JEFF: You think rabbit or ostrich?

TODD: They got ostrich now?

JEFF: I think I saw a sign in the window. "Exotic" something or other . . .

TODD: Man, they'll do anything now, won't they? Damn birds. Look like mutants without those feathers . . . I think rabbit will be better.

JEFF: Softer.

TODD: Yeah. She'll like that.

(Light change.)

SCENE THREE

Gina and Todd in bed.

GINA: You should always hold me like this.

TODD: How can you be so soft?

GINA: I use lotion. It comes out of a pink bottle and just smoothes itself over me.

(He caresses her.)

Stop.

TODD: I can't help it. You're so soft.

GINA: Todd!

TODD: What?

GINA: Don't stop.

TODD: You're on fire.

GINA: I'm happy. (Pause.) Shit.

TODD: What?

GINA: We left the television on. I can hear the static coming in from the other room.

TODD: So? We'll turn it off later. No sense moving now.

GINA: Wasting all that electricity . . .

TODD: You want me to turn it off? I'll turn it off.

(He starts to rise. She holds him back.)

GINA: Leave it. I'll do it later.

TODD: What are you smiling at?

GINA: Nothing.

TODD: I could just stay here, you know. Right here, right inside you, and never leave. Pull me up to bury me, that's my feeling. What, you think I'm funny? You think I'm a funny guy? A little crazy maybe?

GINA: I don't know what to think.

TODD: That's 'cause you're with me. I have that effect on people.

(Gina breaks away from Todd. She gets a shirt, slips it on, and starts to button it.)

What are you doing?

GINA: What does it look like I'm doing? I'm cold.

TODD: You're thinking about him?

GINA: No.

TODD: . . . You're thinking about him.

(He rises, reaches for his jeans.)

GINA: Look, I'm . . . I'm trying, you know.

TODD: Yeah.

(Pause.)

GINA: You want me to rub your back?

TODD: I never liked that shit.

GINA: . . . You want some eggs?

TODD: I'm not hungry.

(She lights a cigarette, smokes.)

GINA: Jeff can't stand my cooking. You know how much food I throw away around here? The rats in the sewers must have the best meals.

TODD: Why can't you think of me?

GINA: I do.

TODD: When? When I'm not here?

(Pause.)

GINA: I'm fading.

TODD: You want to rest?

GINA: No, I'm just . . .

TODD: I can come back another time.

GINA: No. This is good.

TODD: Yeah?

GINA: Yeah.

TODD: You let me know. 'Cause I can do other things. And you don't have to take my word for it either.

GINA: I'll let you know.

TODD: Just thought I'd offer. *(Pause.)* How come the fireplace don't work?

GINA: It's not real. It's decoration.

TODD: Waste.

GINA: At least it's clean. No ashes to take care of.

TODD: What good is it? Might as well look at the TV. At least there you can turn on a channel, and look at a fire all night. Haven't you seen it? They got this channel, it shows you a fire for hours, with flames, I swear, this big. Keeps you company.

GINA: Is that what you do?

TODD: Got to do something, right? I don't say nothing 'bout you.

GINA: I should turn the TV off.

TODD: Don't go. Don't go!

GINA: You're making me crazy.

TODD: Do you love him?

GINA: We're married.

TODD: That's no . . .

GINA: Look, don't ask me, all right? Don't ask!

TODD: You don't want to talk? We won't talk. I can do that. Did that with Marjorie I-don't-know-how-many-years. *(Pause.)* Hey. I'm here. I'm here. It's all right.

GINA: I know.

TODD: . . . I want to spread that lotion on you. Every day.

GINA: I'm sorry.

TODD: What am I supposed to do?

GINA: Stay the night. He won't be here 'til morning. You don't want to?

TODD: Yeah. Yeah. Take what I can get, you know.

GINA: You won't be sorry.

TODD: I'm never sorry.

(Light change.)

SCENE FOUR

Gina is riding her pantyhose up in a hurry. Her clothes are draped over a chair — a pair of jeans and a tank top. Jeff is standing.

GINA: You hurt me. Don't try to explain yourself.

JEFF: It's not like I'm doing it on purpose. I mean, you could be a little more . . .

GINA: *(Looking at pantyhose.)* A run. Great. I hate stockings.

JEFF: *(Begins to comb his hair.)* You don't have to wear them.

GINA: I look better if I wear them under my jeans. Are you through with that comb?

JEFF: Here.

(He hands her the comb. She runs it through her hair.)

GINA: My tits are freezing.

(She stops combing, grabs tank top, slips it on.)

JEFF: You know they said it was going to be cold today.

(She resumes combing.)

The comb. Are you through? I need to cover my bald spot.

(She hands him comb. He combs his hair.)

Looks better now, don't you think?

(She doesn't respond.)

You want to go out or not?

GINA: We're going out now, aren't we?

JEFF: As a favor.

GINA: You like trains. I'm not complaining.

JEFF: We don't have to go.

GINA: A couple thousand lunatics and their model trains. Baby, I wouldn't miss it. Wouldn't miss it for nothing. Toot-toot!

JEFF: Don't call me that.

GINA: Toot-toot! Toot-toot!

JEFF: I mean it.

GINA: Come on, baby. All aboard! Toot-toot!

   (He moves to strike her.)

   Hit me. It's what you want.

JEFF: I'm sorry, Gina. I . . .

GINA: Ah. Hell . . .

   You think the black shoes or the copper?

JEFF: Gina, I don't know what I'm doing.

GINA: You're getting dressed. Come on.

JEFF: I can't think what to do anymore. Nothing goes together.

GINA: Here. Here's your blue tie. You like this one, don't you? It's got the funny little trains on it.

JEFF: Would you . . . ?

GINA: Sure, baby. I've been tying ties since way back. My Daddy taught me. He said "There's nothing to it Bumpers. Just move your hand like this, then like that, and through there, and presto!" *(She finishes tying his tie.)* You look good. Really good.

JEFF: *(Touching tie.)* I like this fabric. What's the fabric on this?

GINA: I don't know. Polyester or something like that. Come on. Get your jacket on. You don't want to be late.

JEFF: Is my bald spot showing?

GINA: Not a bit. Should I hit the light?

JEFF: Yeah.

   (She turns off light.)

GINA: Okay. We're set.

JEFF: Gina?

GINA: What?

JEFF: Gina?

GINA: I'm here, baby. What is it?

JEFF: I'm scared.

GINA: I know.

   (Light change.)

SCENE FIVE

   Jeff is holding the fur coat.

JEFF: Do you like it?

GINA: It's not what I expected.

JEFF: That's what's so great about it. The last thing you'd expect . . . It's authentic. Feel.

GINA: I see.

JEFF: I knew you'd like it. All the drive down I kept seeing you in it. I knew it would fit you. I just knew. Try it on?

GINA: It's so big.

JEFF: It's the style. You can wear it. You can wear anything. You got shoulders. Try it on.

GINA: So many colors. I didn't know they made furs with these many colors.

JEFF: It's all different kinds of rabbits. Believe me, there's not another like it. Just ask Bruno.

GINA: You went to Bruno's?

JEFF: Do me a favor. Try it on. I don't want to fight about it.

GINA: I'm not fighting.

JEFF: You won't try it on.

GINA: Give me.

(He hands her coat. She slips it on. He looks at her.)

JEFF: I knew it would look good. I just knew it.

GINA: You want a beer?

JEFF: Turn around. Let me see. Oh. It's great. It's terrific. Todd was right.

GINA: Todd?

JEFF: It's perfect.

(She takes off the coat.)

What are you doing? It looked good.

GINA: No, I . . . I have to go to work.

JEFF: But it's Saturday. We've been planning this for weeks.

GINA: I have to go out. Overtime, remember? Look, I'll wear it later. You watch TV, whatever . . . I'll be back before dark.

(She exits. Jeff is left with the fur coat. Light change.)

SCENE SIX

Todd, Jeff, and a six-pack of beer.

TODD: So, did she like it, did she like it, did she like it?

JEFF: I guess so.

TODD: Man, I knew it, I knew we'd hit the roof. How much did Bruno offer? Eight, nine?

JEFF: Seven hundred and fifty.

TODD: That's good, that's good. So, did she wear it? How does it look?

JEFF: She didn't try it on.

TODD: What?

JEFF: She didn't want to.

TODD: Why didn't you tell me this? I thought we were a hit. She didn't try it on? She hated it.

JEFF: Maybe later.

TODD: No, no, no. There's no later to be had. She's done with it. She doesn't want the damn coat. Let's face it. We blew it, buddy.

JEFF: I think she liked it, in spite of things.

TODD: Do you? Well, that's encouraging. I mean, that's a good sign. Means your intuition is right, your nose is working. That's good, that's good.

JEFF: She always liked rabbits.

TODD: So you figure if the animal suits the fur, right?

JEFF: Exactly.

TODD: She's gonna wear it. You'll see. *(Pause.)* Hey, you okay, buddy? You sure something's not defeating you? You got that old football face, the one that used to say "The field is wet, my knees hurt, let's get it over with today."

JEFF: I'm okay. Just Gina.

TODD: Well, you picked her. Could've been anybody else but you sought her out. You knew she was tough.

JEFF: If this coat was the wrong thing, I swear . . . what am I going to do? I read the paper. Things are exploding everywhere. If Gina goes . . .

TODD: Hell, you're together, aren't you? How many years of connubial bliss? Come on. Nobody gives that up anymore. Especially not a woman.

JEFF: We used to eat pizza, do you believe that? We used to down a large Angelo's pizza and a bottle of red.

One night. Stay up, watch TV, snooze, talk. It was greasy and fun. We'd wake up in the morning — pizza in my nails and the smell of her pussy and my wuss . . . I never liked it better. Now we order a pizza and it's a meal, you know? We even stopped the red 'cause she has to work odd shifts. We eat, clear the table, do whatever.

TODD: . . . Did you do the movie?

JEFF: Nah. That died.

TODD: The coat took it out of you.

JEFF: The coat took it out of me.

(Pause.)

TODD: I think what's best is if you consider the options. I mean, she could be thinking one thing, but . . .

JEFF: Yeah.

TODD: But you gotta know. Take me and Gina. We went through this sometime after we were married.

JEFF: You and Gina?

TODD: I mean, me and Marjorie. We went through this sometime after we
were married. She wanted to have her nails done every Monday,
Wednesday, Friday. I wanted a bit of bowling every Monday, Wednesday,
Friday. So we talked about it. We talked about it, and what was clear was
that she couldn't stand to have her nails done and I could live without
bowling, so we had an agreement and it was fine.

JEFF: But you got divorced.

TODD: It wasn't working out.

JEFF: What about me and Gina?

TODD: I don't know your exact situation. You seem like a good enough couple. She takes care of you.

JEFF: I bet if we had kids.

TODD: Well, that would honor you. But with kids, you have to be there,
whether you like it or not.

JEFF: *(In thought.)* Jedediah . . .

TODD: Old fortune teller. You went to see him again?

JEFF: He moved away.

TODD: I liked that guy. He knew about the cards . . . He could them in a second, tell you your life story.

JEFF: Told me my fortune once.

TODD: And you believed him?

JEFF: Starting to . . .

TODD: Nothing but lies. That's all they tell you. They tell you what you want
to hear. You think he told you different?

JEFF: He told me to look out for my buddies.

TODD: He was a great man. Great man. Where'd you say he went?

JEFF: Don't know.

TODD: Small town, I bet. Fortune tellers always end up in small towns. Trick
of nature . . .

JEFF: Gina will be home soon.

TODD: You're going to see her down?

JEFF: I thought I'd surprise her. Yeah. Can't hurt, right?

TODD: Keep those surprises coming. The coat, this . . . she'll warm up to you.
I guarantee it.

JEFF: You scramble my mind, Todd.

TODD: It's for your health, my friend. Wouldn't do it otherwise.
(Light change.)

SCENE SEVEN
Gina is dumping old coffee grinds into the trash. Jeff is seated.

GINA: I just made strange sounds and they have nothing to do with you.
JEFF: Well, they have to do with someone.
GINA: I was thinking about me, about my body, how it gets bloated when I get my period and my breasts swell and I have to wear loose tops or else it hurts too much and how my belly gets full of water it feels like a rock and you want to make love to me and all I want is to eat popcorn and chocolate and not even think of your arms or chest or hairy thighs.
JEFF: I've come to disgust you, is that it?
GINA: I wish you'd listen.
JEFF: I don't hear anything. All you're doing is going through menstrual bitching. I can see your jeans don't fit as they should. So what? Am I supposed to fetch you clean rags every twenty minutes?
GINA: My legs are cramping. I'm taking a rest.
JEFF: You're upset, aren't you?
GINA: Sweetheart, my legs hurt. I need to sit down so it'll pass.
(Pause.)
JEFF: Let's play cards.
GINA: Jeff!
JEFF: Straight poker, five cards each.
GINA: Whatever made you decide to play cards?
JEFF: Just thought about it. It's a great game.
GINA: I never knew you played cards. I thought I knew everything about you. When'd you start?
JEFF: Everybody plays. It's a kid's thing.
GINA: You played when you were a kid?
JEFF: I played, all right? Now you're making me crazy here. Cut the deck.
GINA: I want to know.
JEFF: You wanna know? I was a fiend, okay? I stole out at night and went to Dad's pool hall. There was a room in back. Minors only. All of us five year olds would get together and hustle each other out of a few pennies. It was brutal. They even gave a paper cut to one guy for spilling his hand one night.

My brother taught me. It was the cool thing to do. You'd rather I
sniffed glue instead? Now, five cards each, and pick from the pile when
you need a card.

GINA: What if I don't?

JEFF: Then I'll pick one. How's that?

(They each look at their hands in playful silence.)

How about a card?

GINA: No. You?

JEFF: I'm fine.

GINA: Maybe I'll take one.

JEFF: I thought you didn't need it.

GINA: Just one.

JEFF: . . . Anything good?

GINA: You don't want one?

JEFF: I'm fine.

GINA: You're bluffing.

JEFF: You don't want to believe me, that's your problem.

GINA: You got to need at least one. Nobody gets a perfect hand when they start.

JEFF: You'd be surprised.

GINA: Show me.

JEFF: What is this show-and-tell? I can't show you. We're playing a game here.

GINA: Then swear you're not bluffing.

JEFF: That's ridiculous.

GINA: Swear.

JEFF: I swear.

GINA: Liar.

JEFF: You want me to take a card? I'll take a card just to make you happy . . .
Shit.

GINA: I knew it.

JEFF: What? You knew what? You don't have a clue. *(Pause.)* You're so tense.

GINA: My shoulders are killing me. Why does it always bunch up in there?

JEFF: Give me your back.

GINA: What are you doing?

JEFF: You need some hands.

GINA: You're torturing me.

JEFF: *(Massaging her back.)* Squeezing that pain out. You're in knots. . . . I can
smell your blood.

GINA: Do you hate it?

JEFF: I think it's sexy.

GINA: Not every man would say that.

JEFF: That's why you married me.

GINA: A little further up. Yeah. That's it.

JEFF: You need a cut. Your hair's not anything.

GINA: I'll go next week.

JEFF: Your ends are split and everything.

GINA: So, you cut it. Save me eight bucks. Don't stop.

JEFF: Don't want to overdo it. That's just as bad.

GINA: Keep your hands on me.

JEFF: You just want to play.

GINA: So?

JEFF: So . . . we've got a game here.

GINA: . . . You win.

JEFF: What?

GINA: Come on. Let's take a shower.
  (*Lights fade.*)

SCENE EIGHT
  Morning. Jeff is seated at the table. Gina is getting ready to go to work.

JEFF: You're taking a lunch break today?

GINA: Depends on how much work they got lined up. Why? You're thinking
  of picking me up?

JEFF: I thought maybe . . .

GINA: I don't know. This one girl got docked ten minutes for going to the bathroom the other day.

JEFF: I miss you.

GINA: Yeah?

JEFF: When I go to work, I think about you. It's all I can do.

GINA: Going up and down the turnpike, what else are you going to do? I think
  about you, too.

JEFF: . . . Finished the eggs. I like the way you cook things: eggs and shit . . .

GINA: What do you want me to cook tonight? Beans, beef noodle?

JEFF: Let's eat out.

GINA: Eat out, exhausted tomorrow.

JEFF: So, I'll make you something. You rest. Would you like that?

GINA: How come you're so nice all of a sudden? I can't figure you out.

JEFF: We could do pizza and wine.

GINA: I'll be sick.

JEFF: We could pack it in, watch TV. It'll be like the old days.

GINA: I'll think about it. I'll call you from work and let you know.

JEFF: *(Clears newspaper from table.)* You want the paper for anything?

GINA: You don't need it?

JEFF: I'm not gonna find out any more stuff by reading it than not. Might as
     well not know. If there's an emergency, we'll find out. Don't need the
     paper to tell us about it.

GINA: Throw it out then. *(She puts a scarf on.)* Scarf okay?

JEFF: I thought it was pretty good last night. In the shower. You know if there's
     anything you want to tell me . . . you can tell me.

GINA: There's nothing to tell. Kiss?
     (They kiss. He embraces her fiercely. After a moment, she pulls away gently.)
     Scarf okay?

JEFF: Call me later. Tell me what you want.

GINA: Pizza will be fine. Honest.
     (She exits. Lights change.)

SCENE NINE
     The park. Todd and Jeff are jogging.

TODD: Then I went scuba diving.

JEFF: You see anything?

TODD: Saw the waves. It was something fierce. You got those waves coming
     at you and the fish . . . you could lose yourself . . . except the seaweed
     can trap you, and that stuff can burn, scrape your skin right off . . . but
     you hit these reefs.

JEFF: Barrier reefs?

TODD: Ten feet high with rocks coming out of them all different colors. It's
     better than videotape.

JEFF: It's live.

TODD: Very alive. Right there in your face. No commercials, no five and dime,
     just you and the rock: ready to kill you.

JEFF: Wouldn't.

TODD: We're not talking just any kind of rock here. This is dynamite polyurethane
     reef rock. You bang up against that, see where it gets you. Other side of
     the planet is where.

(Todd cuts in front of Jeff, jogs.)

JEFF: You got knocked?

TODD: Reflexes saved me. You come up the air gets so light all of a sudden you have to breathe.

JEFF: I'd like to go next time.

TODD: You think you're ready? You and your nose bleeds, we could have trouble.

JEFF: My nose won't bleed under water. There's too much pressure.

TODD: And if it does?

JEFF: Then I'll let it go. It's going to go into the water anyway.

TODD: What if the eels think the blood's their food? What then? You gonna run away from an eel? You got fins now?

JEFF: No.

TODD: Then what?

JEFF: I'll find my way. You have.

(Jeff picks up the pace. Todd keeps up.)

TODD: We'll see about that.

JEFF: You promised.

(Jeff goes faster. Todd keeps up.)

TODD: Next time I go we'll see about it. You can come with me, but going in . . .

JEFF: But I can come with you.

TODD: You're my buddy. We hit pavement together, right?

(Jeff cuts in front of Todd, stops.)

JEFF: I got a fever. Under the tongue. Is that what they say? You stick your finger under your tongue and you find your temperature?

TODD: Think so.

JEFF: You got a watch on you?

TODD: All I got is a stopwatch.

JEFF: Count me off a half minute, would you? I want to take my temperature.

TODD: A half minute?

JEFF: Yeah.

(Jeff punches Todd in the stomach.)

TODD: Hey. Whatcha doing? You wanna kill me?

JEFF: Yeah.

(Lights fade.)

SCENE TEN

Jeff is seated on the edge of the bed. Gina is beside him.

GINA: So the Big Bad Wolf said to the Little Bad Wolf, "Come on, baby, let's play horse-y."
And the Little Bad Wolf said . . .

JEFF: I don't want to hear this shit.

GINA: I thought you liked my stories.

JEFF: Not when they get asinine.

GINA: You're just jealous 'cause you can't make them up.

JEFF: I can make them up. I just need more time, that's all. I like to think before I speak.

GINA: I think.

JEFF: Yes, but you do it when you speak. There's a difference.
(Pause.)

GINA: I clean up after you. I fold your laundry. But you still keep turning over in your sleep. I try not to listen, but I can't help it. I can't help hearing you turn over and over and then get up in the morning and grunt to the kitchen and grunt out the door.

JEFF: Do I wake you?

GINA: No, but it hurts, hearing you . . .

JEFF: I try to be quiet.

GINA: But you're screaming, aren't you? Like in my dream last night.
There was this field of bare trees and snow, and swirls of fire round and round, but everything was in black and white. Very gray swirls. Sometimes they were snow, and sometimes they were fire . . . And there was this boy, a small boy with a striped shirt, and he was sitting in front of a machine spinning this film which was my dream. And I wanted to steal it. I wanted to steal his film and put it back in my dream. And at the same time these gray swirls of fire kept churning in front of me, and somebody kept running between the trees. Very distant, not even a shadow, and I knew it was you. I know it was you, screaming.
(Silence.)

JEFF: I'm here. I'm not screaming.
(He holds her, rocks her. A soft light comes through the window. Todd is seen, looking in, then disappears. Jeff raises Gina's face to him. He caresses her. They begin to make love. Music comes up: Billie Holiday's "Lover Come Back." Lights fade.)

END OF PLAY

Mistaken for Genius
by Judy Tate

BIOGRAPHY

Judy Tate was a 1997 Manhattan Theatre Club Playwrighting Fellow and winner of the New Professional Theater's emerging playwright award for her full-length play *Fast Blood* which has had staged readings at EST, Playwrights Horizons, Passage Theatre and Hartford Stage. Her short plays *The Point* and *Mistaken for Genius* were both produced by the Women's Project where she was a member of the Playwrights Lab. Her full length play *Slashes of Light,* was commissioned by the Manhattan Theatre Club and read there and at the Ensemble Studio Theatre where she is a member. She is currently on the writing team of the daytime serial *As the World Turns* for which she won an Emmy. A professional actor for many years, Judy has worked in television and theater, traveling throughout the United States and Southern Africa. As a teaching artist, she works with the Manhattan Theatre Club, Lincoln Center Institute, and Theatre Development Fund. She is an alumna of New York University's Tisch School of the Arts Conservatory Program where she studied with Stella Adler, and was an honors graduate receiving the Founder's Day Award, Seidman Award, and Beinecke Award for excellence in acting and academia.

ORIGINAL PRODUCTION

Ethnic, Nonspecific Interviewer . . . . Elise Santora
Three-Name Playwright . . . . Nilaja Sun
Sniveling Sycophant . . . . Melissa Murray

CHARACTERS

ETHNIC, NONSPECIFIC INTERVIEWER
THREE-NAME PLAYWRIGHT
SNIVELING SYCOPHANT

SETTING

Time: The Present.
Place: A Theater/Auditorium in the Southside Public Arts Mecca.

INTRODUCTORY STATEMENT AND DEDICATION

Mistaken for Genius was conceived after reading a particularly unintelligible work and subsequent interview by a multiple award-winning artiste. It is dedicated to all the people who sit in audiences throughout the country going "huh?" and wondering why they weren't invited to the party, and to those who nod and go "ahhh" pretending that they were. Here's to story. Enjoy!

MISTAKEN FOR GENIUS

Spotlight on the Ethnic, Nonspecific Interviewer as she addresses the audience. She is thin, upbeat, well-spoken, sincere, and accommodating.

INTERVIEWER: Welcome. Welcome. Welcome. What a large audience we have here tonight at Southside Public Arts Mecca. For those of you who are new to me, to SPAM, I am the ethnic nonspecific interviewer who is always required to host these gatherings. With my working-class look and upper class articulation, I am the multicultural but well-spoken face that saves this institution, many times on the brink of collapse, from losing its mainstream funding. But this isn't about me. It's about us. Allow me to be falsely modest. Who would have thought that three years ago when SPAM, the most self-important theater company ever to attract a Rockefeller grant, started this series, it would have blossomed into a mega — mega what? Gathering? Roundtable? Salon? Yes. How's that? Salon, where the lost art of conversation has been resuscitated and given new pretense. I am so excited! What a multiculti group we are too! Every blue-haired ancient neatly nestled between someone in black eyeliner. Every gay Jewish intellectual artiste whispering into the ear of his hard-bodied companion. White men in suits snoring. And you, homeboy, you've taken off your shoes. Tired? Why don't you just put your feet up on the seat in front of you? That's right. Good. *(Cell phone rings.)* I hear a cell phone. Why not? Make it a conference call! Well, at this level of art exploration could we expect anything less than genius from our audience? And that's just why we're here, isn't it? — for a glimpse of genius — our own and others — trying our best to unravel the workings of the creative mind; liberating ourselves from the narrow definitions of art, self, and wardrobe. And with us today, is a playwright — I shudder to think that a woman of such stature, such presence, such creative affectation, could be limited by the definition *playwright.* Anyway she is here today. Many of you will remember her play, produced here just last season — Derrière Americain? *(Applause.)* It was a resounding artistic success. A critical masterpiece. A stinging and unintelligible play of mythic proportions. Please give a warm, warm welcome to our guest, accompanied by her Sniveling Sycophant. Please welcome — the Three-Name Playwright.
(Applause.)

(Spot widens and the Three-Name Playwright enters, pauses to make a sacred gesture to the audience, and sits across from the Interviewer in a talk-show-type setup. She wears a high turban of some earthy fabric in gold and russet tones. Her dress is a caftan of bright colors or a loose-fitting top with harem -style pants. Her left breast is exposed. She carries a bell. When she speaks, she looks up at the ceiling a lot as if deep in thought. A slightly built person of indistinguishable sex drools on the floor at her side.)

INTERVIEWER: Thank you so much for coming.

THREE-NAME PLAYWRIGHT: *(Gestures once.)* Je suis le no supa confree zenh fenh.

THE SNIVELING SYCOPHANT: *(Adoringly.)* Aaahhhhh.

INTERVIEWER: I beg your pardon?

THREE-NAME PLAYWRIGHT: No need.

(The Sniveling Sycophant chuckles.)

INTERVIEWER: Thank you. Now I suppose the most obvious question, certainly one our audience would like to throw out of the way in order to get on to more weighty topics is the matter of your nipple — uh, name. You are known as the Three-Name Playwright. Could you illuminate us? What are your three names?

THREE-NAME PLAYWRIGHT: Uhhhhhhhhhhhhhhh.
My . . . *(Gesture.)* . . . three . . . *(Gesture.)* . . . names *(Gesture.)*

INTERVIEWER: Why do you do that?

THREE-NAME PLAYWRIGHT: What?

INTERVIEWER: This. *(She gestures.)*

THREE-NAME PLAYWRIGHT: *(Gesturing as she says it.)* This what?

INTERVIEWER: That. See? That.

THREE-NAME PLAYWRIGHT: Oh, this. *(She gestures.)*

INTERVIEWER: Yes, that.

THREE-NAME PLAYWRIGHT: Because language is a physical reality. *(She rings her bell.)*

THE SNIVELING SYCOPHANT: Ooohhhhhhhh!!

INTERVIEWER: I see.

THREE-NAME PLAYWRIGHT: Did you?

INTERVIEWER: What?

THREE-NAME PLAYWRIGHT: See?

INTERVIEWER: See what?

THREE-NAME PLAYWRIGHT: What we did.

INTERVIEWER: What did we do?

THREE-NAME PLAYWRIGHT: Did do, did do, did do, did do.

INTERVIEWER: Did do, did do, did do, did do, did do?

THREE-NAME PLAYWRIGHT: One less.

INTERVIEWER: Did — ?

THREE-NAME PLAYWRIGHT: No, did do, did do, did do, did do.

INTERVIEWER: Did do, did do, did do, did do?

THREE-NAME PLAYWRIGHT: Yes.

INTERVIEWER: I see.

THREE-NAME PLAYWRIGHT: You see.

INTERVIEWER: Well what? — I mean did do — did we do, I mean.

THREE-NAME PLAYWRIGHT: Like a sandwich.

INTERVIEWER: Like a sandwich?

THREE-NAME PLAYWRIGHT: Your "I means." Like a sandwich around the "did do's."

INTERVIEWER: I see. But before. What did we do before?

THREE-NAME PLAYWRIGHT: Does it matter, this before?

INTERVIEWER: *(Disappointed.)* I guess not.

THREE-NAME PLAYWRIGHT: Ah, but it does.

INTERVIEWER: It does?

THREE-NAME PLAYWRIGHT: To you it does.

INTERVIEWER: Yes.

THREE-NAME PLAYWRIGHT: We explored our mutual sound.

THE SNIVELING SYCOPHANT: Aaaaahhhhhhhh!

INTERVIEWER: I'm dying to discuss that! But let's get back to my original question about your —

THREE-NAME PLAYWRIGHT: — nipple.

INTERVIEWER: Your nipple?

THREE-NAME PLAYWRIGHT: That's what you said.

INTERVIEWER: But I misspoke. I meant to say your name.

THREE-NAME PLAYWRIGHT: But you didn't.

INTERVIEWER: I know.

THREE-NAME PLAYWRIGHT: Now you know.

INTERVIEWER: I knew then too.

THREE-NAME PLAYWRIGHT: But you did.

INTERVIEWER: Say nipple — ?

THREE-NAME PLAYWRIGHT: Nipple. Nipple. Nipple. Nipple. Nipple. Nipple.

INTERVIEWER: No, not you say nipple. I mean me.

THREE-NAME PLAYWRIGHT: Okay, you say it.

INTERVIEWER: I said it.

THREE-NAME PLAYWRIGHT: Say it now.

INTERVIEWER: Okay. Nipple.

THREE-NAME PLAYWRIGHT: Ah, good. Magnificent.

INTERVIEWER: Thank you.

THREE-NAME PLAYWRIGHT: It wasn't a compliment.

INTERVIEWER: No?

THREE-NAME PLAYWRIGHT: It was my name.

INTERVIEWER: Oh. Uh, Magnificent?

THREE-NAME PLAYWRIGHT: *(Slyly.)* A compliment?

INTERVIEWER: No. Your name.

THREE-NAME PLAYWRIGHT: Now this is communication.

(Sniveling Sycophant applauds.)

INTERVIEWER: Magnificent —

THREE-NAME PLAYWRIGHT: It was Margaret —

INTERVIEWER: Margaret.

THREE-NAME PLAYWRIGHT: Well, Margaret blank blank.

INTERVIEWER: Margaret blank blank.

THREE-NAME PLAYWRIGHT: — but somehow Margaret just didn't express my emotional depths nor my monumental elations —

INTERVIEWER: So you changed your name — to Magnificent?

THREE-NAME PLAYWRIGHT: No, it changed me.

INTERVIEWER: "It" being your name?

THREE-NAME PLAYWRIGHT: My three names.

INTERVIEWER: *(Intrigued.)* Oh. How?

THREE-NAME PLAYWRIGHT: Do you know when you're dreaming and the dream is so vivid that you cannot help but wake up with it in the front of your mind's eye?

INTERVIEWER: Yes, oh yes! That's what happened to you?

THREE-NAME PLAYWRIGHT: No.

INTERVIEWER: Oh.

THREE-NAME PLAYWRIGHT: No. "Oh no"!

INTERVIEWER: "Oh no!"?

THREE-NAME PLAYWRIGHT: "Oh no!"

INTERVIEWER: Oh no . . . because?

THREE-NAME PLAYWRIGHT: Because in genius that is how a name revelation should begin! In a waking dream — a vivid waking dream from which there is no escape, no mistake, no retake, no abatement.

THE SNIVELING SYCOPHANT: Ahhh. *(Sing-song.)* No escape, no mistake, no retake, no abate!!

THREE-NAME PLAYWRIGHT: *(Scolding.)* — ment.

THE SNIVELING SYCOPHANT: Ahhhhhhh rapture.

INTERVIEWER: So, where did you go from there?

THREE-NAME PLAYWRIGHT: In search —

INTERVIEWER: — of your name!

THREE-NAME PLAYWRIGHT: My three names!

INTERVIEWER: Your Magnificent three names! I see now. It's so clear. Because only then —

THREE-NAME PLAYWRIGHT: — when you understand the sound, the true sound of your own name, the ancient, pulling, humming, dark, ringing, the rhythmic beating

INTERVIEWER: — like a pulse —

THREE-NAME PLAYWRIGHT: — like the pump of blood through your veins, the steady throb of your being, the monumental waves of spirit crashing against the rocks of your puny ego — *(The Sniveling Sycophant swoons and hums.)* — only then when the rolling, roaring, jumping, jiving, scintillating, scatting, hog maw and chicken foot, blackeyed-pea sound of your name is heard . . .

INTERVIEWER: . . . can be revealed to you . . . uh, . . . only then . . . uh . . . can be revealed to . . . uh . . . us, . . . uh, . . . only then can be revealed to the world . . .

THE SNIVELING SYCOPHANT: Yes! Yes!

INTERVIEWER: What? What? Help me out here! Only then . . . can be revealed . . .

THREE-NAME PLAYWRIGHT: My left breast!!!!!

(The Three-Name Playwright rings her bell and does her gesture as The Sniveling Sycophant begins to cry. The Interviewer's mouth hangs open.)

INTERVIEWER: Well, that was certainly the perfect segue, wasn't it?

THE SNIVELING SYCOPHANT: *(Clapping.)* Aahhh. Your breast. Your wonderful breast!

INTERVIEWER: I get it! Your new play! *Ma Mamelle Gauche.* How did it all begin?

THREE-NAME PLAYWRIGHT: I began, and it's really difficult to say I began, because when I write it's not really me that writes. The I that you know as me stands aside, bears witness to the process that the I who isn't me but rather the transcriber in the process is undergoing. Rather, the I that writes is more another being totally. The I that you know as me is the I whose name I can call, so that it, it being the idea, it being what you finally see when you witness the product of my genius, will come to me.

INTERVIEWER: And your breast —

THREE-NAME PLAYWRIGHT: My left breast?

INTERVIEWER: How did your left breast come to you?

THREE-NAME PLAYWRIGHT: It was always there really.

THE SNIVELING SYCOPHANT: Oh, eternal bosom!

INTERVIEWER: How did you come then to reveal it? If that is indeed what you did?

THREE-NAME PLAYWRIGHT: Yes it is. Uncovered, revealed, released, uncaged. The revelation of my left breast! I came to it once again in a dream-state. A tangible dream in which sound, gesture, and physical form were all one. A state where tastes could be heard and sounds could grow bittersweet on the tongue. I love words. I have a theory that words are related to each other through sound if not etymology. College/knowledge, history/ mystery, grow-up/throw-up.

INTERVIEWER: I see.

THREE-NAME PLAYWRIGHT: So, I dreamed. I dreamed a breast.

THE SNIVELING SYCOPHANT: A mammary memory.

THREE-NAME PLAYWRIGHT: Then I dreamed a crest. Which is not so unusual because I was in search of my name. Or my name was in search of me. And this crest was on a chest. Then I dreamed treasure. A chest of treasure. I saw a wonderful scene in which my breast is the crest of my treasure chest. Then my left breast began to sing. And the music flowed from my left nipple in liquid form. It was intoxicating.

THE SNIVELING SYCOPHANT: A nipple tipple!

THREE-NAME PLAYWRIGHT: And in this milky song my left breast called to me a name. My name. Three names in fact — a treasure chest of names! And the sound of these names tasted sweet. A treasure chest of unlimited sweets. Then I understood. Sweets! Sweets rhymes with teats!

INTERVIEWER: Astounding.

THREE-NAME PLAYWRIGHT: And teats are where it all began. The beginning. The breast! I knew I was on to something unmistakably powerful and stunning. I went to my desk and wrote it down.

INTERVIEWER: And what about left? Why your left breast?

THREE-NAME PLAYWRIGHT: Left, simply because after you've fully explored my breast, indeed what is left? We need to center ourselves but we cannot. Left, because it is a radically altered position. Left because I thought it was right, I thought it was right so it's left!

INTERVIEWER: Fascinating.

THREE-NAME PLAYWRIGHT: Thank you.

INTERVIEWER: Now, I would be totally remiss if I didn't direct some questions to your . . . uh . . . companion . . .

(Sniveling Sycophant turns face uncomfortably to the Three-Name Playwright. Sniveling Sycophant makes a feeble "what me?" gesture.)

THREE-NAME PLAYWRIGHT: My companion?!?

INTERVIEWER: Um . . . er . . . com-pan-ion . . . as from the old French "with bread"?

THE SNIVELING SYCOPHANT: *(Covering discomfort.)* Bread fellows!

THREE-NAME PLAYWRIGHT: *(Shooting Sniveling Sycophant a withering look.)* Indeed!

INTERVIEWER: Indeed. I only assumed . . .
(Three Name Playwright shoots Interviewer a withering look.)

INTERVIEWER: *(To Sycophant.)* Well, you wouldn't mind answering a few questions, would you? *(Sniveling Sycophant turns to Three Name Playwright for help.)*

THREE-NAME PLAYWRIGHT: Delay! *(See Sniveling Sycophant tempted and torn.)* Obey! *(Interviewer gives Sniveling Sycophant a tempting look, Sniveling Sycophant and Playwright hold a battle-of-wills look. Playwright warns:)* BETRAY!

THE SNIVELING SYCOPHANT: *(To interviewer, defiant.)* Not at all! *(Insulted/hurt, Playwright turns away, consoles herself in her breast.)*

INTERVIEWER: Well then, your position as a Sniveling Sycophant . . .

THE SNIVELING SYCOPHANT: You are quite beautiful . . .

INTERVIEWER: . . . Parasite . . . toady, if you will . . .

THE SNIVELING SYCOPHANT: Delight!

INTERVIEWER: What skills are involved? Or would you say you had a calling?

THE SNIVELING SYCOPHANT: You are the epitome of the modern aesthete!

INTERVIEWER: Thank you . . . Now, your training in excessive praise . . .

THE SNIVELING SYCOPHANT: We share a nonspecific soul . . .

INTERVIEWER: Was there an apprenticeship period?

THE SNIVELING SYCOPHANT: You, desired one, "a consummation devoutly to be wish'd" . . .

INTERVIEWER: That's familiar, that line.

THE SNIVELING SYCOPHANT: You are the height of my ambition.

INTERVIEWER: From some old play or something . . .

THREE-NAME PLAYWRIGHT: *(Ringing bell, gesturing wildly.)* Enough, enough enough!

INTERVIEWER: Did you have something to append, amend, rescind?

THREE-NAME PLAYWRIGHT: Oh, Shut up. *(To Sniveling Sycophant.)* I . . . I . . . . I . . .

THE SNIVELING SYCOPHANT: Yes?

THREE-NAME PLAYWRIGHT: I . . . I . . . I . . . she . . . .she . . . don't . . . don't . . . I don't . . . the words . . . no words . . . *(Three-Name Playwright cries.)*

THE SNIVELING SYCOPHANT: *(Takes Three-Name Playwright's hand.)* May I? *(Three-Name Playwright nods.)* Add meaning.

THREE-NAME PLAYWRIGHT: *(Skeptically.)* To the words?

THE SNIVELING SYCOPHANT: But who am I to say?

THREE-NAME PLAYWRIGHT: I . . . need . . . you . . .

INTERVIEWER: "A consummation devoutly to be wished . . ."

THE SNIVELING SYCOPHANT: *(Shyly.)* Hamlet, Act III, Scene 1 *(Apologetically.)* It's a . . . story.

EVERYONE: *(Repulsed by the hideous notion.)* Eeeewwwwwwwwww.
  (Beat. Three-Name Playwright and Sniveling Sycophant begin to hold hands and coo adoringly.)

INTERVIEWER: Well, we'll be seeing our friend's enlightened work at the South-side Performing Arts Mecca festival in the bandshell.

THE SNIVELING SYCOPHANT: A SPAM jam!

INTERVIEWER: And I understand that your Sniveling Sycophant will actually be portraying your left breast in that production.

THREE-NAME PLAYWRIGHT: Yes. And I will be playing myself.

THE SNIVELING SYCOPHANT: The best part. The most complex. I love you.

THREE-NAME PLAYWRIGHT: *(Affectionately.)* You servile flatterer, you!

INTERVIEWER: Well, thank you all for coming. Feel free to come up on the stage. Talk to us. Berate our work. Continuing our theme of language abuse, next time we'll be discussing new works with a panel of writers who refuse to use connective words. Sounds fun, could bore! *(She giggles.)* See you next time.

(Lights fade on the three as they chat and examine the playwright's breast.)

END OF PLAY

Relative Strangers
by Sheri Wilner

To my mother

BIOGRAPHY

Sheri Wilner's play *Hunger,* produced by the Contemporary American Theater Festival in Shepherdstown, West Virginia, was chosen for the Smith and Kraus anthology *New Playwrights: The Best New Plays of 1999. Hunger* has also received readings at the Williamstown Theatre Festival, Women's Project & Productions, the Cherry Lane Theatre Alternative, Rattlestick Productions, New Dramatists, and Ensemble Studio Theater. Her play *Labor Day* was a co-recipient of the 1998 Heideman Award granted by the Actor's Theatre of Louisville, which produced the play during the 1999 Humana Festival. Other productions and readings of her plays include: *Bake-Off* at the 2002 Humana Festival; *Labor Day* at the Bailiwick Repertory Theatre and the 2001 Boston Women on Top Festival; *Relative Strangers* at New Georges, the Organic Theater Company, 2001 Boston Women on Top Festival, and the Pittsburgh New Works Festival; *Joan of Arkansas* at Actor's Theatre of Louisville, New York Performance Works, and New Georges; *Little Death of a Salesman* at the 2000 Boston Women On Top Festival; and a new adaptation of Carlo Gozzi's *Turandot* at La Mama. Her plays have been published in other various Smith and Kraus anthologies, as well as by Samuel French, Applause Books, and *Dramatics Magazine.* She received her MFA in Playwriting from Columbia University in 1999 and was named a 2000–01 Dramatists Guild Playwriting Fellow.

ORIGINAL CAST LIST

Relative Strangers was first presented by Women's Project & Productions in *Relative Strangers: Playwrights and Directors Together,* an evening of plays by members of the Women's Project's Playwrights Lab, directed by members of the Women's Project Directors Forum. Presented at La Mama Galleria, May 1, 1994.

Marie Harvey . . . . Geraldine Abbate
Marie Barrett . . . . Ellen Korbonski
Virginia . . . . Wanda Wiesler
Voice of the Pilot . . . . Michael Keck
Director . . . . Elaine Smith

SETTING

On board an airplane flying from New York City to Charleston, South Carolina.

TIME

Present day.

CHARACTERS

MARIE BARRETT: Twenty-five years old.

MARIE HARVEY: Mid-fifties.

VIRGINIA BARCLAY: Thirty-five to forty-five. Head flight attendant. Speaks with a Southern accent.

VOICE OF PILOT

AUTHOR'S NOTE

Once aboard an airplane, when I was imprudently reading in the dark, a passenger reached over the aisle to tap me on the arm. "Excuse me," she said, "but the mother in me wants to tell you to turn the light on when you're reading. You're destroying your eyes." I thanked her, turned on my light, and we shared a smile over the results. End of story.

Well, not completely. I had found her gesture remarkable. She had taken care of me. She actually cared about my eyesight and acted on her concern. And this notion, that my welfare actually mattered to a total stranger, set off a string of complex reactions that resulted in this play.

I first lingered on the comforting thought that perhaps — unbeknownst to me until now — there was a legion of mothers out there, like guardian angels, or soldiers sent into the field, who rescue us from such dangers as reading in dim light, swimming too soon after a meal, or licking a metal pole in the winter. The world just appears to be a dangerous place; in reality, there are invisible hands all around us, poised to break our falls.

Such wishful thinking next lead to an idea for a play — about a motherless young woman who was taken care of — essentially raised — by a secret band of angel-mothers who watched over her wherever she went. They passed her gently from one to the other, making sure she was safely delivered before letting her go. Perhaps she knew of their existence or perhaps she didn't, I never worked that part out, because of the interruption of . . .

The realization of why I needed to write a play about this in-flight encounter. Of course. The mother who was waiting at the airport for my plane to land (who had often told me to turn the light on when reading) had come perilously close to not being there. Not being there at all. A recurring illness, whose modus operandi was the surprise attack, could have taken her from me several times throughout my childhood. It is only through some form of divine luck that I even have a mother and have not had to depend on the kindness of strangers. And so there and then, in the midst of this recognition, I began to write the play that follows, still benefiting from the light recommended to me by the adjacent stranger who had no idea I was now creating our continued, imagined exchange.

And now, each time this play is performed, I stand in the back of the theater and fantasize that this kind passenger is in the audience and will see how her simple suggestion, her single gesture, meant everything in the world.

How fortuitous it is as well that this particular play of mine is included in a Women's Project Anthology. It is a play about mothers, and for the past twenty-five years Julia Miles has been a mother to just about every women playwright in America. She gave me my first job in New York City — "manning" the Women's Project's box office, and I feel honored and blessed to have grown up in her care.

RELATIVE STRANGERS

In the black the voice of an airline pilot can be heard over an intercom.

VOICE OF PILOT: Once again, ladies and gentlemen, from the flight deck, it's our pleasure to welcome you aboard National Airlines Flight 1738 from New York City to Charleston, South Carolina. Flight time is approximately one hour and forty-four minutes, which means we should be landing at 12:44 PM.

(Lights gradually rise to reveal two women seated next to each other in an airplane. It is a few minutes after takeoff. There are vacant seats around them, however, in the world of the play, the seats are occupied by other passengers. Marie Barrett, mid-twenties, seated on the aisle, reads a book without the overhead light on. Marie Harvey, mid-fifties, seated by the window, reads a magazine. She appears uncomfortable and frequently looks at Marie Barrett.) I'd like to take this opportunity to thank you for selecting National Airlines. We bring people together.

MARIE HARVEY: You *cram* people together.

MARIE BARRETT: I'm sorry. Am I crowding you? Here, I'll move my jacket.

MARIE HARVEY: They really pile us on top of each other . . . *(Indicates seatbelt.)* and strap us down. If they truly wanted to ensure our comfort, they wouldn't strap us down.

MARIE BARRETT: Don't they have to? For safety's sake?

MARIE HARVEY: Do you feel safe bound up like a prisoner? I sure as hell don't.

MARIE BARRETT: Planes scare me no matter what.

(Marie Harvey returns to her magazine. She is not interested in conversation, but tries to remain polite.)

MARIE HARVEY: Don't worry. You're safer up here than you are down there.

MARIE BARRETT: Do you live in New York?

MARIE HARVEY: I live about an hour's drive from Manhattan. Twenty minutes if you walk.

MARIE BARRETT: I've only lived there for three years. I'm originally from Rhode Island.

MARIE HARVEY: Quite a change.

MARIE BARRETT: Yeah, it was. The biggest I've made.

MARIE HARVEY: There'll be bigger.

MARIE BARRETT: What's the biggest change you've made?

MARIE HARVEY: I used to be your age. Now I'm mine.

MARIE BARRETT: Are you going to Charleston for anything special?

MARIE HARVEY: Not special. No.

MARIE BARRETT: Just visiting?

MARIE HARVEY: Just divorcing. My divorce hearing is tomorrow.

MARIE BARRETT: Your family lives in Charleston?

MARIE HARVEY: Just my husband. Divorcing me isn't enough. He also needed to move to a different climatic region.

MARIE BARRETT: I'm sorry.

MARIE HARVEY: Don't be. We had ten happy years of marriage . . . which isn't bad out of twenty-five.

MARIE BARRETT: You were married that long?

MARIE HARVEY: Yeah, well, what's twenty-five years?

MARIE BARRETT: Me. My birthday was last month.

MARIE HARVEY: Well I hope the past twenty-five years have brought you more happiness than they've brought me.

MARIE BARRETT: I don't know that they have.

MARIE HARVEY: Unless the only things you have to show for them are bills from your lawyer and a tan line on your ring finger, I'd say they have.

MARIE BARRETT: Are those really the only things you have? Bills and — ?

MARIE HARVEY: And in a couple of weeks I won't even have a tan line.

MARIE BARRETT: You don't have any children?

MARIE HARVEY: I didn't say that.

MARIE BARRETT: Oh. So you do have something.

MARIE HARVEY: Divorces don't allow for much neutrality. At least not in my family. Good news is, if you know anyone at Hallmark, you can tell 'em to make one less Mothers' Day card this year.

(Marie Barrett stares sympathetically at Marie Harvey. Marie Harvey tries to ignore her for as long as she can and then:)

MARIE HARVEY: Yes?

MARIE BARRETT: If you want to talk about anything, I'm a great listener. I wouldn't mind at all. Really. I don't know much about divorce, but I know a lot about being alone. Would you like to talk about being alone?

MARIE HARVEY: Not at the moment. Maybe when we reach cruising altitude.

MARIE BARRETT: Well you know where to find me.

(Marie Barrett returns to her book. Marie Harvey tries to read her magazine, but keeps looking at Marie Barrett as if she wants to say something.)

MARIE HARVEY: Ah . . . Excuse me —

MARIE BARRETT: Yes?

MARIE HARVEY: Nothing, I'm sorry.

MARIE BARRETT: No, no. Did you want to talk about something?

MARIE HARVEY: No. I —.

MARIE BARRETT: Go ahead. I'm listening.

MARIE HARVEY: It's just, well, I can't help it, the mother in me wants to tell you to turn the light on while you're reading.

(A call button "bing" is heard, indicating a "passenger" requesting service.)

MARIE BARRETT: What did you say?

MARIE HARVEY: You should turn the light on. You're destroying your eyes —

MARIE BARRETT: No, no before that. What did you say before that?

MARIE HARVEY: Nothing.

MARIE BARRETT: No. Something. "The mother in me." Right?

MARIE HARVEY: Yeah . . .

MARIE BARRETT: That's what I thought. Wow.

MARIE HARVEY: What?

MARIE BARRETT: Wow.

MARIE HARVEY: What?!

MARIE BARRETT: I'm just going to seize the opportunity, OK? Because who knows when it will ever come my way again.

MARIE HARVEY: I don't know what you're talking about.

MARIE BARRETT: I'll throw out a bunch of questions and you can answer them one at a time . . . or pick and chose the ones you want — whatever feels right . . . Just go wherever the mother in you takes you, OK? All right, this is it.

(Taking a deep breath.)

Would you definitely say it's better to breast-feed a baby? Does the fork go on the left or right? . . . Um . . . Oh yeah — is it true you can't wear white until after Memorial Day? and should you really wait an hour after eating to swim? Um . . . damn, why haven't I been writing these down? I literally have hundreds — thousands of — Oh, I know, if an invitation says "and guest" —

MARIE HARVEY: I just thought you should turn your light on.

(She reaches above Marie Barrett's head and turns on her light.)

That's all.

MARIE BARRETT: I know you must think I'm a weirdo, but I'm not. I don't have a mother, you see. It's something I'm aware of every second of the day. Like if I didn't have any arms or legs . . . or skin. She died during child-birth. They say as soon as I emerged — as soon as I took my first breath, she took her last. She really was only a vessel for me if you think about it — just like this plane. She received me, took me to a destination and then I emerged, disembarked and she was gone. Lame metaphor I know, but the mind — my mind — needs ways to understand, to make sense. I'm always feeling so . . . lost — like everyone in the world has a map that I don't have. Sometimes, I find I just don't know how to get around. Like there's vital information I don't have access to. Letters missing from my alphabet, you know? But now, all of a sudden . . . here you are. I know this is lousy timing given your situation, but there's too much I need to know. So I'm just gonna grab a hold of this before it floats away. *(Beat.)* OK?

MARIE HARVEY: *(Sympathetically.)* I don't think so.

MARIE BARRETT: But you offered —

MARIE HARVEY: I didn't offer anything.

MARIE BARRETT: Yes you did.

MARIE HARVEY: No I didn't.

(Beat.)

MARIE BARRETT: How many children did you say you have?

MARIE HARVEY: *(Trying to remain pleasant.)* I didn't.

MARIE BARRETT: Sons?

(Marie Harvey shakes her head no.)

Daughters. How many?

MARIE HARVEY: Enough.

(Marie Harvey flips through her magazine. Pause.)

MARIE BARRETT: My name's Marie. What's yours?

(No response.)

OK — I'll guess.

MARIE HARVEY: *(Before she can guess.)* Marie.

MARIE BARRETT: Yes?

MARIE HARVEY: No. That's my name too. Marie.

MARIE BARRETT: Is that the truth? Is it?

MARIE HARVEY: Yes.

MARIE BARRETT: That's . . . phenomenal. My God! Can you believe it? Maybe that's how they seat us.

VIRGINIA: Ladies and gentleman the pilot has just turned off the "fasten seat-belts" sign indicating that you are free to move about the cabin.

MARIE HARVEY: *(Unfastening her seatbelt.)* Hallelujah.

MARIE BARRETT: It's an amazing coincidence, don't you think?

VIRGINIA: However, for your safety, we recommend you keep your seatbelt fas-tened while you are seated. Also, please remember that due to federal regulations, smoking is not permitted on this flight. If you choose not to obey these rules, you all might not get that midday snack you were promised. Just a joke. We will be around shortly with our complimentary beverage service. Please refer to the *Flight* magazine in the seat pocket in front of you for your selections. Thank you.

MARIE BARRETT: Marie, there's something I really need to ask you —

MARIE HARVEY: Look, I don't know you —

MARIE BARRETT: My name is Marie Barrett. I live in Brooklyn, I'm twenty-five years old, I'm Episcopalian, I work for a small but reputable publishing company and . . . um . . . I'm allergic to birch trees. What else do you want to know?

MARIE HARVEY: I shouldn't have said anything about the light.

MARIE BARRETT: The mother in you couldn't help it.

MARIE HARVEY: Marie, in twenty-four hours I have to stand in front of a judge and a bunch of other strangers and bicker with my husband about how much of an allowance he'll give me per month, so at forty-nine years old, and having acquired no marketable skills, I won't have to beg anyone to give me my first job —

MARIE BARRETT: You've never had a job?

MARIE HARVEY: I paint.

VIRGINIA: Hello, ladies. What would you like to drink today?

MARIE BARRETT: *(To Marie Harvey.)* You paint? I work for a children's book publisher. I could help you find a job.

MARIE HARVEY: *(To Virginia.)* Are there any empty seats?

MARIE BARRETT: Please don't.

VIRGINIA: No ma'am, there are no vacancies. And as far as I can tell, that seat you got there is perfectly fine, so let's not make complaints just to hear the sound of our own voices, OK?

MARIE BARRETT: Is your name Marie?

VIRGINIA: No. It's Virginia. Why?

MARIE BARRETT: We're both Maries.

VIRGINIA: Really? Isn't that a tremendous coincidence?

MARIE BARRETT: It sure is.

VIRGINIA: So. What can I get you two Maries to drink?

MARIE BARRETT: Orange juice, please. Wait. No. My stomach feels a little weird. All this excitement's got it doing somersaults.
(To Marie Harvey.) Is it OK to have the acid? What does the mother in you say about that?

(Marie Harvey does not respond. She continues to flip through her magazine. Virginia and Marie Barrett stare at Marie Harvey for a few beats.)

VIRGINIA: Ma'am?

MARIE HARVEY: What?

(Marie Harvey realizes they are staring at her.)

VIRGINIA: What's your call on the OJ?

MARIE HARVEY: Oh good God — have ginger ale.

MARIE BARRETT: Excellent. Ginger ale please.

VIRGINIA: Peanuts?

(Marie Barrett and Virginia look at Marie Harvey, as if asking her a question. Marie Harvey sighs heavily.)

MARIE HARVEY: Are they salted?

VIRGINIA: Yes.

MARIE HARVEY: Skip the nuts.

VIRGINIA: And what would you like for yourself?

MARIE HARVEY: A Bloody Mary.

(Virginia looks at her watch.)

Believe me, I'm entitled to it today.

MARIE BARRETT: She certainly is. Her divorce hearing is tomorrow.

VIRGINIA: *(Sympathetic.)* Do you really think alcohol is an answer?

MARIE HARVEY: No. Alcohol is a beverage. You asked me if I wanted one and that's the one I chose.

VIRGINIA: Suit yourself. But remember, I do have the authority to cut you off at any time.

MARIE HARVEY: Don't worry, I found a designated driver to fly the plane.

VIRGINIA: I'm only doing my job. Four dollars, please.

MARIE HARVEY: I don't suppose I can start a tab.

VIRGINIA: That's not in keeping with our policy.

(Marie Harvey pays her. Virginia pours ginger ale into a glass.)

When I was a little girl, and my tummy felt funny, my mother would stir up my ginger ale until all the bubbles were gone.

MARIE BARRETT: Oh yeah? Why?

VIRGINIA: Strangely enough, I never asked.

(Marie Barrett looks at Marie Harvey.)

MARIE HARVEY: I am not stirring your ginger ale.

VIRGINIA: Would you like me to stir it for you?

MARIE BARRETT: Yes please.

(Virginia stirs and then stops suddenly.)

VIRGINIA: Whoops. There is no tomato juice on my cart. Be right back.

(Virginia hands Marie Harvey the ginger ale and walks to the front of the plane. Marie Harvey looks at ginger ale for a moment, sighs heavily, and then begins to stir.)

MARIE HARVEY: It prevents gas.

(Marie Harvey hands Marie Barrett the ginger ale. A call button bing is heard.)

MARIE BARRETT: Thank you.

(Marie Barrett sips her ginger ale and watches Marie Harvey read her magazine.)

Could I ask you just one thing? Just answer this one question and then you can go back to your magazine, which I can tell you're only pretending to read. Marie? Could you put that down, please? Please?

MARIE HARVEY: Are you working for my husband? Did he hire you to drive me mad?

(Virginia returns, handing Marie Harvey a Bloody Mary.)

VIRGINIA: You sip this slowly now, understand?

(Pointing to Marie Barrett's glass.)

Did you stir that for her?

MARIE HARVEY: Yes.

VIRGINIA: Good. Lord knows I can't do it all.

(Virginia exits. Marie Harvey takes a big gulp of her Bloody Mary.)

MARIE BARRETT: I wouldn't bother you like this if I hadn't been waiting what feels like my whole entire life to ask someone this quest . . .

MARIE HARVEY: In approximately five minutes, this Bloody Mary will kick in, allowing me to pretend I don't have to do tomorrow what I have to do tomorrow. So if I enlighten you with some motherly advice now, you'll leave me alone for the rest of the flight, agreed? Minimal interaction only, right? Right?

MARIE BARRETT: Well, I might —

MARIE HARVEY: I'll sweeten the deal. Stop asking questions and the entire armrest is yours. OK? Maternal advice. Here goes —

(Taking a drink.)

If you have to get married, marry a lawyer . . . surround yourself with people you can tolerate but don't particularly like and most importantly — never, never have any children. Lovely meeting you — have a good trip.

(She turns away.)

MARIE BARRETT: Why shouldn't I have kids? Because I didn't have a mother of my own? Am I missing something essential that all other women have? Like some internal instruction book?

MARIE HARVEY: Just do what I did — read Dr. Spock and then hire a nanny. *(She takes another gulp of her drink.)*

MARIE BARRETT: *(Laughs.)* Did your daughter inherit your sense of humor?

MARIE HARVEY: No, just my nervous condition.

MARIE BARRETT: I see.

MARIE HARVEY: You see? Really? What do you see? Do I have an "I've-driven-my-child-to-seek-extensive-psychotherapy" look to me? I've also driven her to an aromatherapist, a scalp masseuse, an herbalist, a dog psychologist . . . an astrologist . . . and a marriage counselor. *(Beat.)* And every goddamn one of them tells her it's all my fault.

MARIE BARRETT: Even the dog psychologist?

MARIE HARVEY: Apparently even little Snowcake isn't immune to the tension my visits create.

MARIE BARRETT: *(Laughs.)* You're really very funny.

MARIE HARVEY: Well, I'm glad you've enjoyed our little time together. *(Lifting her glass in a toast.)*
Good-bye.

MARIE BARRETT: I have enjoyed it. That's actually what I wanted to ask you about. You see, I always hoped I could find someone . . . like you . . . who I could talk to from time to time. You know, like if I have any questions, maybe I could call you —

MARIE HARVEY: What?

MARIE BARRETT: I'm just so tired of never knowing where to find answers. I need someone . . . a woman . . . an older woman, who I can go to when I need help.

MARIE HARVEY: Are you asking me to be your mother?

MARIE BARRETT: No. *(Beat.)* It would be more like freelancing.

MARIE HARVEY: Good God — don't give yourself away to a stranger.

MARIE BARRETT: See — you're giving me advice already — you're a natural.

MARIE HARVEY: *(Uneasily.)* You're going too far. Now leave me alone.

MARIE BARRETT: I don't mean to imply that I'd call you constantly, just on occasion.

MARIE HARVEY: *(Overlapping.)* I'm not listening to this.

MARIE BARRETT: We both live in New York. We could meet for coffee from time to time.

MARIE HARVEY: Stop it.

MARIE BARRETT: — your own daughter would have first dibs of course, but we could all work out a schedule I'm sure —

MARIE HARVEY: Not another word.

MARIE BARRETT: Only when it's —

MARIE HARVEY: I mean it!

MARIE BARRETT: I'm sorry. This isn't a good time for you.

(Marie Harvey finishes her drink, shakes the ice around her glass, then looks up and down the aisles.)

I spend so much time trying to acquire family I can't imagine having to give any up. I'm sorry.

MARIE HARVEY: Don't be. My husband and I were happy for twenty years. And then we met.

(Marie Barrett does not laugh.)

MARIE HARVEY: *(Imitating a rim shot.)* Ba-dump-ump.

MARIE BARRETT: Would you like to talk about how you're feeling?

MARIE HARVEY: I'm feeling annoyed.

MARIE BARRETT: I mean about your divorce. Would you like to talk about that?

MARIE HARVEY: Yes. But to someone I've known for longer than five minutes.

MARIE BARRETT: Well that's unfair.

MARIE HARVEY: What is unfair?

MARIE BARRETT: Shutting me out like that. It's not my fault we've only known each other for five minutes.

MARIE HARVEY: You shouldn't take it personally. I don't like talking to strangers.

MARIE BARRETT: Why?

MARIE HARVEY: Because they end up asking you to be their mother.

MARIE BARRETT: This has happened to you before? Has it?

MARIE HARVEY: I was speaking figuratively.

MARIE BARRETT: That's a relief. You're the first person I've asked. It would be just my luck if you had like a waiting list or something.

MARIE HARVEY: *I'm* the first person?

MARIE BARRETT: Yes.

MARIE HARVEY: Why on earth would I be the first person you've asked?

MARIE BARRETT: Because of what you said — "the mother in me." You saw me reading in the dark and the nurturer in you was so strong you couldn't resist reaching out to me. I'm a perfect stranger but you wanted to take care of me, to protect me. You're who I've been searching for. You've got the right stuff.

MARIE HARVEY: I don't have any stuff.

MARIE BARRETT: Exactly. You're alone like me. I mean, you're going to get divorced tomorrow, and no one's coming with you. It seems like . . . maybe . . . you have no one to ask. *(Beat.)* Hey — would you like me to go with you?

MARIE HARVEY: What?!

MARIE BARRETT: You don't want to be there alone, do you?

MARIE HARVEY: Thanks, but no thanks. Maybe next time.

MARIE BARRETT: I think you're looking for someone as much as I am.

MARIE HARVEY: Oh God, I'm in Hell, I'm in sheer Hell.

MARIE BARRETT: Truthfully, I don't believe for a second that you want me to stop talking to you.

MARIE HARVEY: Then make believe. Please.

(*Virginia enters carrying plastic bags containing earphones. She passes them out to the other passengers.*)

VIRGINIA: Now don't y'all push these too far into your ears. With the cabin pressure being as high as it is, we don't want any of your heads exploding. Just a joke.

MARIE HARVEY: Excuse me —

VIRGINIA: (*Pointing at Marie Harvey's empty glass.*) You shouldn't drink that fast.

MARIE HARVEY: I wouldn't drink at all if you could suggest another way to get it down.

VIRGINIA: Sarcasm will not get you better service.

MARIE HARVEY: I want to change my seat.

VIRGINIA: One at the bar perhaps?

MARIE BARRETT: Don't change your seat. I —

(*A call button bing is heard.*)

VIRGINIA: Duty calls.

(*Virginia abruptly tosses Marie Harvey a package of headsets and quickly exits.*)

MARIE HARVEY: Hey!

(*She pushes the call button, but gets no response.*)

Oh, for crying out loud.

(*She rips plastic bag open, puts the earphones in her ears, and stares out the window.*)

MARIE BARRETT: Please don't do that. I wasn't finished talking —

(*Marie Harvey closes her eyes and leans her head back. Marie Barrett stares at her.*)

I'm sorry to bother you, but there are things I have to talk to someone about. You see I'm really scared about something and there's no one else who I — Are you listening? Marie? . . . Come on . . . Talk to me. I don't think what I'm asking is so bad . . . I only meant that I'd call you every once in a while . . . just when I need an answer, or some advice. That's all, really. I just want to know there's someone out there I can talk to when I don't know what to do. Like about dating, or getting rid of strep throat . . . or cooking roasts . . . or buying flatware . . . or . . . or about . . . about lumps. You know, as in what if you feel something in your body you know wasn't there before?

(Marie Barrett becomes more emotional; Marie Harvey removes her headsets and listens to her.)

And you don't know a single thing about what a lump could be, except . . . And you're too scared to find out because you don't think you could go through anything that bad without someone . . . a mother to help you through it. Does it always mean something bad? Does a lump always mean cancer? Does it? Marie? Answer me. ANSWER ME PLEASE!

(Virginia rushes over.)

VIRGINIA: Is there something I can help with here?

MARIE BARRETT: *(To Marie Harvey.)* Does a lump always mean cancer?

VIRGINIA: Excuse me?

MARIE BARRETT: Does a lump always mean cancer?

VIRGINIA: Ma'am, I think I'll defer to you on that one.

MARIE BARRETT: Excuse me. I feel sick.

(She exits to lavatory at the back of the plane.)

MARIE HARVEY: Oh, brilliant. Is that how they teach you to handle crises in stewardess school? To defer?

(Virginia sits down in Marie Barrett's seat.)

VIRGINIA: Does she have cancer?

MARIE HARVEY: I don't know. She said she found a lump.

VIRGINIA: Does a lump always mean cancer?

MARIE HARVEY: Why is everybody asking me that?

VIRGINIA: Does it?

MARIE HARVEY: No.

VIRGINIA: Well go on and tell her that.

MARIE HARVEY: I don't know who she is.

VIRGINIA: She seems to have formed an attachment to you.

MARIE HARVEY: Yes. However, I can't have her attached. *(Beat.)* Look, before she comes back, I need you — I want you to change my seat.

VIRGINIA: Tell her she's all right, and then we'll discuss the seating arrangements.

MARIE HARVEY: Look, I bought a ticket for this plane so I could get from point A to point B. That's it. As far as I know, I'm not required to adopt anyone. So move my seat, please.

VIRGINIA: That's against policy.

MARIE HARVEY: No it's not.

VIRGINIA: And how would you know? I don't see any wings pinned to your chest.

MARIE HARVEY: Don't force me to make demands —

VIRGINIA: Oh, we're threatening to make demands, are we? I guess our morning cocktail wasn't such a good idea after all, was it?

MARIE HARVEY: She won't leave me alone despite numerous requests —

VIRGINIA: Requests? No demands? I see, it's only airline personnel that are threatened with demands.

MARIE HARVEY: I apologize if I've offended you. I'm asking you, politely, could I possibly change seats with someone?

VIRGINIA: What would you like me to do? Walk up to a passenger and say, "Excuse me, that woman up there is sitting next to someone who is driving her crazy. Would you mind switching seats with her?"

MARIE HARVEY: Surely you can find another way to phrase it.

VIRGINIA: *(Earnestly.)* Go tell her she's all right.

MARIE HARVEY: I'd prefer it if you told her.

VIRGINIA: You know, I chose this profession so I could help people on a daily basis. But all it usually entails is passing out drinks and pillows. I know that. However, you have a real opportunity here to help someone. And for that I envy you.

MARIE HARVEY: If you want her, you can have her. She's currently accepting applications for a mother.

VIRGINIA: *(Patting Marie Harvey's lap.)* Not any more. So. What kind of arrangement did you all work out?

MARIE HARVEY: We didn't work out an arrangement. She's a total stranger —

VIRGINIA: But "stranger" is a relative term. Compared to say, that gentleman right there, she isn't such a stranger, is she? You know her name, where she works . . . her current medical situation.

MARIE HARVEY: She's allergic to birch trees.

VIRGINIA: See there? Seems to me the two of you could have a nice little relationship.

MARIE HARVEY: There's no such thing as a nice little relationship.

VIRGINIA: Ma'am, I'm a recent divorcée myself, and personally the amount of people exiting my life is greater than the amount of people boarding, if you know what I mean. Lucky for you if that's not your situation. Oops, she's coming back. Try talking to her. You never know — .

(Marie Barrett returns to her seat.)

How are you feeling, dear?

MARIE BARRETT: Fine, thank you. Could I have a pillow please?

VIRGINIA: Would you like a pillow also?

MARIE HARVEY: Just another Bloody Mary.

VIRGINIA: Are you su — .

MARIE HARVEY: I'm sure.

VIRGINIA: *(To Marie Barrett.)* A lump doesn't always mean cancer, you know. *(To Marie Harvey.)* Does it?

MARIE HARVEY: No.

VIRGINIA: *(Indicating to Marie Barrett.)* Tell her.
(Virginia exits.)

MARIE HARVEY: Are you OK?

MARIE BARRETT: Yes.

MARIE HARVEY: I'm sure there isn't anything wrong. But go to a doctor as soon as you get home.
(Marie Barrett nods. Beat.)
Usually, a woman your age has nothing to worry about.

MARIE BARRETT: Usually. The women in my family aren't really known for their longevity. So . . . I get scared.

MARIE HARVEY: *(Gently.)* Don't get so scared.

MARIE BARRETT: If this is bad, I won't be able to do it without . . . a mother.

MARIE HARVEY: I'm not who you want for a mother. The truth is, that's an item my own daughter is currently debating.

MARIE BARRETT: There's something unbelievable to me about a mother and a daughter not getting along.

MARIE HARVEY: It's unbelievable to me that any do. If the truth be told, you've asked me more questions in the past ten minutes than my daughter has asked me in the past ten years. I'm not as adept at mothering as you'd think.

MARIE BARRETT: I don't care. In fact, I prefer it that way. If you've been waiting ten years for someone to ask you for advice, you must have a lot of it to give. Right?
(Marie Harvey laughs.)
Hey, and just think, you'd be getting me at the best possible time. No teething, no toilet training . . . I've had all my shots.
(Virginia returns with a pillow and a glass.)

VIRGINIA: Here's your second drink. FYI, regulations do not permit us to serve more than three.

MARIE HARVEY: Thank you.
(Marie Harvey pays Virginia for the drink.)

VIRGINIA: My hands are full. Would you put this behind her?
(Handing Marie Harvey the pillow.)
(To Marie Barrett.) Lean forward, honey.

(Marie Barrett leans forward. Marie Harvey puts the pillow behind her, fluffing it up first. Virginia watches happily.)

So, is it settled? Are you two gonna go out and buy matching outfits?

MARIE HARVEY: Go away. Shoo.

VIRGINIA: *(Whispering to Marie Harvey.)* Don't blow this.

MARIE BARRETT: You did tell me that all you have are lawyer bills and a tan line. When you said that, you reminded me of this quote I use to describe how I feel: "Life has not yet offered me a trinket of the slightest value." It's from Virginia Woolf — *Mrs. Dalloway*. Except for the yet. I added that — I try to be optimistic. "Life has not *yet* offered me a trinket of the slightest value." That's how you feel too, isn't it?

MARIE HARVEY: Well, like I said . . . I paint. That's my trinket.

MARIE BARRETT: *(Disappointed.)* Maybe I'll buy some watercolors.

MARIE HARVEY: I'm sure you have something.

MARIE BARRETT: Books, I guess. Virginia Woolf, Willa Cather, George Eliot. Anything written by a woman, I've read. But Virginia, Willa, and George, God bless 'em, have little to say about yeast infections and monthly mood swings. I can't find my mother in a book.

MARIE HARVEY: So now you're looking for her on airplanes?

MARIE BARRETT: I'm looking for her everywhere. I search for her the way you look for something you've dropped in the grass. Parting every blade . . . I used to dream that she didn't actually die. Instead a team of evil doctors kidnapped her from the operating table because she had a rare something or other — like three fallopian tubes. Or a five-chambered heart. I liked that idea the best — that she had a tremendous heart. Anyway, they kidnapped her to study her, so she's not really dead and it's only a matter of time until she escapes. And I find her . . . That's why I start conversations with strangers.

MARIE HARVEY: I don't have a tremendous heart.

MARIE BARRETT: How about three fallopian tubes?

MARIE HARVEY: I'm sorry. This arrangement you want, it's not possible.

MARIE BARRETT: Is there anything that could make it possible?

MARIE HARVEY: Marie, I need to get through the divorce tomorrow before I can think about any . . . acquisitions.

MARIE BARRETT: I understand. *(Beat.)* Could I just ask you one more thing?

MARIE HARVEY: Yes?

MARIE BARRETT: A lump can really be something else besides cancer?

MARIE HARVEY: Yes. It can be just a cyst. Which I'm sure it is.

(Beat. A call button bing"is heard.)

Anything else?

MARIE BARRETT: What's a duvet?

MARIE HARVEY: It's like a giant pillowcase — for a comforter. When you want a new look.

MARIE BARRETT: Does it hurt to breast-feed a baby?

MARIE HARVEY: It sort of feels like jogging without a bra.

MARIE BARRETT: Will I ever enjoy sex as much as the man?

MARIE HARVEY: Probably not. But sometimes.

MARIE BARRETT: What's parboiling?

MARIE HARVEY: It's when you boil something for a short time — to prepare it for roasting

(Lights begin to fade.)

MARIE BARRETT: I keep getting canker sores on my gums.

(Marie Harvey maternally inspects Marie Barrett's gums.)

VOICE OF PILOT: Ladies and gentlemen this is your captain. We're experiencing some minor turbulence. Please remain in your seats with your seatbelts fastened while we find you a smoother ride.

(Marie Barrett and Marie Harvey fasten their seatbelts.)

MARIE HARVEY: You probably have too much acid in your diet.

(Fade to black.)

END OF PLAY

at 1501 Broadway, Suite 2310, New York, NY 10036, without whose permission in writing no performance of the play may be made.

Bread © 1995 by Margaret Hunt. Reprinted by permission of Margaret Hunt. All inquiries should be addressed to: Noel Silverman, Esq., Silverman, Shulman & Baker, 136 E. 57th St., New York, NY 10022. 212-758-2020

Old Wives Tale © 1995 by Julia Jensen. Reprinted by permission of Julia Jensen. All inquires should be addressed to: Karin Wakefield, Epstein-Wyckoff & Assoc., 280 W. Beverly Drive, #400, Beverly Hills, CA 90212.

The Encanto File © 1991 by Rosa Lowinger. Reprinted by permission of Rosa Lowinger. All inquiries should be addressed to Rosa Lowinger, 8643 Chalmers Drive, Los Angeles, CA 90035.

Freakish Times © 2000 by Lesli-Jo Morizono. Reprinted by permission of the author. All inquiries should be addressed to Anne M. Hamilton, Hamilton Literary Management, 718-937-9155. hamiltonlit@hotmail.com

The Only Woman General © 2001 by Lavonne Mueller. Reprinted by permission of Lavonne Mueller. All inquires should be addressed to: The Women's Project, 55 West End Ave., New York, NY 10023.

Betty's Garage © 1999 by Carmen Rivera. Reprinted by permission of Carmen Rivera. All inquires should be addressed to: Carmen Rivera, 286 Court St., #6, Brooklyn, NY 11231.

the life before/reconstruction/reconstructing whiteness © 2001 by Alva Rogers. Reprinted by permission of Alva Rogers. All inquires should be addressed to: The Fund for Women Artists, Inc., PO Box 60637, Florence, MA 01062. 413-585-5968, Fax 413-586-1303. info@womenart.org

Look What You Made Do © 2001 by Lynda Sturner. Reprinted by permission of Lynda Sturner. All inquiries should be addressed to: The Women's Project, 55 West End Ave., New York, NY 10023.

but there are fires © 1991 by Caridad Svich. Reprinted by permission of Caridad Svich. All inquiries should be addressed to: New Dramatists, 424 West 44th St., New York, NY 10036.